The Human Side of Music

Da Capo Press Music Reprint Series

GENERAL EDITOR

FREDERICK FREEDMAN

VASSAR COLLEGE

The
HUMAN SIDE
of MUSIC

by
Charles W. Hughes

 DA CAPO PRESS • NEW YORK • 1970

A Da Capo Press Reprint Edition

This Da Capo Press edition of Charles W. Hughes' *The Human
Side of Music* is an unabridged republication of the first edition
published in New York in 1948.

Library of Congress Catalog Card Number 70-107871

SBN 306-71895-2

The Human Side of Music

The

HUMAN SIDE
of MUSIC

by
Charles W. Hughes

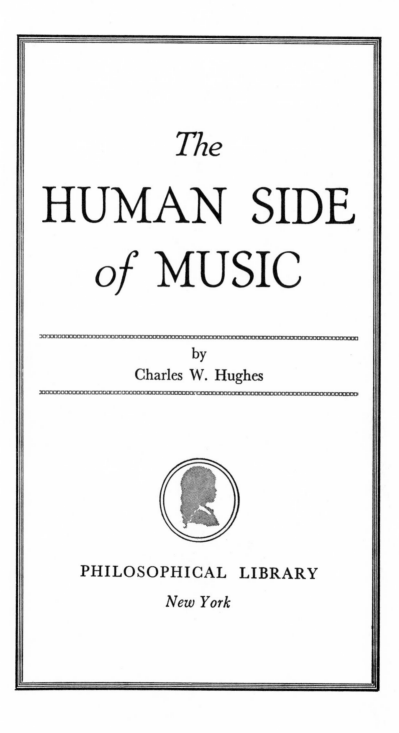

PHILOSOPHICAL LIBRARY

New York

To
My Wife

Acknowledgements

Among the many who helped in the making of this book the author wishes to express a particular indebtedness to the following: to his wife, Fannie Lippman Hughes, for unfailing helpfulness; to Dr. Max Schoen for friendly advice and encouragement; to his friends and colleagues Prof. Vincent Aita, Prof. Herbert Inch, and Mr. Saul Novack for reading and criticizing the text; to members of the staffs of the Music Division of the New York Public Library at 42nd Street and of the Music Library at 58th Street for invaluable help on occasions too numerous to mention.

Table of Contents

Introduction

We are all aware that a great change has taken place in music, but few of us are conscious of the far-reaching implications of that change. Since the earliest times there have been two basic ways of experiencing music: listening and performing. The listener and the performer might be one and the same. The shepherds piped in the meadows, the plowboy sang as he labored in the fields, the mother as she worked at the hearth. In a more complicated society like our own the musician might be a pianist who performed the Mozart sonatas. As long as he played them for his own comfort and satisfaction, he was conforming to an ancient pattern.

Since all gifts, including the gift for music-making, are given in a greater measure to some than to others, there have always been singers and players who were listened to with delight. In very ancient times we find that some of these gifted singers devoted more of their efforts to music-making than did their fellows. When the singer was able to exchange his songs for his food and clothing and shelter, the professional musician appeared. From the period of Homer to the present century, however, the musician could only sing to the listeners gathered around him. If he wanted to reach new audiences he must travel to new places. This the early minstrels, the scalds, and the troubadours did. The great performers of the later nineteenth century spent much of their active lives in travelling from one musical center to another.

The opportunities for hearing a performer of national or international reputation were thus limited to those who lived in centers large enough to possess and fill a suitable hall. Under such circumstances the great problem was to provide a musical experience for the largest possible number of people. The solution, however, was to come from an unexpected quarter.

This solution was twofold. It involved the discovery of

ways in which the performance of music could be preserved and repeated and a method of transmitting music from place to place. The ingenious mechanics who worked at this problem were able to produce automatic harpsichords as early as the sixteenth century, but they were chiefly interesting as wonderful and ingenious toys and played no significant role in the spread of music. The player-piano was a descendant of the automatic organ which had adorned the pleasure gardens of the eighteenth century. Although it is almost obsolete now after attaining an enormous vogue in the early years of this century, it played a not inconsiderable role in making music available to a wider audience. Such books as "The Complete Pianolist" by Kobbé which hail the musical possibilities of the player-piano may surprise readers who remember the instrument chiefly as an adjunct of the corner saloon. Though Kobbé pinned his faith on the wrong instrument, he was nevertheless quite right in realizing the critical importance of the reproduction of musical performances.

When the phonograph reached a practicable form, it became still more possible to sell a musical performance to a customer in such a form that he could take it home and repeat it as often as he wished.

The second element in the solution was found in the radio. If the phonograph and player-piano made it possible to repeat a performance at a later time, the radio represented a conquest of space. The audience of a musical artist was no longer represented by the number of people who could be packed into a single auditorium. The audience was expanded in an amazingly brief period until it included any American sitting by his radio-set and even listeners in other continents.

Musical experience has thus become possible for anyone who has a radio and the time to listen to it. These limitations are not as slight as they might appear. Many American citizens are so poor that they cannot buy a radio. Many are forced to work so long and so hard that they lack both the leisure and the energy which they might devote to music. The problem here, however, is not a musical or technical problem but one which must be solved by better social planning. We have reached a point where an experience of music is technically possible for a whole people without demanding any performing skill beyond the ability to turn a switch and push a button or adjust a pointer on a dial.

One might expect that such a state of affairs would promptly result in a musical Utopia. We may indeed claim that music has been democratized and made available to a degree that can only be compared to the spread of knowledge as a result of the mass production of cheap books and newspapers. But just as the daily newspaper and the cheap book have failed to make wisdom universal, so the wide availability of music has not made us all discriminating music lovers.

The availability of music has, however, provoked many discussions on the meaning of music on a popular level which are themselves typical of our period. They result in part from the interest of individuals who have a practical stake in the development of a large and interested musical public, in part from a feeling that music, like all other good things, should belong to all the people and not merely to a privileged few. We assume the existence of a large public for symphonic music at the present day. The number of symphony orchestras, of symphonic broadcasts, of recorded programs of symphonic music, all show that this is so. Yet it is only necessary to turn back to the period when Theodore Thomas was active as a conductor to see how small were the American audiences for such music in the mid-nineteenth century. Thomas put the matter very concisely in an interview in 1880. "Ah! Very few can realize what the struggle of twenty years ago was. Then the people here knew little about classic music, and the presentation of programmes of the best class met with little or no recognition. It was disheartening work to play again and again before small unappreciative audiences who seemed to care nothing for the end we had in view . . ." It would be easy to give examples in other musical fields which would show a similar advance. But the fact that it was possible to hear music did not mean that the public would indeed come to hear it. It did not mean that those who came would understand it or be moved by it. The "People's Concert Society" which organized free symphonic concerts for working men (in 1884) may have naively under-estimated the extent of the task to which it addressed itself. The task was a noble one which still has not been completed.

It was not until the nineteenth century that writers on musical subjects began to address themselves to the great public. It was in 1830 that the learned Monsieur Fétis published his "*La musique mise a la portée de tout le monde*" ("Music placed within the reach of everyone") which promptly went through a number of editions. In England John Hullah popularized singing with such success that, in the period between 1840 and 1860, twenty-five thousand pupils were said to have attended his classes. In our country W. S. B. Mathews published the first volume of his "How to Understand Music" in 1880, which was followed in 1896 by Krehbiel's "How to Listen to Music." Clearly the companies which dealt in records and player-piano rolls had a stake in the musical education of the public, and many publications along these lines were directly or indirectly due to their influence. Psychologists began to study the process of hearing and the emotional reactions of the listener.

The whole problem which these and many other works attempted to solve was a new one which had arisen solely because music was reaching a new, a more diversified, and a less experienced audience. In an eighteenth century court music was regarded as one of life's luxuries. One listened with pleasure, or, if the music ceased to amuse, it was always possible to talk or indulge in a little flirtation with a pretty neighbor. Musical aristocrats undoubtedly did understand music very well indeed, but no one was serious-minded enough to worry about the unmusical aristocrats except, perhaps, the unfortunate musicians who had to minister to their wishes. Our own concern for the musical understanding of the great public is a characteristically mixed blend of idealism and shrewd business enterprise. Our eighteenth century aristocrat was so generously provided for by the labor of others that he could afford to add a few musicians to an

already large retinue without considering the expense. But
if we, the people, do not buy concert tickets or pianos or
books on musical subjects, the gentlemen who produce these
useful objects will have to retire from business. Our willingness to do so depends on the pleasure that we find in music.

Musical enjoyment depends first on the quality of one's
hearing apparatus and on the ability to remember what one
hears. It depends on an abundant experience of music. As
we have seen, this experience is now constantly available.
The study of music, moreover, is enormously facilitated by a
knowledge of music notation. Notation serves as a basis for
comparing one passage with the other, for discovering how
effects of harmony and of instrumental color are obtained,
for studying the themes on which compositions are based.
Yet, vital as this knowledge is to the musical amateur as well
as the professional musician, it is still so far from being general
that it will not be taken for granted in the chapters which
follow.

Probably music can only be fully enjoyed when it is valued.
It is often the lack of a deep conviction of the value of music
which stands as an obstacle to our enjoyment. It is, however,
quite understandable that this should be more of a problem
here and now than at an earlier period. Music was accepted
in earlier times because it was part of the apparatus by which
the prestige of a social order and of its rulers was made
manifest. It was accepted, not only because of its own inherent values, but also because it was a symbol of desirable
luxury and prestige. In our own time and country music is
no longer the property of a ruling class. Since it belongs not
to a few but to many people, it has lost its symbolic value
as a mark of desirable prestige and must be judged by its
own merits, by its effect on us. As a result many listeners
have been unable to stand on their own musical feet and
make their own judgments. This is an effect of a lack of experience, which more experience will remedy, or of a lack
of discrimination, which will be more difficult to repair. To
say that the rewards of listening simply, quietly, and attentively to music are great is true, but it is not a useful statement. Music lovers will need no such assurance. Those who

have never really listened to music will hardly be convinced since conviction depends on experience, not on words.

The direct experience of music is the basic fact. What can this book, any book, add that will be of any value? The books on music published for the general reader fall into a number of general classes. There are popular biographies and collections of biographies which attempt to satisfy an interest in the personalities of famous composers and performers. This is a natural interest, but one of the most remarkable features of many biographies of composers is the rather small amount of light they cast on the music written by those composers. It is easy to feel the energy, the decision, the pride of Handel in his music, but what in his life prepares us for the tender pastorals which are so characteristic of his music? What in the life of Delius would hint at the brooding reveries of his scores? The life of a composer and his music bear a varied relationship. Some life-characteristics of the composer appear in the music, Beethoven's vehemence, Schumann's poetic and fanciful reveries. Sometimes the music seems to express a side of the composer which was repressed or frustrated in actual life. The tender love songs of Brahms, the heroics of the Wagner music dramas perhaps served as compensations. They may portray what these composers longed for but not what they were. A more recent example of compensatory music is the *"Musique de Table"* of Maurice Rosenthal which, though it portrays the gastronomic delights of French cookery, was composed in the hard days of 1942.

A second and frequent type of popular book on music deals largely with the way in which music is organized, that is with musical form. There is no doubt that some knowledge of musical form makes for clearer listening. The cumulative effect of longer works can only be fully experienced if one sees what the composer is doing in terms of what he has done earlier and what he will in all probability do in the future. Such a foreknowledge is possible if one has heard the work before, or if one knows what the organization of such a piece is likely to be. A frequent difficulty in this connection arises from the different needs of the composer and the listener. In order to build a clear and well-integrated tone structure the composer needs to analyze his music in a more detailed fashion. Even a composer is likely to listen to the compositions of other composers in a more general fashion. Inevitably the member of a concert audience will comprehend formal construction in still vaguer, less precise terms. In accordance with this conviction, the treatment of musical form in this volume is treated in the light of general principles. In this field a clear outline is of more importance to the listener than a detailed analysis, and more in accordance with the way music is experienced.

This book is divided into two parts. The first deals with music as an expression of certain needs of society. It attempts to show, not only that music interpenetrated life in the most varied way, but also that the society which music expressed had a reciprocal effect on music and determined its moods, its forms, and its functions. It asks what demands were made on the musician, what he was asked to do, and how he responded, how he was able to satisfy the demands of society. One may object that music is a matter of personal feeling rather than anything which concerns a social group. Personal emotions, however, are not self-generated but conform more or less to a social standard which is illustrated in the lives of our fellows, which is dramatized on the stages of our theatres and exemplified in the pages of our novels. The idea of romantic love which is so prominent in our literature and our songs hardly antedates the Middle Ages. In certain Greek dramas we find it difficult to understand character behavior because romantic love was not the usual motivating force. Its place was taken by some factor which plays a smaller role in our emotional world such as fate or filial piety. In a similar fashion musical emotion conforms to or rebels against the prevalent emotional tone of its society. In either case it is conditioned by social factors.

It is quite apparent that most materials manipulated by man have possibilities peculiar to themselves. This is not less true of sound because it is the most impalpable of all mediums. Accordingly the second half of the book deals with the way music is organized from sounds, and how these sounds are so arranged as to be expressive. These are the inner workings of music which enable it to perform its social function. Perhaps a real insight into the true relationships of melody and harmony and rhythm are only attainable by the trained musician. The attempt to explain in words what is so clear and so definite when expressed in tones must always fall short of complete success. Yet certain general remarks can be made which will be useful to thoughtful readers.

Music for most modern listeners is emotional expression. The fundamental question for the listener is not how a given scale is constructed, but rather how the construction of that scale lends itself to the expression of certain moods and effects, not in the analysis of a flute tone, but in the realization that its quality is suited to a certain range of emotional expression. It is from this angle that the discussion of musical instruments, of rhythm, of melody, of harmony and form, has been conducted. There are many books which deal with these subjects from the approach of the musician and the composer. There are few which show a realization of the fact that just as writing a symphony and listening to a symphony are two different processes, so the knowledge which is helpful in listening to a symphony is not only less profound but different from that which is necessary in composing it.

Conclusion — The first requirement in listening to music is to value music. The second is to give oneself up to the music during a performance simply and completely. The third is to hear with complete clarity, with complete understanding.

These requirements, so simple to state, are rarely met in real life. Hearing can only be learned by hearing. The most that can be expected of a book for listeners is to furnish general ideas as to what to listen for. It is the hope of the author that this book may serve the purpose.

CHAPTER I

THE LISTENER AND HIS WORLD

MUSIC is a meeting between sound and human consciousness. This, like any other concise statement, is inadequate. It implies many things, both about the sounds heard
and the human being who hears them, which cannot possibly
be packed into a sentence. Indeed, this entire book can give
only a partial and necessarily incomplete description of this
relationship. Yet music had to be created by man. It did
not antedate him. It developed with him. And when the
dubious record of man's progress is finally evaluated, not
the least of the accomplishments which may be placed to his
credit will be the fact that he was a music-making animal.

Even the sounds which are the materials of music had to
be created. The sustained tone of an opera singer is a most
artificial performance resembling nothing in nature or in
human speech. Scientists describe a musical tone as characterized by regular vibrations. We perceive such a tone as
constant in pitch. In the speaking voice, however, the pitch
is vague and the fluctuations are ill-defined. We may speculate that early human creatures probably howled at random,
then in a more or less stylized fashion, and that finally one
tone, then two tones were produced more or less clearly
though the voice moved in a sliding glissando between or
around these points of reference. At this stage our theory
gains some support from a study of the music of primitive
peoples. There are many folk tunes where two tones emerge
so prominently that it seems clear that they were more clearly
differentiated by the singer and were regarded as more important than the others. No doubt such early instruments
as conch shells and trumpets of animal horns served to fix
the idea of sustained tone, since such an instrument, when

blown as a trumpet, would respond most easily at its natural pitch. But this would be much later in human development. In some such fashion as this, man learned to produce a musical tone with his voice and upon simple musical instruments.

The air stirs in regular vibrations. The vibrations spread in all directions from their source. They reach the protruding trumpet which is the human ear and are guided to the ear drum. The ear drum responds to these pulsations and vibrates in sympathy. They pass into consciousness and become human feeling. What was a purely mechanical agitation of the atmosphere has become sensation. The pattern of the air wave is so perfectly reproduced that the hearer perceives not merely a tone, but a flute tone or trumpet tone. This conversion of atmospheric vibration into warm human experience is a miracle, the marvels of which increase with our knowledge of them. Yet a single tone is only a letter of the musical alphabet. To make music this tone would have to be followed by others, each gaining in emotional richness and significance by its relation to the sounds which precede and follow it. The tones of such a series would be accompanied by other tones with the result that at each moment our ears respond to the combined assault of three, four, or more sounds. With each added factor the emotional burden of the music becomes more complex and more precise. Sound has been organized into melody, and to melody harmony has been added.

The mechanism of the ear serves as an intermediary between us and the world outside. It is our window opening on the world of sound. The ear is a marvellous instrument, yet it is neither so entirely reliable nor so sensitive as might be desired. We cannot improve the sensitivity of our receiving mechanism. Accidents may and old age will impair its efficiency. Yet simple sensitivity to tone is only one element in musical experience.

The perception of unorganized sound may itself be enjoyable just as the warmth of the sun in spring or the smell of violets may give pleasure. Such pleasures are reinforced by association. The poets continually remind us of pleasant auditory sensations, the sighing of the wind as it passes through the trees, the babbling of running water. Yet this simple pleasure in agreeable sound enters into and may even dominate the complex pleasure of listening to a Kreisler or a Traubel. Many people probably enjoy music much as a baby enjoys a warm bath. Saint-Saëns in his "Musical Memories" insists on the purely sensual effect of music for the average listener when he says, "For most people it (music) is, as Victor Hugo said, an exhalation of art—something for the ear as perfume is for the olfactory sense, a source of vague sensations, necessarily unformed as all sensations are." Surely Mallarmé's faun as Debussy portrays him in his tone poem, "The Afternoon of a Faun," would listen to music in terms of simple sensation.

We need not confine our observations to Mallarmé's faun. The warmth and beauty of a singer's voice are her greatest assets. Though it is possible to point out singers of great intelligence and artistic sensibility who have succeeded in spite of vocal limitations and to others whose personal charms have excused the fact that they sang badly, it nevertheless is true that beauty of voice is of supreme importance. Yet the idea of what is beautiful in vocal tone varies with one's place of birth and one's musical experience. To many Westerners the nasal white tone of the Chinese singer is so unpleasant that it prevents them from enjoying the music performed or even keeps them from perceiving that such a performance is music. This, however, is purely a matter of habit and education. A prominent educator, who was born in Constantinople and who spent his boyhood there, came to this country to complete his education. Shortly after his arrival he heard a performance of "The Messiah." He was deeply moved by the music, but found the voice quality of the soloist strange and unnatural. To this lad the vocal

[3]

quality of the East had become natural and our Western singing voice strange and disturbing.

Beauty of tone is not less important to the violinist. All the volumes which have been written about the violins of the old Italian masters, Stradivarius, Guarnerius, Amati, all the investigations into the nature of the varnish used by these makers, spring from the passionate conviction that these old master-violins produce a warm, vibrant, and rich sound. All great violinists of the present day possess a technique sufficient to play the literature of their instruments. In the case of well-established concert works the correct style and manner of performance have been fixed within fairly narrow limits. The tangible quality which differentiates violinist from violinist is tone. Perhaps the most personal factor in tone is what is known as vibrato, a rocking motion of the finger, wrist, and arm of the violinist as he presses the string down on the fingerboard. The early violinists did not employ this device but played a dead tone, simply pressing the string against the fingerboard and drawing the bow. In the seventeenth century the vibrato appears as an expressive accent, as an ornament, used only on important notes of a composition. As the art of performance developed, the violinist began to employ the vibrato on all notes of sufficient length as an expressive effect. The success of Fritz Kreisler and Mischa Elman was to no small degree due to the richness and warmth of their tone. Indeed, Elman has been reproached for using luscious tone even in passages where it was inappropriate. The public was pleased, however, thus furnishing one more testimony to the importance of sensuous beauty in the art of music.

One final example may be pointed out. The symphony orchestra owes a large part of its hold on the public to the fact that it is capable of a greater variety of color and nuance than any other musical instrument. Moreover, the fact that the stringed instruments are massed produces a kind of sound which is quite different from that of a solo instrument. Something is lost in terms of individual expressiveness, but anyone who has heard the cellos of the Philadelphia Orchestra playing a sustained melodic passage will realize the magnificent effects of which the massed strings are capable. We may regard the orchestra as an aggregation of soloists on all the instruments. The composer can announce a melody on a violin, let it pass to a flute, and then reiterate it with all the force of the full orchestra. It is this richness of tone color which makes it possible for the composer to write works for orchestra which have a longer duration than those for a solo instrument. Yet orchestral effects rest largely on sensuous beauty, the beauty of tone produced by the individual instrument and by the various instruments in combination.

Music is a time art which can only be comprehended by remembering what was heard in relation to what is heard. When we hear Beethoven's "Ninth Symphony," we must remember the opening theme of the first movement in order to recognize it when Beethoven introduces it into the final movement. This peculiarity of music is comparable to the cinema. In a screen play we must remember the characters and incidents of the earlier scenes in order to understand the development of the plot. The all too frequent plight of the movie-goer who arrives in the middle of the dramatic action only to be confronted with a series of apparently unrelated actions is not without a certain likeness to the music lover who is unable to remember the themes of a symphonic work and who therefore finds the work vague and pointless. In both arts immediate comprehension is not possible. It is necessary to wait while the work unfolds itself: It cannot be grasped at one moment but must be unified and understood by remembering the past and by relating the past to the present. Only when the work is completed can we be said to possess it. The importance of memory to the listener is thus clear. It is even more vital to the professional musician.

Musical memory is, however, a capacity which varies to

an incredible degree. Perhaps Mozart is the master who possessed this faculty in the highest measure. On one occasion he played at the piano a string quartet of Cambini from memory although he had to invent certain passages which he had forgotten. Even more remarkable was the feat of writing down the famous *"Miserere"* by Allegri from memory after one hearing. This work had been jealously guarded by the Sistine Choir which performed it during Holy Week. Mozart returned with the manuscript tucked into the crown of his hat in order to make pencilled corrections. He then sang the work to the chief sopranist of the choir who testified to the accuracy of the transcript, even to the traditional passages (*abbellimenti*) which were added in performance.

Complete musical memory implies the ability to repeat exactly what was heard, or at least a mental impression so clear that the music could be reproduced exactly if the listener possessed the necessary performing skill. Perhaps it is fortunate that a less exact form of musical memory can serve a useful purpose in listening to music. This is the stage at which a melody is not remembered completely but is recognized as familiar when it is heard again. Sometimes the listener, once the beginning of the tune is played, can anticipate what is to follow. This recognition of a tune is pleasurable by itself, and pleasure in recognition has in turn profoundly influenced the development of musical form.

Closely related to complete musical memory is musical imagery, the power of imagining sounds which are not actually heard. With the composer this may take the form of elaborating and combining melodies which are first imagined, then written down, and only then are actually played and heard. Some composers have possessed this quality to such a degree that they habitually composed "in their minds." Thus Camille Saint-Saëns writes of his childhood days, "As has always been the case with me, I was already composing the music directly on paper without working it out on the piano." In this case his conceptions exceeded his performing ability, for the waltzes which he wrote at this time were too difficult for him to play and had to be performed by a friend. It was the possession of this "inward ear" which enabled Beethoven to compose when he was completely deaf. The same capacity comes into play when we hear in imagination the sounds of the music as we look at the printed notes. This ability, which sometimes seems so mysterious to music lovers who lack systematic education in music, is in reality not mysterious at all. The same individuals would find nothing remarkable in the fact that the symbols forming the word "cat" convey a clear idea of the sound of the spoken word. In both cases we associate a symbol and a sound. The necessary drill in reading words, however, is more diligently practised, because of its practical value, than the comparable drill which is necessary if we are to read musical symbols with understanding.

One must keep in mind that the will to remember is a factor in determining whether music is or is not retained. Musical enthusiasts and many composers have developed the power of concentrating on the world of music to a remarkable degree. A charming letter of Mozart to his sister reveals that he was able to compose at Milan on his Italian tour under circumstances which would have driven most musicians to distraction. "Above us we have a violinist, below us is another, next to us a singing-master, who gives lessons, and in the room opposite, a hautboy-player. This is famous for a composer—it inspires so many fine thoughts." The promiscuous spraying of music over listeners by the radio has produced the listener who defends himself by willing not to hear. A recent survey shows that an astonishing percentage of the listeners to a commercially sponsored radio program did not know the name of the product which the program was designed to sell. The listener in self-defense has developed an immunity to commercials.

As a matter of fact, this question of the power of paying

attention to music goes still deeper. It required a long evolution before many individuals realized that music should be listened to. It required courage which often verged on desperation for the musician to insist on an attentive audience. Huygens was a learned man as well as a skilled lutenist. He was nevertheless flattered and honored to be invited to play for James II of England. The king hardly interrupted his card-playing from time to time to listen to his performance, and dismissed Huygens with the usual compliments when he had heard enough. An opera performance in Italy during the eighteenth century was a social affair which did not involve even the rather desultory amount of attention vouchsafed to the performance by the average opera-goer at the present time. "The Italians play at cards, receive visits, and take all sorts of refreshments in their boxes; they resemble little rooms, rather than boxes at a theatre. . . . The King's box is in the second row, and fronts the stage: it is 30 feet wide, and the back part is covered with looking-glasses, which reflect the stage, so that those who happen to have their backs turned to the actors, being either conversing or at play, may see the performance at the glasses."

Handel seems to have been the first musician who imposed himself on his audience and demanded silence. Even the presence of members of the royal family did not deter him from cursing vehemently and from calling the offending conversationalists by name. These outbursts were indulgently received by Frederic, Prince of Wales, and by the Princess, but they made him enemies who lost no opportunity of injuring him. Smaller and less violent men than Handel had to give in.

Nicola Matteis, a famous violin virtuoso active in England at the close of the seventeenth century, "did not please, and he was thought capricious and troublesome; as he took offence if any one whispered while he played, which was a kind of attention that had not been much in fashion at our court." Two or three admirers, however, undertook to bring him to a more complaisant state of mind with such success that "he became generally esteemed and sought after and having many scholars, though on moderate terms, his purse filled apace which confirmed his conversion."

Such were some of the slow and painful steps in a process which is still far from complete: the education of the audience to listen attentively and quietly to music. At least something has been accomplished, for, though present-day audiences are frequently noisy and distracting, most auditors realize that silent listening is considered desirable. The privileged audiences of an earlier day acknowledged no restraints of this kind. This is not to say that attentive listening did not exist at an early period. In contrast to the card-playing audiences of the opera houses were the fiercely passionate music lovers who dwelt on every note of an aria. There were the concerts of Louis XIII who listened to music with a few intimates. The ladies were excluded "because they always talk." During the song contests of the mastersingers "the other members of the Guild must abstain from conversation and noise in order that the singer may not be confused." By and large, however, audiences listened with desultory attention and often, in the case of exalted personages, with complete indifference to the fate of any melomaniacs who might prefer to listen to the music rather than to the conversation.

Continuous attention is very important in relation to musical memory. It also plays an important role in determining whether a given listener will respond to the more extended musical forms. The attention span of young children is short. This is generally recognized, and songs for the kindergarten are therefore short and easy to remember. Many adults also have very limited powers of concentration. A stanza of a popular song demands a minimum of attention. The remaining stanzas are sung to repetitions of the music for the original verse and chorus. In Italian opera of the eighteenth century which is composed of arias preceded by more dramatic passages of recitative, though the entire opera is lengthy, the individual numbers are not. It is possible to listen with satisfaction to a favorite aria and to neglect the passages which precede and follow. In such a case the dramatic element suffers; but, since the score is a mosaic of short detached compositions, each of these may be enjoyed as an independent unit. The music-dramas of Richard Wagner, on the other hand, lack the stops and fresh starts so characteristic of the older forms of opera. Much of the difficulty experienced by music-lovers when they make their first acquaintance with the Wagner music-dramas is due to the fact that a full understanding of them demands concentrated attention over a very considerable period of time. Wagner, indeed, probably erred in writing continuous developments which exceed the attention span of the average music-lover. Instrumental music might be studied in similar fashion to show not only that there is a gradual development in the power of the individual to listen attentively as he matures, but also that there has been an increase in the attention span of the audience as music has evolved forms which are progressively more extended and more complex.

A little reflection will convince us that this is so. Many of the dances composed by the violinists of the seventeenth and eighteenth centuries were tiny indeed and might be engraved on a line or two of the score. It is true that a performer would usually play a series of such dances arranged as a suite. Nevertheless, the continuous attention required of the listener was of small duration since each dance was complete in itself. Although the performance of a suite or sequence of dance movements might take several minutes, the individual dances were short and self-contained. If we examine a "lesson" or sonata by Domenico Scarlatti, we may find that it fills only two or three pages. A sonata by Beethoven would represent an enormous increase in playing time. (The *"Waldstein* Sonata" Op. 53, requires over thirteen pages for the first movement only in one edition.)

The development was thus twofold. The musician learned

to construct coherent musical units of increasing length. This went hand in hand with the development of the attention span of the audience. The musician moved in advance of his audience. The audience listened, lost the thread, yawned with boredom, tried again, and, if individually gifted and well-disposed, eventually learned to follow and even to anticipate the features of a familiar form. We can sometimes see that earlier efforts in a given form aim at clarity, at emphasizing the divisions of a composition, while later composers assume that the audience has the form in mind and allow melodies to develop with more freedom and fewer pauses for clarity. Thus, in a sonata by Haydn, the end of the first section is not only made clear by playing and repeating a closing formula of the most unambiguous kind, but the whole section is repeated to give the hearer every opportunity to become familiar with the themes employed. A work like the opening movement of the "First Symphony" of Brahms is almost monolithic. Where in Haydn each element is carefully set off from the other, in Brahms the stream of melody is almost uninterrupted from the magnificent kettle-drum pulsations of the introduction to the closing chord.

In such ways the audiences in successive generations learned to grasp compositions which were more extended and more fully developed. The art of the composer evolved in a parallel fashion so that the composer was able to conceive compositions of ampler breath with some confidence that they would be understood by his audience. Thus, at least one important aspect of music history is the gradual evolution of the power to pay attention to music for longer and longer periods of time. There are indications that this is not a development which will continue indefinitely. Music for a wealthy and idle but cultured leisure class could occupy more time than a modern concert. An audience which was subject neither to economic limitations nor to the fatigue which dulls the edge of our attention at the end of a working day could obviously enjoy operas of great length or extended concerts.

THE HUMAN SIDE OF MUSIC

The appetite for music in the courts of the seventeenth and eighteenth centuries was indeed enormous. We cannot compare such court music with the modern concert because court music was a part of the luxury of living, not an occasional event. If we turn to the oratorios of Handel, we find them too long for modern taste. As a result, even the "Messiah" is normally presented today with substantial cuts. Handel, however, frequently added music of a more appealing character between the parts of his oratorios. Mrs. Delany, Handel's friend and admirer, referred to this practice when she wrote to her mother, "My sister gave you an account of Mr. Handel's playing here for three hours together. I did wish for you, for no entertainment in music could exceed it, except his playing the organ in *Esther,* where he performs a part in two concertos, that are the finest things I ever heard in my life." The Handel practice was thus to exploit his great reputation as an organ virtuoso to induce light-minded listeners to accept his choruses.

The dilettanti of the classic period were so eager for music that they sometimes had a complete set of symphonies played at a single concert. Though such symphonies were diminutive compared with later works in this form, it was a robust appetite which could enjoy six in succession. We read, for example, that Gyrowetz "sold his first six symphonies to his Serene Highness Prince Kraźalkoviz who was a great amateur of music and maintained his own full orchestra, the director of which was Mr. Zissler. The Prince had the six symphonies performed at a concert which he arranged to which his Serene Highness Prince Esterházy and other great amateurs of music were invited who praised these symphonies highly and considered them good." Dittersdorf relates a similar anecdote. An aristocratic amateur was interested in a set of violin concertos. "Why not [have] the whole twelve [played] today?" he enquired. His friend explained that this would be exhausting for the artist. "Well that does make a difference. I never thought of it," replied the nobleman. Beethoven's concerts were not all of formidable length, but the one given at the *"Redoutensaal"* on February 27, 1814 included three symphonies (the "Seventh," the "Eighth," and the "Battle Symphony") in addition to selections from the composer's music to "The Ruins of Athens." At the present time a Sunday afternoon broadcast of the Philharmonic takes less than the alloted hour and a half, since much time is lost by preparatory and closing remarks and intermission features. An overture, a symphony, and a concerto would constitute a typical program.

On the other hand, the music for the laborer has always been the popular ballad and the folksong. This was not at all because the laborer did not have the capacity to appreciate music of large dimensions, but because his daily labors and his small earnings did not permit the leisure which the enjoyment of art music demands. His own voice was his instrument, his music a simple melody which was repeated till the words of his song were at an end. Yet all who know the folk music of any land will realize what poignancy may be compassed in these few measures.

The final meeting of music and consciousness is conditioned by two factors, the nature of the individual and the nature of his society. The musical nature of the individual is very largely determined by the society in which he lives. That society is molded to some infinitesimal degree by what each individual is and desires to be. On the one hand there is the solitary and inviolable meeting of the individual sensitivity with music, on the other, the group pattern which impels towards likeness, conformity, a common experience.

It is relatively easy to understand how we come to value and like certain compositions, the music of certain composers; how the cycle of taste operates. That, indeed, is the subject of the following chapter. It is far less easy to answer the question which is so frequently asked, "What is good music and what are musical values?" Yet in the answer to that question is the key to what the individual is musically and what he will become.

The heart of the difficulty lies in the fact that the valuing of music is a matter of emotional conviction, not of reason. A musician can easily show that a given piece is more complex than another, that one piece, because of its construction, demands a more sustained act of attention than another. Thus a fugue by Bach is, almost by definition, more complex than a song by Schubert. This is an objective difference and, indeed, is one of the factors which serves to separate music into categories. It does not necessarily follow that we will experience a Bach fugue more intensely than Schubert's brief but wonderfully concentrated song, "Death and the Maiden."

It is the nature and intensity of our emotional experience which makes us value music. Even this is not universally true. Indeed, it is possible to divide music-lovers into those who wish to be deeply stirred and those who prefer a milder experience on the level of distraction or entertainment. Thus certain of the Chopin "Nocturnes" and "Waltzes" display a politer and more elegant emotion than the grander lines of the "Ballades" or the wild fantasy of the "Scherzi." For those who still find the nostalgia and the melancholy of certain of these pages too intense there is the pretty sentimentality of a Friml, a Nevin, composers who echo with diminished intensity the idiom of the great romantics.

There are listeners who prefer to find in music merely an agreeable diversion. The intensity of musical experience (as far as it can be judged in the case of another individual) does not always seem to be closely related to the intensity of the music. The most banal pages of a song sung by a Frank Sinatra (to choose one ephemeral example out of many) seem capable of producing a reaction which is out of all proportion to their musical content. It must always be remembered that a musical experience is composed of two variable factors, the music itself and the sensitivity of the listener at the moment when the music is heard. Most musicians would agree that music does indeed vary in intensity. The Andante of Beethoven's "Fifth Symphony" is conceived in a nobler mood than Dvořák's "Humoresque." A listener who wished to be titivated, a frivolous listener who sought entertainment might be more moved by the less intense music, might, indeed, entirely fail to respond to the more deeply stirring strains.

It is precisely this double variability which makes it so difficult to establish musical values. Since intensity of emotional response is the key to our conviction that a given piece of music has value, the responses of a friend, of a professional musician do not always carry conviction. At the most such a difference in response can indicate that others find values where we do not. It may lead to repeated hearings of debatable works, and perhaps in the end to an understanding of and a feeling for musical works which had previously awakened no such response. This is the only service which one music-lover can render another, the enthusiasm which leads others to seek what one has discovered. But the final test has to be sought within the individual consciousness.

The problem is further complicated by the simulated response to music. There are always many listeners who find it simpler and safer to trust to the reactions of others than to look within and judge as best they may by their own feelings. Though their own responses are thus made valueless (perhaps because they are not very pronounced in any case, perhaps because the desire to be in style is stronger than the desire to know oneself musically), such listeners do have a pronounced effect on musical taste. Though they could never initiate a trend, they are always on the alert to find out what they should like. Once they are assured that a given composition is approved of by connoisseurs, they become doubly enthusiastic. Thus they may be said to perform a certain function by reinforcing or hastening the peak of popularity of a work which would have succeeded in any case. They also join lustily in the hue and cry which leads to the re-

[15]

placement of a symphonic conductor or the decline of a former musical idol.

Yet perhaps it is wrong to insist too exclusively on individual experience. Musical experience is indeed an individual matter, but not exclusively so. We must still account for the considerable amount of likeness in musical taste displayed in any historic period. We must assume the transmission of musical enthusiasms from individual to individual which produces a certain likeness of sensibility among the music-lovers of a given generation.

One factor which has made such a likeness surer and more complete is the fact that music (in the sense of concert and ceremonial music) has been predominantly a social experience. We sit, each in our own seat, at Carnegie Hall, yet we are conscious of our neighbors. The applause at the end of a composition is a symbol of the influence which we exert on each other. Applause generates applause. We find ourselves joining in, unwilling to withhold what our right-hand neighbor is performing so vigorously. It is a bold soul indeed (as well as an unmannerly one) who would venture to boo or hiss a composition which has aroused the other members of the audience to the heights of enthusiasm.

Applause is, of course, a convention, and one which is frequently a tribute to the persistence of habit rather than an indication of any real internal fire. But it is only the most apparent indication of the common verdict which we render at any concert. The obvious boredom of the fat gentleman who reads the advertisements in the program instead of listening to the music, the tense attention of a schoolgirl, the whispered critical comment, are only a few of the thousand criticisms, implicit or expressed, each a personal expression, each a factor influencing others.

There is also our link with the performer. He marches out on the platform. He seats himself at the instrument, adjusts the piano bench, glances at the audience, glares balefully at late-comers and finally begins to play. His gait, his gestures at the keyboard reinforce the sounds which he produces from the piano. Perhaps he does not disdain the coquetry of a spotlight, the darkened auditorium which merges the audience into a uniform twilight and leaves the artist in solitary radiance, the dramatic gesture, effective from a histrionic point of view but perhaps not a necessary act in piano playing. When he bows, he bows compellingly. There he is, his task completed. We must do ours. We respond to his unspoken appeal, moved by a warm enthusiasm for the work which we have just heard, by sympathy for the artist and a delight in his performance, by a natural wish to clap as loud as our neighbors. These reactions, and a thousand currents of mutual sympathy, pleasure at a happily turned phrase, hero worship, boredom, distraction, build this threefold relationship which, with the exchange of comments in the intermission and the heated discussions which follow, build a certain characteristic reaction, though one which appears much more unified in historical perspective than at the moment. Though our reaction to music is inevitably solitary, unique, it is experienced in a social setting which modifies it from the moment of its inception.

Daniel Gregory Mason in an essay on "The Depreciation of Music" points out a fact which all thoughtful observers have noted, the fact that the radio does not compel our attention to the same extent as an actual performance in the concert hall. Professor Mason, however, who dislikes machines and dislikes business as well, blames this effect on the "standardized, wholesale, impersonal quality" of "music from the machine" and on the "well-nigh insoluble psychological problem of the passivity of the listener." But are these really the reasons for the conditions which he describes?

One might with entire justice reproach the machine because it fails to reproduce music accurately. The player-piano with "the exuberant spirits of a machine-gun," the phonograph with its needle scratch, its pauses which inter-

[17]

rupt the current of our musical thought as the record-changer does its work are defective machines. They are a part of a mechanical technique which is already obsolescent, which will be improved, which has to some extent already been improved. It is, however, hardly fair to oppose the machine because it is a machine.

Mr. Mason insists on the "uniqueness, particularity and personal reference" of musical experience. Would he claim that such an experience was more personal, unique in the midst of a great crowd at Carnegie Hall than in a solitary vigil beside the radio? Is not the real difference the fact that when we listen to a broadcast we are confronted with musical tones, shorn of marginal associations, deprived of the visual showmanship of the concert (though the announcer works hard to supplement this lack with vocal enthusiasms and descriptions, and television will perhaps restore these factors once more), lacking that subtle interchange of enthusiasms, sympathies which corroborate our own musical passions or rouse us to opposition? We are a little uneasy without these echoes and reverberations of the moods and convictions of fellow-listeners. The personality of the artist can only be perceived by the sounds we hear (perhaps dulled somewhat by the imperfections of transmission), and this is too severe a test for us. We are alone with music.

First there is the individual, then the circle of listeners in the concert hall, then the nation, the larger cultural unit of which we are a part. What are we musically that differentiates us from other peoples, other times?

Much of what we are is implicit in our musical history. Psalm tunes intoned in the forest clearings of New England, echoes of French folksong on the banks of the great northern rivers, Moravian chorales, Scotch and English ballads sung in log cabins, plain-chant resounding in isolated missions, under the vaultings of baroque cathedrals. Arts diverse, scattered, surviving in isolation.

The first of our own music-makers appeared. A cultivated

amateur, Francis Hopkinson learned to speak the musical language of the eighteenth century and left us a slender sheaf of songs. William Billings, bumptious and independent, tanner, singing master, composed hymns of a charming and naive simplicity. The mystics of Pennsylvania, closely united with their fellows in the bond of a common language and a common religious belief, laboriously transcribed a voluminous literature of chorales.

We became a commercial people with ships which crossed and recrossed the Atlantic. Those ships brought back harpsichords as well as textiles and tools. With leisure, with the increase of wealth, we bought the products of English cabinetmakers, brocaded silk dresses and the services of dancing masters, of singers, and of instrumental performers.

Our art music, at first frankly provincial, a distant echo of European culture, gained impetus. By the mid-nineteenth century we were sending our talented musicians to Europe, importing great European artists to play for us. The stages of our cultural development were foreshortened. We rapidly acquired all that Europe could offer. The most violent contrasts obtained. Pianos were shipped to the West to stand on wooden platforms in dirt-floored cabins.

Americans flocked to hear artists only if they were famous enough. We adored personalities. Ole Bull, Jennie Lind, gigantic musical festivals occupied us in turn. The skillful manipulation of public opinion, a childish delight in the extraordinary, the tremendous, the sensational was symbolized in Barnum who promoted Jennie Lind and the Fegee Mermaid with equal success. Theodore Thomas, who brought the music of Wagner to American audiences, played a tune for a group of armed cowboys on a Western station platform. We sent a Lowell Mason, a Gottschalk, a MacDowell to Europe but listened with delight to the homespun ditties of minstrel troupes, to the ballads of the Hutchinson family, to the Stephen Foster songs. While wealthy patrons were transplanting composers from Europe to America, European-trained American composers were wondering how an American should compose.

Our mechanical inventiveness, our business acumen, our achievement of mass production made music a general possession to a degree that no industrial civilization had yet realized. We made the piano a symbol of prosperity. We broadcast copies of the Foster songs over the whole nation. We hesitated and then admitted music into our public schools. This was a symbol of the reaching out of a whole people for music which had revealed itself in a thousand less formal ways, in the play party, the camp-meeting, the singing school, the choral society.

The great pioneering projects of the nineteenth century made endless demands for labor, and great waves of immigration swept across the continent bringing with them folk-tales and folksong, musical tastes and preferences which formed cultural islands here and there. These islands were only partly obliterated by the drive to erase the contributions of these varied cultures in favor of a chauvinistic and provincial Americanism, an Americanism which often forgot or never knew the true breadth and greatness of the foundations of our land.

Music ceased to be something imported. Our symphony orchestras, even the Metropolitan Opera Association, moved partly by the shortage of artists during two World Wars, partly by the appearance of promising native artists, depended less on imported European talent. Our musical life, nourished by a still unsurpassed industrial potential, outshone a Europe broken and weakened by two World Wars, though Mexico and South and Central America steadily increase in importance. Our composers, many and gifted, hardly achieve the individual significance and prominence of their predecessors of the nineteenth century. Their diversity of style and the divergence of their expressive aims betray the stamp of a period of transition, the search for a new great style commensurate with that formed by the giants of nineteenth century Europe. But if we cannot claim dominating figures, we can lay claim to a richness and diversity of creative activity which is probably unmatched and which may remain so. In Europe a few great figures survive from the interval between two great wars. Many of the potential singers, instrumentalists, composers are dead. Much depends on us and on our neighbors to the south who remained relatively untouched by the devastation of World War II. Much depends on us as members of the audience, the final court of appeals for artist and composer. What are we like and how do we differ from other audiences?

We may answer the question quite simply by saying that our clearly marked characteristics are our wealth, with all its obvious inequities of distribution, our tremendous material and cultural resources, our diversity of thought and background, and our incipient democratization of music.

It is unnecessary to labor the first point. European and native critics have reproached us with material mindedness and our worship of wealth, and, no doubt, they had a sufficient justification for the strictures. Other nations have admired our abundance of electric refrigerators, autos, bathroom fixtures, radios, pianos, phonographs.

What is not always made so clear is the intimate dependence of things of the spirit, of music, on wealth and on technology. Without these things, music as we know it would cease to exist. A folk culture which grew up under poverty and material bareness could survive under those conditions. Such a culture, though it persists as a symbolic and fertilizing influence, can be said to flourish only in marginal areas of the United States. In England folksong has already passed. Only perhaps in the Soviet Union do we have the immediate contact of living folksong and the developed music of a modern industrial society.

Jazz and swing have been claimed as our folk arts, but they are so only in origin and perhaps in informal "jam sessions." Their milieu, night club, movie theatre, dance hall, their extremely competitive business character, their highly colored publicity, their assembly-line methods of composition and orchestration belong to the modern industrial world. Modern popular song, like Disney's cartoons, can justly be called a popular art but not a folk art unless we are willing to inject a totally new content into an accepted term. Nevertheless, they are both infinitely characteristic of us, not only in content, but even more in their highly industrialized and commercialized modes of production and distribution.

We have tended to admire the composer, the artist who was willing to sacrifice material gain for artistic integrity. We should do so. At the same time we should realize that the elements of the culture of which this composer is a part are twofold in nature,—on the one hand wealth and technology, on the other spiritual and emotional life, musical imagination and craftsmanship.

But where in more primitive cultures the need for wealth or manufacturing skill was small, our society makes enormous demands on both. A Beethoven symphony required a Beethoven, but it was inconceivable without a concentration of wealth, a technology of some complexity. Thus our wealth, our industrial capacity are to be regarded as the prerequisites for a highly developed musical art. The question is rather whether we are making them serve our highest interests.

The United States is unique in the fact that its cultural diversity is a recently transplanted diversity—from many peoples one nation speaking one language. This unlikeness of culture, a tradition of individual independence which was in part a product of economic self-sufficiency and isolation, has given place to a collective interdependence.

The immigrant (whether he arrived recently or in colonial days) carried with him something of the culture of his natal land. These ties brought us the song of the voyageur, the brisk lilt of the Creole song, the graceful melodic curve of Latin-American melody, the plaintive cadence of the spiritual. There was, especially in more recent years, the over-enthusiastic desire of the immigrant to conform, a carelessness or indifference to the loyalties of parents or grandparents. This was made more intense by the contempt of the American herd for anything different or foreign. It was made doubly complex by the fact that our composers went to Germany, later to France only to return and imitate European models at the same time that most of us scorned the folkways of those humbler Europeans who had come to our shores. Yet something persisted, some echo of the songs sung by peoples of many tongues, something that we can hear in Farwell's "Sourwood Mountain," in Goldmark's "Negro Rhapsody," in Chavez' *"Sinfonia India,"* in MacDowell's "Second (Indian) Suite," in Gottschalk's *"La Savane. Ballade Creole,"* something which is regional and American and at the same time English or Negro, Mexican, Indian or Creole, something which shows that we are richer for that wealth of folksong which is part of our national heritage.

Our industries have developed selling techniques which have interpenetrated every phase of our lives, a technique which is employed to sell music as well as automobiles. An advertisement, whether of a piano, a symphony, or a fireless cooker is an interested statement. It is designed not so much to reveal truth as to sell goods. It is more convenient, more in accordance with the requirements of mass production to standardize products, to make as general an appeal as possible, but to do so on the assumption of a low and elementary sensitivity and intelligence rather than on the highest possible level. This trend is most evident in the field of the movie, the radio broadcast, the popular song. Since all these are educative factors, they tend to hold popular taste at their own level rather than raise it, to stimulate a demand for musical goods at a level which lends itself readily to mass production.

Music in the United States may one day be for the people, not for some but for all, not a symbol of the power of wealth but a common heritage. We are far from the realization of such a condition, yet we have gone far enough to make musical democracy more than a fancy. The old singing master who wandered from place to place teaching the young people their notes made one step. Lowell Mason who pronounced, almost with an air of surprise, that more people were capable of learning to sing than was generally realized, marked an advance which was to bring music into the schools with the three R's. The publishers who kept two (sometimes three) printing presses busy turning out copies of "Old Folks at Home" did their part as did Edison who invented a strange little hand-cranked phonograph in his laboratory.

Theodore Thomas took his orchestra on tour and brought symphonic music to many Americans who had never heard it before. The musicians of the W. P. A. Music Project were able to create new audiences even in a great music center like New York. All the factors which made material America entered into the development of our music: our wealth, our idealism, our industrial production, our love of the arts, and above all a sound feeling that the good things are for all, not for a few. This, however, is an ideal still unattained. Masses of our people, badly housed, inadequately fed, underpaid, are still deprived of music, for they lack the economic basis on which alone a good life can be built. Until they attain that security, music can hardly reach them, and until it does, musical democracy remains an ideal still unattained.

CHAPTER II

THE MECHANISM OF TASTE

TASTE implies choice. Choice is only possible when several alternatives are present. In this sense perhaps no period has presented a greater opportunity for musical choices than the present. The variety of music available now is greater than at any other period in history. This is not only true in terms of the amount of contemporary music of all kinds which is performed. It is also true of music of the past. Zealous scholars have been extending our musical horizons. As a result, a curious listener may have a considerable knowledge of the music of Bach in the eighteenth century, of that of Lassus in the sixteenth century, even of that of Machaut and of Perotinus at still more remote periods. Indeed, historical curiosity is one of the characteristics of our time, limited though that curiosity may be to a mere fraction of the listening public and a few scholars and enthusiastic performers.

At the same time anthropologists and folklorists have been busy collecting the music of primitive peoples, their folksongs and folk tales. Such material reaches the concert hall only when a composer selects a theme of this kind for treatment. Chavez, for example, treats indigenous Mexican motives and rhythms in his *"Sinfonia India."* Yet in spite of this, such music does have a limited circulation among specialists and, in certain categories, with a wider public. "Hawaiian music," hill-billy music, cowboy songs, barn-dance tunes are heard over the air, often in forms which are dull caricatures of their originals. Yet they do have a relationship, however tenuous, with styles which are at the periphery of the concert world, with styles which, a generation ago, would have been familiar only to isolated regional groups. Thus the present century, in spite of the material and spiritual destruction caused by two world wars, has witnessed a tremendous widening of the scope of music in terms of the variety, the amount, the geographical and chronological range of the music heard.

It is only possible to see such a picture in its true perspective if it is placed against other situations, other cultures. An American Indian of pioneer days would know the traditional songs of his people. If he went to visit a neighboring tribe, he would very probably learn some of their social or dance songs and would sing them on his return. If they found favor, some of them might become popular among his own people. Since the Indians had a strong conviction that a song belonged to someone, he would be careful to mention the original owner. Though a certain exchange of music might take place in this way, the style of the new songs was similar to those which the Indian already knew. Only where missionaries came in contact with them would Indian singers become familiar with music of a markedly different character, the chants of Catholic missions, the hymns of the Protestant Church.

Yet even this situation is relatively flexible compared to those where music is regarded not so much as a pleasurable part of social intercourse as a part of an elaborate system of magic designed to insure good crops, adequate rainfall, to avert or to mitigate possible disasters. Here the whole basis for musical choice, as we know it, is absent. A magic song was sung, not to produce a pleasurable effect, but (in conjunction with the proper text and ritual) to secure certain desirable effects or to avert those which were undesirable. If the song were changed, it lost its efficacy. What was sought was the exact repetition of a formula which was regarded as powerful.

Thus the mere possibility of musical choice is the result of a long historical evolution. Yet it is possible to see that the area of choice was always less where magic or religion was concerned, greater where music was used for individual or group solace or amusement.

Choice not only involves the presence of alternatives. It also implies, if the decision is to represent anything personal, that the social pressures exerted on the individual are not so overwhelming as to preclude all choices but one. But from childhood to old age every individual is subject to influences which determine to a large extent what music he will hear. Such influences are exerted by members of the family group, by friends, by religious groups, by national and political organizations, by business interests.

The normal reaction of the individual is compliance. Yet, since human nature is as it is, music-lovers sometimes seize avidly on an inconspicuous element in their environment and reject what is most abundantly offered to them. Thus an amateur musician may go to concerts of Elizabethan music by preference in an environment which offers a hundred performances of Brahms' "First Symphony" to one of Dowland's "Lachrimae." Loeffler spent his mature years in Boston and Medford yet produced music which has echoes of Celtic lore, childhood memories of Russia, music which reflects the subtle melancholy of the French impressionists, but which surely drew no nourishment from his immediate environment. In general, however, the cradle songs a child hears, the hymns and chants of the church which he attends, the patriotic songs which he learns to sing, all these form him musically before he is able to make conscious choices for himself.

Thus every music-lover is bounded by a circle. Within all is familiar, the well-loved composers, the familiar compositions. Outside is strange and alien music, old music, new music, queer and disturbing music of all kinds. This boundary, however, is a shifting one. We continually take in and absorb new experiences, we reject the over-familiar, the strange and remote. Our musical experiences tend to establish certain musical patterns as usual for us, and by this very fact erect psychological barriers against music of other kinds.

[27]

The Chinese child will hear music in the pentatonic scale, will relish the nasal voice quality of the oriental singer, the shrill tones of the Chinese fiddle. The boy of the southern Appalachians will hear the dulcimer and the banjo and learn the traditional ballad airs, "Barbara Allen" and the "Raggle-Taggle Gypsies." City children in our own country are likely to develop an ear attuned to the swing band and the juke box unless their parents exercise a censorship of an extraordinarily effective kind.

Such limitations are at once desirable and undesirable. Just as local peculiarities of thought and behavior can crystallize into a pattern of life which presents interesting and desirable features, so also can it harden into barbarism or intolerant provincialism. In a similar fashion, the limitations of one's musical environment may be accepted and may harden into fixed habits which make a sympathetic approach to novel music impossible, which stand as a barrier to personal development. On the other hand, an early contact with music of special characteristics may enrich one's experience without lessening an appreciation of music of quite a different kind.

Nevertheless, basic musical experiences, without precluding the possibility of choice, establish an area within which choices are likely to be made. Thus an English villager of the last century might sing in the church choir and learn the hymns and psalm tunes practiced there. He might acquire some skill on the violin and play for the local morris-dance team or for country dancing on the village green. He might repeat the ballads and the folksongs which he had heard his father sing. He would not be likely to hear the Beethoven symphonies since they were not a part of his environment. If by chance he heard them, he would have lacked the background of experience which alone could make them comprehensible.

The musical choices of a young man growing up in New York at the present time would be wider because the different kinds of music available are infinitely more varied and also because there are marked oppositions and conflicts within the environment itself. In some cases such conflicts are largely musical in nature. Are the later works of Stravinsky revelations of new facets of his genius or are they slight and brittle pieces which reveal his deterioration as a composer? In other cases the music is a symbol of conflicting ideas. The voices raised to praise or condemn the Shostakovich "Seventh" or "Leningrad Symphony" were influenced not only by the sounds they heard, but by the convictions and feelings which were embodied in those sounds. Nor is this association of music with political ideas as new as some would have us think. One can readily grant that a man whistling "Yankee Doodle" in the year 1776 or "We will hang Jeff Davis to a sour apple tree" during the Civil War was expressing more than a taste in melody. But it is precisely the presence of opposition and conflict which makes choice possible, indeed, inevitable.

Our imaginary New Yorker must decide whether to listen to Frank Sinatra, Bing Crosby, Harry James, Jascha Heifetz, Vladimir Horowitz, Arturo Toscanini. His experiences of religious music might be gained in a Methodist Church, a Catholic Cathedral, a Jewish Synagogue. He would surely hear a great variety of music at the movies or at the radio no matter whether he wished to listen or not. He might go to the Philharmonic at Carnegie Hall, to the Goldman Band in Central Park, or he might listen to Harry James at the Paramount. He might develop into a lover of symphonic music or a fancier of swing. He would be rather unlikely to develop a taste for Chinese opera or for the motets of Victoria though even such relatively esoteric tastes might be satisfied in such a multicolored environment.

In most instances the framework within which musical tastes will develop is well established before the individual has become very conscious of it. What are the factors which determine conscious musical choice? They may be divided into two groups. The first will consist of factors which con-

[29]

trol the amount of repetition which music receives. The second is a resultant of the personal tastes, beliefs, prejudices, enthusiasms, dislikes of the individual listener and of the members of his circle.

Music, however, has passed into a stage of development in which business motives are perhaps stronger than at any earlier period. The musician has passed from a society in which his living was granted him in return for his assistance in courtly and religious functions to one in which he must sell his wares as a business man or disappear. At the same time the alliance between music and advertising has become closer than ever before. The obnoxious "singing commercial" over the radio is only the most obvious example of a tendency that spreads far and penetrates deeply into our musical life. Since music is a chief aid in radio advertising propaganda, it is to the interest of the advertiser to announce the performers and the compositions on sponsored radio programs in such a way as to convince us of their excellence. The praise of music and other goods for ulterior motives is hardly new. Never, however, have the forces of advertising and propaganda been so powerful, so highly organized, and so centralized as they are at present. Never has it been so difficult for an individual to feel and to judge with precision without being influenced by partisan statements.

In the previous section repetition was stressed as a crucial factor in influencing our musical tastes. It is, indeed, true that the very basis for our appreciation of a musical composition is the repeated experience of that work. Yet the effect of repetition is complex. A piece of music is heard with increased satisfaction as it becomes familiar. Increase the amount of repetition sufficiently, and it ceases to please. An intolerable amount of repetition may incite the victim to rage and even violence. The rate at which music ceases to give pleasure varies with the complexity of the music. The more complex the music, the more repetitions are required for it to reach its peak of popularity. Thus a popular song may rise to dominate the air waves in a matter of weeks and with the passing of a few more weeks may disappear more or less finally and completely. A fugue of Bach or a symphony by Mozart may be more popular with audiences a hundred years later than with contemporary listeners.

In our daily musical experience, however, the amount of repetition which any work receives is conditioned by a number of factors. One is the date of the work, its remoteness or nearness to our time. The reasons for the infrequent performances of early music are easy to understand. Music as it recedes into the past becomes unfamiliar. Its traditions are less clear than those of more recent works whose composers still live and can explain and demonstrate their intentions. Early music presents to the uninitiated listener a similarity and uniformity of style which is largely a result of a lack of familiarity. A common and thoughtless observation states that all Chinamen look alike. In a similar vein a skilled pianist once remarked that all eighteenth century pieces sounded the same. A more intimate acquaintance with music of that period will reveal a great variety of style, though this does not preclude that general resemblance which music of any one historical period will possess.

Gradually, as we go back into the shadows of history, the musical language changes, the sounds of the instruments and their forms differ from those which we use today. Finally the music itself no longer stirs us. It no longer communicates emotion but becomes merely a subject for curious speculation. It is not difficult to see why pianists prefer the more certain rewards of recent music with an occasional polite excursion back to Scarlatti and Couperin. Yet much music of the past lives in the present. The works of Bach surely seem more rich, more vivid today than they did to his own contemporaries. A lifetime of repetition was not enough for his music. More time and a different cultural climate were needed, for with the passing years his compositions have gained in eloquence. The music-lover should recognize that it is because scholars and students have served as intermediaries between the past and the present that the music of the Renaissance, for example, seems more real and vivid to us than to audiences of fifty years ago.

The amount of repetition which music receives lessens as the music is older. It increases as we approach the present. It is, however, the music of yesterday rather than that of today which is most warmly received. Very recent serious music has not yet had time to become familiar. Audiences are timid, and performers and conductors must choose their repertories with an anxious eye on the audience. Most members of their audiences resent real novelty because it requires an effort at comprehension which they would prefer not to make.

One of the amusing things about music criticism is its uniformity. Haydn wrote noisy music. Beethoven must be pardoned for his later compositions which were the result of his deafness. With Wagner the indignation of the critics reached a climax which considerably exceeded the limits of gentlemanly behaviour and makes curious reading for the present generation. Each generation of composers writes music which is unmelodious and confused. One should not infer from these statements that adverse criticism is a sure stepping-stone to fame. What it does prove is the painful and bewildering effect on the audience of a relatively slight change in the musical language, a condition which could be further illustrated by the indignant subscribers who rose and tramped down the aisles at the sound of the wild music of the 1920's.

Another kind of remoteness is spacial or geographical. This factor, which was formerly of the greatest importance, has been drastically diminished in significance by the development of modern systems of transport and communication without entirely disappearing. Medieval courts and monasteries were musical islands, visited now and again by travellers, but affected only gradually by outside changes. Travel was slow, tedious, and dangerous. A composer's reputation might well repose with his manuscripts on the shelves of some remote library. The quickening of trade, the improvement of roads, the building of larger and better ships created as many channels for the spread of music. The fusion of musical cultures went hand in hand with the development of better means of communication and travel.

Telemann, a contemporary of Bach, visited Poland and, according to his own account, arranged the Polish themes which he heard there in Italian style. Handel, Saxon by birth, received profound musical impressions in Rome but spent most of his life composing for a London public. In the eighteenth century Europeans were pleased with "chinoiseries" in the decorative arts and by Eastern effects in music, the "Turkish Rondo" of Mozart, for example.

To this cosmopolitanism which was so typical of the eighteenth century we must oppose the nationalism of the nineteenth century which tended to develop music within the border of a single nation and to use its power as an incentive to national patriotism. The Germanic element in Wagner's music and writings, the devotion of Chopin to the rhythms of his native Poland, the "Hungarian Rhapsodies" of even so cosmopolitan a figure as Franz Liszt, all testify to this growing consciousness of musical nationality.

The development of music within the United States has deviated from this pattern. The United States is diverse culturally since it has been from the beginning a fusion of many peoples from many different parts of the world. Our instrumentalists, our singers stem from a multitude of nationalities as do the audiences of our great cities. Thus our musical tastes are varied, and many of our composers have tended to speak musically with an accent or have sought rather anxiously for an authentic American style.

This process touched the masses of our people very little if at all. Most of them were too poor or too remote to have much contact with professional music. The phonograph and the radio represented successive advances in cultural diffusion. They poured out music of all kinds over the whole nation, ballads, ragtime and jazz, folksongs, negro spirituals, Viennese waltzes and operettas, classics of the eighteenth and nineteenth centuries. All this and much more pour from the loud speaker. Geographical barriers have, to a very large degree, been removed. Yet they have not entirely vanished. Though the music we hear owes many of its peculiarities to the conditions of its origin among different peoples in different places, we still do not have any real contact with many musical styles; nor do we hear all the available styles with equal frequency. Balinese music and the native music of North Africa, for example, play an extremely small (though perceptible) role in our musical life. What we seem to have is not only a wider diffusion of more varied music but also the predominance of the type which evidently suits the means of diffusion best. We may call this the triumph of the juke-box. A glance at the tunes listed on the record selector of a well-serviced juke-box would give a very fair idea of the music which is most widely played in our country today and which will be heard in the South Seas, in Japan, and Germany tomorrow or even this afternoon. The next decade will see the forces which make for internationalism in music tested against those which produce regionalism and nationalism. The simple fact that radio waves do not stop at town lines or national boundaries will be a powerful factor operating for a world idiom in music.

Space has ceased to be an obstacle to the spread of music. When Olin Downes, the music critic of the "New York Times," visited Tiflis in the Caucasus in 1932, he had considerable difficulty in persuading a café orchestra to stop playing American popular music long enough to play their own folk melodies. Downes received in return a request from the orchestra. "Although the company here prefers jazz, the orchestra has done all it could under the circumstances to play as much Caucasian music as it dared for the gentleman's entertainment. . . . Provided the American gentleman is pleased

. . . will he please on returning to New York, send them the music and the parts of the latest fox trot? It is a long and difficult task to get it here!"

This may be contrasted with the eighteenth century when Bach had to make a laborious journey on foot to become acquainted with the style of an organist in a city only thirty miles away. It may be compared with the folk music of the Pyrenees where the peasants in one valley have preserved local customs and songs quite different from those in the next since the channels of communication run along the valleys, not across the mountain ridges.

What the airplane has accomplished for travel, the radio and the phonograph have done for music. Yet the musical invasion of one culture by another is no new thing. The contact between Spanish and Moorish music, the intermingling of Eastern and Western music at the time of the Crusades, are only two of many examples. The phenomenal spread of opera all over Europe from its original focus in Italy is one of the chief facts of musical development during the seventeenth and eighteenth centuries. All these cultural transfers took place while transportation was relatively primitive.

By the time the phonograph had become an important factor in musical development, enterprising business men had penetrated to Russia and the Orient and had recorded the voices of Russian opera singers and of the singing girls of the East. Radio completed the conquest of space, spanning the American continent, then transcontinental space.

Yet in spite of these developments cultural remoteness still lingers. It exists because millions of people still do not have the phonograph or the radio to listen to. It exists because of national antagonisms, the hostility of those within a group to those outside it. It exists because few individuals have the power or the will to enter perfectly into two cultures. In addition, the spread of a culture is usually no equitable exchange but rather the conflict of a conquering and a vulnerable way of life.

[35]

THE HUMAN SIDE OF MUSIC

Although a people may be exploited in an economic sense, they may still exert a great influence on music. This is true of the American Negro. Here a group of people who are discriminated against, who are largely relegated to the performance of undesirable and menial tasks, have been able to influence musically the culture under which they live. Negro spirituals and work songs, the minstrel show, jazz, swing, the blues, all have left their imprint on our musical culture, yet all were to some degree Negro in character. It is even possible to see Negro influence on certain of the folksongs collected from white singers in the Appalachian regions, on such white composers as Gottschalk, Chadwick, Dvořák, Gruenberg, and Gershwin. Indeed the latter was to find in "Porgy and Bess" one of his most congenial subjects. That he was able to treat such a subject with complete naturalness was due not only to his own gift for assimilation but also to the fact that American popular music has made the Negro's contribution its own.

In the long run the problem of cultural isolationism may be replaced by the question as to how much local and regional music can survive the gigantic process of hybridization which has been in progress during the present century. This is not to say that the phonograph or the radio necessarily works for any particular culture. An American composer was present in Syria when a native appeared with a phonograph on which he played recordings of Indian music in exchange for small coins from interested listeners. Generally, however, it may be said that the music of Western industrial civilization is one music with only slight local variations in France, England, the United States, and the other industrial powers and that it is the dominant music of our period.

The result on the one hand is the extinction or hybridization of all other musical cultures. Thus South African Negro music has assumed a pronounced European character. In China pupils of Alexander Tcherepnin have produced music for piano which, though Chinese in melodic character, utilizes Western conceptions of melodic combination and piano writing. In Japan we find a most curious imitation of our own popular music in the form of Japanese jazz.

The forces influencing regional cultures are in some cases powerful, in some cases insignificant, in all cases worthy of note. In our own country the older idea of the "melting pot," in which our new citizens were to be purged of all foreign influences to emerge as 100% Americans, has been followed by an attempt to preserve whatever color and beauty the immigrant may have brought with him. In the Soviet Union official encouragement has been given to the collection of the folksongs and folk-dances of the constituent republics, and composers have been encouraged to use such material in their scores. The American Negro has to some degree realized the importance of understanding and studying the African peoples from which he had his origin. Mexican students have been penetrating beneath the veneer of Spanish music to distinguish the Indian traits which are so basic in Mexican life. These are a few of the many aspects of the struggle between the forces working towards cultural unity on a world-wide scale and those which make for the preservation of regional characteristics. What balance will ultimately be achieved can only be revealed by the future.

Two final observations may be made. The means for a world-wide diffusion of cultural traits are in effective existence. The music of Western industrial civilization is in the ascendent. There are, however, clear indications that other forces which would encourage regional music are growing in strength and may play an important part in the final decision.

The barriers of space may be overcome. Time preserves its secrets better. This is true for two reasons: the imperfection of the historical record and the alterations in human sensitivity to music. It is common knowledge that our information about ancient man is based not necessarily on the most important evidence, but rather on what was most durable.

Since stone is enduring, we know much about early sculpture. But nothing in the arts is so evanescent, so fleeting, as sound. As a result, though we know something of early musical instruments, we know almost nothing about the music which was played on them. Before man was able to imprison sound by inventing a notation, Babylonian civilization had developed. Or are the puzzling cuneiform characters incised on an ancient clay tablet truly a musical notation? Have we really learned to reproduce the Gregorian chants as they were sung from the earliest notations, notations which indicated the pitch of the various tones only in a vague fashion? Can we be certain of the rhythmic interpretation of troubadour songs when the written record often consists of a series of uniform notes? Do we interpret the dynamics of Mozart correctly from the sparsely scattered symbols in his manuscripts?

Probably only when the sounds of music could be captured on phonograph record, on photographic film or wire did we reach the point where a music tradition could be really preserved, not in bare outline (and no notation preserves more than this) but as a living performance. This has happened within the present century. Nevertheless we do hear Gregorian chant, troubadour songs, and Mozart symphonies. If these renditions do not reproduce the exact inflections of the original performances, some, at least, conform to historical probability. What is more important is the fact that this music still can move us, still remains music.

The subtler factor which influences our attitude towards the music of the past is the alteration in our own musical sensibility which distinguishes our response from that of the audiences which first heard the music which we now hear. It might be difficult to find an auditor of our period who would be deeply touched by the music of Gottschalk's "Dying Poet" or "Last Hope". This is not because we are untouched by music but because we differ from our Victorian ancestors in our feeling for pathos and sentiment. The music remains fixed on the printed page, but its effect on us has changed. What was touching and pathetic has somehow become vapid or even comic.

Perhaps no music has undergone more amazing vicissitudes in succeeding generations than that of Bach. It is difficult to assess contemporary reactions to his music because, though we possess eloquent tributes to his skill as a performer, we know little of how his own audiences reacted to his music. A comparison of his music with that of his contemporaries would indicate that he was a conservative composer clinging to the past, that he could have had little sympathy with the new trends which were to lead to the music of Mozart and Haydn.

The Bach revival dates from the romantic period, and it was a new Bach whom they discovered, a romantic Bach. His music for harpsichord became piano music. His music was retouched (notably by such masters as Mendelssohn and Robert Franz). Mendelssohn and Schumann did not appreciate the unique quality of his works for unaccompanied violin and furnished them with piano accompaniments. At a later period Busoni produced transcriptions of the chorale preludes in which the music has somehow become warm and sensuous even though the essential tones of the composition are preserved. From our point of vantage the methods of the nineteenth century show a woeful lack of historical knowledge and a lack of respect for the composer's text. They considered that they did only what was necessary to make Bach presentable in the concert hall. The essential fact to be noted here is that Mendelssohn's Bach differed from Bach's Bach and our Bach not only in style but in actual sonority.

Today's Bach is diverse. The modernists have adopted him because of the boldness of his harmonies. He is even credited by one writer with an approach to polytonality, the device which presents the listener with music in two different scales at the same time. William Walton showed us that Bach could be a very gay and smart composer in the ballet score

"The Wise Virgins". Stokowski has shown us that Bach is more romantic, more dramatic, more exciting than anyone had realized. He and many other contemporary arrangers demonstrated how well Bach sounded when played by the modern symphony orchestra. But in doing so the uniform colors and clearly exposed contours of his organ compositions were replaced by over and underemphasis, by melodramatic stresses, and the resplendent coloring of the symphonic palette.

At the other extreme, the gradual accumulation of historic studies has had its effect, and we are able to attain a position and a perspective which enable us to understand more clearly the historical Bach. Parts written for the high pitched and fluent Bach trumpet are played on a specially constructed instrument which makes it possible to play the exact notes which Bach wrote. Accompaniments are played on the harpsichord, not the piano. Obbligato parts conceived by Bach for the ancient viola da gamba are performed on that instrument, not on the cello.

Yet even so, the revived Bach is not the original Bach. It is not possible to forget the two hundred years of music-making which have left their impress on us, but which the performers of his day were never to hear. Neither are our harpsichords exact equivalents of the baroque harpsichord. If we repair an old instrument, we are employing a sound-board which no longer responds as it did, which has surely lost its resonance. New instruments are frequently built with heavier strings and a stronger sonority, with an action which differs from that employed in Bach's time. Even when the instrument faithfully reproduces every detail of an authentic instrument of the period, we cannot be sure that it speaks with the exact tone-color of the instruments which Bach played.

Yet it is well that we should approach the historic Bach as closely as is possible. Music so presented provides its own satisfactions. It also furnishes us with a standard by which the Bach of the modernists, the frivolous Bach, the romantic Bach may be judged. Such are some of the difficulties in reviving the music of a composer who, considered in a broad historical perspective, is relatively close to us. Our difficulties in restoring music of a still earlier period to actual performance are greater. Notation becomes less exact, traditions have been largely lost, documents of all kinds are rarer and more difficult to evaluate.

Often a musical decision is motivated by nothing more than a desire for conformity, on the one hand, and a willingness to like what others have agreed to like, on the other. Conformists are more numerous than non-conformists, or group opinion could not exist. Non-conformity marks a departure from an established norm which may be the starting point of a new shift in taste or perhaps only a sign of an ill-adjusted temperament. The cynic might decide that the critical factor determining the success of a musical movement was the fact that it was well enough advertised to secure a following.

A fairer view would recognize that both conformity and rebellion in musical matters may range from sheep-like acquiescence and meaningless faddishness to a thoughtful and convinced championship of a composer or a tendency.

In a sense, indeed, the whole development of music has been a series of successful revolts against an established tradition. It is true that such breaks with tradition seem in retrospect to be less radical in character than they appeared at the time. We have only to regard the spectacle of Bach hustled off the musical scene to make way for the music of his sons and that of the other precursors of the classic style, the passionate rejection of the balanced symmetries of the classics by the more convinced romantic composers, the varied revolts against romanticism by Debussy, by Stravinsky, by Hindemith.

Yet in each case the change was less complete than the changed label would indicate. The reason for this is twofold. Every composer, no matter how completely he may desire novelty, is tied to the past by his whole experience, by the music he has heard, the music he has played, by the very changes in his organism which these impressions have caused. He cannot entirely reject that heritage. Bach's son Friedemann wrote fugues though he also wrote a set of polonaises. There is much of Mozart in certain works of Beethoven, in Rossini, in Gounod. Stravinsky did turn from romanticism, but not before he had paid a most charming tribute to its spirit in his ballet "The Fire Bird." Even where the break seems most decisive and most complete, the past furnishes the point of departure for the adventurous composer. Composers whose later works seem to show little relationship with those of their predecessors usually leave behind early works which betray their sources and their early enthusiasms. The early songs and the "Transfigured Night" of Schönberg, the "Rêverie" of Debussy, the earlier piano compositions of Scriabine, mark the beginnings of developments which might seem altogether novel if we were not able to follow their evolution.

There is a second factor which tends to limit the extent to which a composer may cultivate novelty. It is well known that many changes in national affairs may be desirable, and be recognized as desirable by leaders and thoughtful citizens, and yet be unattainable because they represent too great a departure to gain adequate public support. Music is a medium of communication. New music moves people because they are able to detect in it resemblances, clues, which relate it to music which has moved them in the past. If it presents none of these resemblances, or rather if the members of the audience are unable to detect them, they are bewildered. In most cases the music does indeed have perceptible relationships with the past which repeated hearings would make evident. In this way the audience acts as a brake on the development of the composer. The more the composer is dependent on his audience the smaller will be the element of novelty in his work. Nothing is clearer than the fact that earlier composers who were completely controlled by their masters differ less at a given period than later composers whose lives were relatively free. The music of Haydn resembles that of Mozart more than the music of Brahms that of Tschaikowsky. But only a composer who was able and willing to write without an audience could escape some degree of audience control. The composer Ives in our own country is perhaps the clearest example of a composer who was financially independent, who wrote his music as a personal expression without regard to its chances of performance. The natural result of this was the simple fact that, although his gifts were very pronounced indeed, he was not performed until he was "discovered" by composers of a later period who were pleased to find in him a sort of spiritual ancestor of whom they had been unconscious. At the other end of the scale is the composer of popular songs who studies nothing so carefully as the last success. His entire effort is directed at writing something which will gain complete and immediate audience approval.

Thus musical change is motivated partly by aesthetic impulses and convictions, partly by a shrewd observation of audience reaction on the part of the composer. The reaction of the press and the audience is also partly directed by a discriminating and alert response on the part of the more sensitive listeners, partly controlled by those who will gain by audience approval.

Music history hardly has time to record the advocates of trends which have proven to be blind alleys, insignificant deviations from the main line of development. It is, however, precisely the right choice among all the multi-directional tendencies of modern music which marks the sensitive and sincere music-lover. Here also the cynic would object that the course of music is chiefly determined by clever opportunism. The smart listener and the clever composer choose a style which seems likely to gain a following and ride this trend until it shows signs of faltering. Certainly the restless changes of style on the part of certain composers of the present century, notably Casella and Stravinsky, suggest something other than organic development.

Is there indeed such a thing as organic development of music; or is the historic "direction" of music like that of a flock of birds where the direction taken is an average of the deviations of the birds in the lead, a direction which could quite easily have been different in the absence of some definite attraction (food for the bird, economic advantages for the musician)? Here, as so often elsewhere, it would appear that composers move in a line which represents a compromise between music which is likely to succeed and music which they regard as artistically satisfying. It would be possible to assemble a most varied collection of instances which bear on this point. Bach, for example, produced in his gigantic "B minor Mass" a work which, though it defies all the usual limitations set on a compōsition of this character, represents his own personal reaction to the ideas of the text. Yet it is quite clear that the *Kyrie* and *Gloria* of this score were presented to the Elector of Saxony to secure Bach in his disputed prerogatives at Leipzig.

Mozart has been called the musician's composer. Indeed no music gives us such an impression of ideal beauty as his. Yet Mozart was keenly aware of his audience, and passages from his letters show that he calculated his effects with this in mind. In a letter which tells his father of the success of his "Paris Symphony" (Köchel 297) he writes: "Just in the middle of the first Allegro there was a passage which I felt sure must please. The audience were quite carried away . . . and there was a tremendous burst of applause. But as I knew, when I wrote it, what effect it would surely produce, I had introduced the passage again at the close—when there were shouts of 'Da capo'." He was also very conscious that his audiences, like those of the present day, were composed of individuals who varied in their capacity to understand and enjoy music. A passage from one of his letters reveals this very clearly. "These concertos are a happy medium between what is too easy and too difficult; they are very brilliant, pleasing to the ear, and natural, without being vapid. There are passages here and there from which connoisseurs alone can derive satisfaction, but these passages are written in such a way that the less learned cannot fail to be pleased, though without knowing why."

Up to this point only the drama of the conflict of individual likes and dislikes has been considered as they affect the shifts in public taste. Music, however, is a business as well as an art, and in this as in other businesses it is desirable that the hazards due to customer reaction should be controlled as far as is possible. The business of influencing public taste in the interest of greater and surer profits is a complicated one. The musician, his friends (and his enemies!), his manager and press agent, officials of radio chains, representatives of publishers and recording concerns, and finally the audiences who hear him, all have a share in the decision.

The progress of a single work might be summed up under the following heads: 1. Build-up. "Mr. So-and-So is engaged in the composition of a symphony. A noted conductor is said to be considering this score for performance during the coming season." 2. Audience reaction. The great day of the claque is past. There was a day when the chief of the claque of the Paris opera conferred before the performance of a new work with the director of the opera to indicate the points where applause seemed desirable. His services in insuring the success of a new work were regarded as indispensable. They were rewarded by regular payments from all the artists involved, payments which varied according to the importance of the individual. The well-known French writer Théophile Gautier comments with apparent seriousness on the utility of such a system in helping the audience to make up its collective mind. "The claqueur," he says, "renders as much service to the public as to the administration. If he has sometimes protected mediocrity, he has often sustained a new, adventurous work, swayed a hesitant public, and silenced envy. Moreover, in delaying the failure of pieces that have necessitated much expense, he has prevented the ruin of a vast enterprise and the despair of a hundred families. . . . In short, the claqueur represents the thoughtfulness of the director for the public that one supposes to be too genteel and well-gloved to applaud by itself." The halcyon days for the professional applauder are past, but no rule prevents friends from attending and applauding one's recital. Perhaps the lowest stage of spontaneity in applause is reached in broadcasting studios where it is turned on and off by signs reading "Applause" and "Silence." 3. Follow-up. The influence of music criticism has been much debated. The fact that it continues would indicate that it is read, and that it is not altogether unheeded. "Mr. So-and-So's symphony was well received by a large and enthusiastic audience. The composer came on the stage to respond to the ovation. Mr. So-and-So's symphony which was first performed last season will be repeated by several major orchestras during the present winter."

Mr. So-and-So will probably not be richer for all of this attention, but he has been played and his reputation has been fortified by the reception which his work has received. He may benefit indirectly by a commission which will bring in a substantial sum or a contract to compose movie music or a ballet. However he may fare, the reading and the listening public has been swayed, if ever so slightly, by the efforts of this composer and the multitude of voices raised in praise or disapproval.

A popular song possesses at least the possibility of earning a large sum for its creator, and, since this is so, the efforts to make it successful may be of some magnitude. The song, once published, must be placed in the hands of a popular performer, played by a "name" band. It must be broadcast. At this juncture its fate is in the balance. If it displays any possibility of achieving success, it is seized on by other performers, with a consequent rise in popularity. It is recorded, it goes out to the juke-boxes and is then heard by everyone within earshot of a radio until it is wrung dry of the last possibility of pleasurable audience response. When the critical point has been reached, the next song has already been written and the cycle begins anew.

A generation ago the sale of sheet music would have been an important source of revenue. Now it is a secondary factor. What was once a slow increase in popularity, as a song was sung on one vaudeville stage, around one parlor organ after another has become an almost instantaneous process. Millions of radios simultaneously blare the latest tune from coast to coast. In hot-dog stands, filling stations, restaurants, the youth of the nation deposits its nickels in juke-boxes, presses the appropriate button of the record-selector, and listens. Thousands of portable phonographs repeat the same melody to thousands of teen-agers. The composer is understandably pleased, and his bank account increases.

Since considerable sums are involved in this process, no stone is left unturned in the effort to convince the public that a given song is a good one, one that must be heard. These efforts rest quite simply on the belief that a good song is one which makes money. Such a view is too naive for serious acceptance, but it is omnipresent and may always act as a distorting agent when we ask ourselves the worth of a song.

Self-advertisement and self-praise for the sake of gain are not new arts. They are indeed so ancient that one would hesitate at suggesting their date of origin. What is new is the omnipresence of music in our civilization, the tremendous power concentrated in a few hands, and the consequent possibility of shaping public taste and opinion almost at will.

The auditor is first stirred and vaguely attracted to music. Then he begins to recognize that music is of different kinds, infinitely varied in quality, in purpose, and in the means of effect. Eventually, with music as with books, the listener is able to select consciously the music that most deeply moves

[47]

and sustains him. Never have the opportunities for a rich musical experience been so easily available. Never have the factors which deflect judgment and distort values been so formidable. Music depends on the vision of the composer. If it is to have more than a paper existence, it depends equally on the receptivity of the audience. No composer can write for himself alone. His future audience is present as he writes, and his knowledge of that audience guides his pen. Thus the role of the audience is no passive one. Its decisions, its intelligence, its ability to discriminate are determining factors in the development of music. Its taste level acts as a drag or an incentive to the composers who write for it.

Chapter III

MUSIC AS MOLDED BY SOCIETY

THE development of music has been influenced by three great factors: the capabilities of sound itself, the human need for emotional expression, and the nature and the requirements of the society which music serves. Some of the possibilities of sound are so simple that we all understand them. Some are completely understood only by the most gifted composers. The amazing effects which are obtained by causing sounds of varying duration to follow one another are the secrets of melody. The increasing richness obtained by simultaneous sound impressions or by simultaneous melodies is even more remarkable and constitutes the province of harmony and counterpoint. Finally, the organization of music on a large scale involves questions of proportion, of contrast, of repetition, of the characteristics which are different aspects of musical form.

Such are some of the considerations which the composer must ponder, considerations which grow very largely out of the nature of sound itself. That part of the audience which has not been exposed to courses in music appreciation does not, in general, worry about these matters at all. If they are emotionally stirred by the web of sounds, they listen with eager attention in order to spin out the mood until the musician's final chord. If they do not respond to the music they lapse into day-dreaming, reflect on unrelated matters, or indulge in a variety of activities which are most annoying to their more attentive neighbors.

Music is a medium which has been created. Although the painter may introduce a personal nuance into the landscape which he transfers to the canvas, he produces something which is recognized as the counterpart of the original. It is precisely the early painters, whose conventions, distortions of nature, and personal idiosyncracies are so obvious to us, who would probably have assured us that their sole object was to give an accurate reproduction of their subject.

No art develops in total isolation, not even music which is the most remote from natural prototypes. A dancer takes two steps forward, then two steps back. Any music which may be devised for this dance is likely to consist of two equal melodic phrases to match these balanced movements. To this degree the construction of such a melody is controlled, not by internal laws, but by the construction of the dance. In the old French verse form, the *rondeau,* the opening words recurred twice as a refrain. Naturally, a composer who adjusted music to such a text might devise a melodic phrase which would be repeated whenever the refrain appeared. This, again, would be a hint taken from the verse form, not a principle which was solely musical in nature.

Music is an incredibly flexible art responding in the most varied fashion to the needs of the individual and to the needs of the group of which the individual is a member. One of the great difficulties with many discussions as to the meaning of music is the fact that they commonly assume that music has one instead of diverse meanings. It has meant what the individual or the group intended it to mean. There have always been two broad categories of music, however, which served two different purposes: music which expressed individual emotion, and music which was ceremonial in character.

The human being cries when sad, laughs when happy, shouts when jubilant. He is not content to sorrow in silence. His sadness must be made manifest. This at the most elementary stage may be sobbing or moaning. At a more advanced stage these sounds may become rhythmic, may organize themselves. Our instinctive vocal inflections are crystallized in melody. A football yell or the speech of children at play illustrates a stage where word repetition and rhythm play their part to turn a simple phrase into a sort of chant. "Keening" or lamenting may reach a point where emotional speech becomes song, as in the traditional lament (the *vocero*) of a Corsican mother for her dead son. Human emotion has become song. Though all humanity experiences the same basic emotions, they are expressed in songs which vary according to the habits of the social group to which the individual belongs.

A large number of folksongs, even if their text is not immediately applicable to the folk singer, are at least so familiar to him in sentiment and in meaning that they can be adopted as a natural expression of his own feelings. A native of the Andaman Islands engaged in hollowing out a log to make a canoe may chant, "Knots are very hard to cut with an adze. They blunt the edge of the adze. How hard I am working cutting these knots." A woman of the Hebrides might sing as she turned the stone which ground the grain, "Put round the quern and spare not." The cowboy may tell of the fatigue of the roundup and of lonely nights on the prairie. The basic theme is labor, but it is subject to an infinity of local variations.

Many songs in English folk literature praise country occupations.

> "My song is of the ploughboy's fame,
> And unto you I'll relate the same,
> He whistles, sings, and drives his team,
> The brave ploughing boy."

Mr. Kidson has pointed out that it is precisely in the southwest of England where agriculture is a dominant occupation that these songs in praise of the "bold young farmer" and his fellows are most frequent.

In a seafaring nation we expect and find an abundance of ballads of adventure on the broad ocean as well as many chanties which the sailor roared out as he heaved on the capstan bars or pulled at the ropes. Particularly bold and confident is the seaman's farewell in a foreign port. "Farewell

[51]

and adieu to you, Spanish ladies, Farewell and adieu to you, ladies of Spain," continuing, "But we hope in a short time to see you again," and concluding "From Ushant to Scilly is thirty-five leagues."

A more tragic note is sounded by songs of the press gang which in the eighteenth century sometimes seized every able-bodied man of a sleeping village and sent them to sea in the King's ships. Many of them were never to see their cottages again. If we may believe the folk singer, many an irate father found that a bribe in the right quarter would ensure the removal of some ploughboy who had won his daughter's heart. The highwayman and the poacher were closer to the folk than to the gentleman in his coach and four. Accordingly, many of the ballads dealing with the highwayman represent him as a sort of Robin Hood who stole from the rich to give to the poor. "Brennan on the Moor" is one gallant highwayman among many.

Thus many folksongs deal with familiar figures of the countryside or of the port. This is, however, the simpler part of the relationship between folksong and the folk singer. The union of music and text in an expression which is true and, on occasion, vividly poetic must be felt rather than analyzed. Yet these less obvious characteristics are true mirrors of the pride and poetry of a people. Folksong, properly speaking, was the voice of the cottager, the farmer, the shepherd. It expressed the folk, not, as some folk enthusiasts have imagined, because they were composed in a communal collaboration, but because they were true to the feeling of the singers who remembered and repeated them. Folksong survived longest where there was the least formal education, where there was the greatest poverty. The rich gifts of the American Negro as a singer are well recognized. The Negro is still underprivileged and underpaid.

European folksongs might be performed for a reward by a harper in a baronial hall or a ballad singer in the market-place. More frequently they were sung by the people for their own satisfaction. The decay of folkways, the increasing influence of urban culture, the triumph of an emerging industrialism led to the disappearance of the folksong. The void was only partially filled by the popular song.

The popular song was a commodity. It was often circulated in the form of ballad sheets which were sold by peddlers. Though at first many old traditional songs were preserved in this way, these melodies (which might serve as a basis for many texts) were gradually replaced by dance tunes, popular airs from operas and operettas, and tunes composed for the purpose. It might be unfair to say that the folksong was an emotional expression which a people had accepted as its own, the popular song a reflection of known popular tastes concocted with a view to an easy sale. Nevertheless such a statement possesses an element of truth and, indeed, might be quite accurate in many instances. It describes two different ways of producing and distributing songs which were characteristic of two different stages of society. The popular song belongs to an industrial society where money is the usual medium of exchange, with printing presses, with wandering packmen with ballad sheets among their goods, with stores where music is bought and sold, with professional singers on the street corners, in theatres and music halls.

Early examples were the *brunettes* and *chansons à boire* in the seventeenth and eighteenth century France. Since basic enjoyments have not altered a great deal since the seventeenth century, we must not be surprised to find that most of these effusions were devoted to love and wine, with occasional lyrics which praise the delights of the table. The narrowing of scope and focus, the restriction of the song to hours of amusement have tended to prettify and to limit the emotional range of popular music. Songs of labor have vanished. Songs in praise of the vine are not intoned as publicly nor as frequently at present as in earlier periods. Thus the night club and radio artists of the present day are restricted to two variants of a basic theme: the maiden who has lost her man and regrets it, and the man who has won his maiden and is understandably elated. The conventions governing popular song demand a light touch which results in gay and carefree compositions, intentionally superficial. Our Western civilization possesses no body of contemporary song which truly represents the common man, his dignity, his work, his loves, his devotion to his fellow workers. The "Ballad for Americans" by Earl Robinson is indeed an expression of the feelings of the common man, an expression perhaps less important for what it is than for what it may foreshadow.

2 (Man early discovered that music was one of the means for increasing the unity of a group.)The simplest kind of unity was simultaneous movement, and this was obtained when music acted as a regulating element. The object might be a practical one, in order that the group might exert the maximum force at the same moment. The halyard chanty is a simple example of this type. Here the sailors have the task of hoisting a sail by hauling on a rope which was passed through a block on the deck. The task was easy at first until the wind caught the sail and bellied it out. Then one of the hands nearest the mast would start "lining out" a chanty such as "Reuben Ranzo." The chantyman would sing, "Oh poor old Reuben Ranzo," and the crouching line of sailor-men would respond, "Ranzo boys, Ranzo!" with a pull together on the first syllable of "Ranzo" followed by a shift to a fresh grip on the rope in preparation for the next pull.

Probably the last survivor of the work song is the marching song. Perhaps no army of the present day has so rich a literature of marching songs as the Soviet army, and certainly no government has been so successful in promoting a singing spirit among army personnel. The performances of the Red Army Chorus under Alexandrov demonstrate what can be achieved in this direction under skilled leadership. The effect of music in helping men forget to some extent the fatigue of long marches has long been realized whether the song was the inspiration of some singer in the ranks or was played by a regimental band. Many tunes have been sung: "British Grenadiers," the *"Marseillaise,"* "Yankee Doodle," the "Battle Hymn of the Republic," "Over There," "Forward Together," but each has the cadence of marching feet.

On less serious occasions, instead of pulling a rope or screwing a cotton bale, music might be used to unify the steps of dancers. This use of music was a very ancient one. The scene might vary, a clearing in the midst of a circle of primitive huts, an English village green, a barn floor in early New England. The circle of dancers and their song would be a common feature. The tune might be "Sourwood Mountain" in our own South, "Come Lasses and Lads" in England, *"Viens mon beau laboureur"* ("Come my handsome husbandman") in France, the *"Hopak"* in Russia. The movement of such tunes was light and rhythmic, and the words were chosen as much for rhythm as for sense. The mood was one of careless gaiety, the object fun and courtship. Music remained the unifying force, but it gained a reputation for frivolity which made it the butt of stern moralists and of puritanical preachers.

Some folk-dances, which in later periods were performed only for the satisfaction of performers and spectators, preserve traces of a more ancient usage. They testify to the age-old connection between music and ritual and between dancing and ritual. Thus, sword dances of England culminate in the mock decapitation of a victim. Even in our own country we may point to the dance-songs and to the religious dances of the Shakers. The carol, which in more recent times has become a popular Christmas song, was a circular dance in earlier days. The text of an English folk carol collected by Sandys hints at this connection. Beginning, "Tomorrow will be my dancing day," it narrates the events leading to the birth of Christ.

In a similar fashion, popular marching songs might have religious significance. Particularly in Catholic countries, out-

[55]

of-door processions of religious societies, which sing processional hymns as they march are a customary feature of certain holy days. The Spanish processions have become famous for their picturesque beauty as well as for their music.

Popular religious song, of course, includes a much wider field than the carol or the processional hymn. Many folksongs, other than carols, have a religious character. The French *"Noël,"* the Spanish *"villancico,"* the Italian *"laudi spirituali,"* all had a more or less popular character. The chorale of the Protestant Reformation as well as the *"laudi spirituali"* were frequently spiritual paraphrases of folksongs which were originally sung to less edifying texts. This device was utilized by religious leaders who realized the popularity of secular songs and sought to adapt them to the ends of religion.

In our own land camp-meeting songs and revival hymns had a marked popular character. We are just beginning to realize the importance of evangelical hymns, both for their own sake and for their influence on Negro folksong and the spiritual. The songs of such revivalists as Moody and Sankey were written to melodies of the utmost simplicity with a striking but obvious rhythm. The enormous success gained by such hymns as "There were Ninety and Nine" was resisted by those who clung to music in a more dignified and traditional style. The very simplicity of construction of many of these tunes made them fatally easy to imitate. We must recognize that they appealed to great numbers of people and that they still form a major part of the musical fare of many Americans.

The Negro spiritual has attained a wide popularity among Americans and Europeans of every shade of religious belief. This is due in part to the sincerity and real poignancy of the finest examples, as well as to a long series of gifted interpreters from the Jubilee Singers to Marion Anderson. A tendency in certain quarters to treat spirituals in a spirit of caricature is to be deplored. On the other hand, it must be granted that the enormous popularity of the spiritual has obscured a wealth of Negro secular song. The spiritual originally consisted of a solo phrase followed by a group response, a form which we have already noted in the case of the chanty.

Much music associated both with religion and with the state has what we may call a ceremonial character. In group song what is expressed is the feeling of the group. Ceremonial music is planned to impress its audience, to arouse feelings of awe, reverence, inferiority. This is at variance with our modern concept of music. We expect music to be the product of personal emotions. We take it for granted that the transmission of feeling is the purpose of the musical performance. Much ceremonial music is objective in character. Its aim is to impose itself on us, to overwhelm us, and so to convey to us our smallness and the greatness of the monarch or the deity who is praised. This may be accomplished by a multitude of performers, by an overwhelming volume of sound. Thus, the Venetians of the Renaissance let chorus answer chorus under the sonorous vaults of St. Mark. Thus, the visit of a monarch was hailed by fanfares and by the voices of singers and minstrels. The king made his entry to the accompaniment of trumpet fanfares and martial rhythms on the kettledrums, instruments which were traditionally a symbol of rank. Such an assault on the ears was an announcement of his arrival, an audible symbol of his greatness. Music was, however, used in many other ways, and royal musical establishments grew in complexity as their functions multiplied.

The chapel of the ruling monarch always included singers and players for the performance of religious services. Long before the emergence of modern European nations, there had been specialized musical groups engaged in the performance of religious rites. We have only to look at Egyptian wall paintings or read of the services in Solomon's temple to realize how highly organized some of these ceremonies must have been. Music took its place in the earliest periods as a necessary adjunct of magic incantations. In later days the musical part of religious ceremonies seems sometimes to have been intended to over-awe, to impose itself upon the listening worshippers. This is evident in primitive rites where strange sounds or an unnatural use of the voice is designed to create in the auditors the fear of ancestral voices or the supernatural. Such an effect is suggested by an awesome account of the music produced on an organ in medieval England: "Like thunder the iron tones batter the ear, so that it may receive no sound but that alone. To such an amount does it reverberate, echoing in every direction, that everyone stops with his hand his gaping ears, being in no wise able to draw near and bear the sound, which so many combinations produce."

Admittedly, one way of expressing the greatness of God is by performing music of such grandeur as to convey an idea of unlimited power. This Bach did in the *Sanctus* of his "B Minor Mass." The grief of Mary, the mother of Jesus, might be expressed in music of such poignancy as to mirror the sorrow of a mother at the death of her son. This Pergolesi (1710-1736) did in his *Stabat Mater*. This is a dramatic method, and one which is, in reality, an application of the methods of opera to church music. Composers of the sixteenth century, on the other hand, wrote music which treats even the most dramatic texts without any external drama.

Mendelssohn has stated the contrast between a meditative and a dramatic approach to the sacred texts very clearly, though with an obvious bias in favor of the latter. In writing of the music for Holy Week as sung in the Sistine Chapel at Rome he compares the setting of the "Passion according to St. John" by Victoria with the setting of the same narrative by J. S. Bach: "Music . . . is a distinct language speaking plainly to me; for though the sense is expressed by the words, it is equally contained in the music. This is the case with the 'Passion' of Sebastian Bach; but, as they sing it here, it is very imperfect, being neither a simple narrative, nor yet a grand solemn dramatic truth. The chorus sings *'Barrabam'* to the same sacred chords as *'et in terra pax'* ('and peace on earth'). Pilate speaks exactly in the same manner as the Evangelist." This is an extremely instructive passage. Mendelssohn was not so close to the pure contemplative style of the religious masters of the sixteenth century as we are at the present day. He sympathizes with the dramatic approach. He has only criticism for the early composers who treated the sacred texts in a manner which suggests reverent contemplation rather than drama.

The music of Palestrina speaks a language of collective aspiration, of collective worship. He does not dramatize his texts but meditates on them. The solo voice which must inevitably speak to us in terms of individual emotion is absent here. Palestrina's music is expressed by the blended voices of the choir, pure, impersonal, yet instinct with a kind of feeling suitable to its subject and its purpose.

Thus, it would be possible to arrange a series of religious rites beginning with ceremonies which attempt by crude devices to influence the forces of nature, to make the uninitiated fear the supernatural. These might be followed by ceremonies which glorify God in a fashion comparable to the manner in which a great king or emperor might be glorified. These ceremonies would naturally be most appropriate to a stage in human development in which the king was a high priest himself, or to the later period in which religion was a state function. Finally it is possible to point out music which embodies a mood of prayer and meditation, which neither dramatizes nor overawes, but embodies a kind of ideal aspiration.

The personnel of the court music of the earlier kings in England or France consisted of a more or less haphazard group of musicians whose tasks were ill-defined and whose functions varied according to the caprice and the musical taste of the ruling monarch. In general their task was to amuse the ruler and his attendants and to impress visitors with the wealth and the luxury of the court. The banquet of the "Oath of the Gilded Pheasant," presented at the court of Burgundy in 1454, was so appallingly expensive as to shock even contemporary chroniclers. This banquet was enlivened with such pretty devices as an enormous pasty which contained twenty-eight musicians who entertained the guests with their music. This is only one of many examples of the vulgar and tasteless displays of wealth with which the chronicles are studded. With time, however, these state musical establishments assumed a more definite form. The personnel was chosen and balanced in order that the court musicians might furnish instrumental music for court balls, vocal or instrumental music for the hours of relaxation of royalty, music for religious services, and musical instruction for the princes and princesses.

With the development of opera an unexcelled instrument for display was placed in the hands of pleasure-loving monarchs. Court musical establishments were accordingly expanded in order to make operatic productions possible. Diplomatic agents all over Europe manoeuvered deftly to secure the services of the most famous singers for their masters. The birth of an heir, the wedding of a prince or princess were the usual excuses for the performance of a festival opera. The allegorical prologue in which Jupiter and Mars proclaimed their inferiority to the ruling sovereign was a necessity in a performance of this kind. The fact that opera concerned itself only with the fate of mythological deities or the heroes and monarchs of classic antiquity was only natural under the circumstances. Common people made a very tardy appearance on the operatic stage; when they did so, it was as comic servants or rustic clowns. Tragic endings frequently were altered to avoid lacerating royal feelings. Readers who are familiar with the Gluck *"Orpheus"* will recall that Amor intervenes at the critical moment to restore Euridice to the arms of Orpheus. Under limitations such as these, it is remarkable that such outstanding figures as Monteverdi (1567-

1643), Handel (1685-1759), and Gluck (1714-1787) succeeded in achieving the intense expression and the deep emotion which animate their greatest scenes.

Though by far the larger part of the ceremonial splendor of a court existed to delight the members of the court itself and to impress visiting dignitaries, there were occasions when the monarch did show himself to his subjects. Thus music was called upon to add glorious sounds to coronations. Perhaps the earliest example which we possess is the Mass by Guillaume de Machaut which may have been composed for the coronation of Charles V of France (1364). The four anthems which Handel composed for the coronation of George II (1727) were wonderfully suited to their purpose. Ceremonial music of this kind is typically pompous and grandiose. This mood was reflected in certain instrumental forms. The overtures which prefaced the operas of Lully stride on with a majesty which reflects the pomp and the ostentation of the court of Louis XIV. Bach reflects a similar musical mood in the overtures of his orchestral suites.

Court music was designed to amuse the courtiers, to impress foreign diplomats, to awe the populace when a ruler made a public appearance. Patriotic music was dual in function. It might be an individual expression which was accepted by the people. It might be sponsored by the government, and its performance might be enforced as a symbol of loyalty. Its range of expression might vary from patriotic idealism to a glorification of war for its own sake, from a call for self-sacrifice to the more realistic sentiments of the foot soldier.

One striking fact about many patriotic songs is the fact that they were not deliberately composed for the purpose but were seized upon by an aroused people as a symbol of their ideals and purposes. Nothing could be more fortuitous, for example, than the way in which a trivial ballet air *"Daghela avanti un passo"* became a symbol of the aspirations of the Italian people for national independence. The performance of a dancer to this air proved unsatisfactory to part of a Milanese audience (in 1858). When the police intervened against the dancer, Italian patriots immediately took her part, and her melody became the symbol of national aspirations. When war broke out between Austria and Lombardy, the bands of the Austrian armies played the tune derisively as they advanced on Italian soil. The tide of war turned against Austria, and the same tune became a hymn of victory in the mouths of the Italian soldiers. Perhaps never was there a development of a patriotic song which was so completely unpremeditated.

The obscurity which shrouds the origin of such a tune as our own "Yankee Doodle" is another indication of the casual way in which it became one of our national songs. A gay and trivial dance tune became by chance the famous *"Ça ira"* of the French Revolution. Sometimes the symbol seems more adequate to the thing expressed. The hymn "Chester" by William Billings in its direct and simple way seems an appropriate symbol of the American Revolution, though it was perhaps its text which caught the attention of his contemporaries:

> "Let tyrants shake their iron rod,
> And Slavery clank her galling chains;
> We'll fear them not, we'll trust in God;
> New England's God forever reigns."

A song could not only unify and heighten a great wave of national feeling, it was also a formidable weapon against an adversary. When Shakespeare in "Henry IV" (first part) makes Falstaff threaten Prince Henry that he will have a ballad made about him which will be sung in the streets, he was voicing no idle threat. A song played an important role in enforcing the flight of James II from England. This was "Lilliburlero" which attacked both James and Talbot, his deputy-lieutenant in Ireland. "A foolish ballad was made at that time, treating the Papists, and chiefly the Irish, in a very ridiculous manner. . . . The whole army, and at last the people, both in city and country, were singing it perpetually. And perhaps never had so slight a thing so great an effect."

The French street singers played their part in the downfall of the monarchy when they sang of the aged Louis XIV and of his family:

> *"Le grand-père est un fanfaron,*
> *Le fils un imbécile,*
> *Le petit-fils un grand poltron,*
> *Ohé la belle famille!"*

"The father is a braggart,
The son an imbecile,
The grandson a great coward,
My, what a fine family!"

If songs could thus emerge from obscurity and become the symbol of some popular aspiration, it was also possible for those in authority to use the force of song for their own advantage. They could make sure that songs expressing loyalty to themselves or to the government which they served were sung in public places. They could establish a censorship which would prohibit the singing of songs or the staging of performances which were hostile either directly or by implication. Perhaps the most terrifyingly complete control of the songs of a people was achieved by the Nazi regime in Germany with its ruthless suppression of all music which did not accord with Nazi ideology and the persistent repetition of songs composed to inculcate the war lust which their plans demanded, *"Volk ans Gewehr"* ("People, to arms!") and *"Wir fahren nach England"* ("We sail against England").

Rollo H. Myers, the author of a thoughtful book entitled "Music in the Modern World," ventures the remark that "music could not possibly be used, shall we say, to make us vote in a municipal election." Unfortunately, Mr. Myers speaks without a knowledge of the ingenuity and guilefulness of politicians on this side of the Atlantic. We have not only hired bands and marched in torchlight processions, but have sung out our political enthusiasms and antipathies ever since we have been a nation.

The campaign for "Tippecanoe and Tyler Too" was marked by an especially vigorous outburst of political song. As the publishers of the "Harrison and Log Cabin Song Book" stated in their preface, "The enthusiasm of a happy people always did and always will break forth in song." The Hutchinsons, the singing family of New Hampshire, expressed that desire for social reform which was one of the characteristic drives of their period in lyrics supporting the temperance cause and the abolition of slavery. They sang in support of Lincoln and published campaign song books, "Hutchinson's Republican Songster" as well as "The Connecticut Wide-Awake Songster." The first collection alone contained the words of fifty songs.

The political power of song has not been forgotten in more recent campaigns. A comic closing note on a subject, which might profitably be discussed at much greater length, is furnished by a recent newspaper clipping. In discussing primary elections in Alabama it states that "Folsom led the race because he has a popular hillbilly band, à la Sen. W. Lee O'Daniel (Tex.) and Gov. Jimmy Davis (La.)." These other gentlemen had previously proved the merit of this method of winning votes.

In closing, it may be well to place the popular concept of music as an expression of a personality against the view that music is a social product. Anything made by man reveals the character of its maker. Its form and purpose have been gradually evolved that it may effectively serve its user. Thus a pot may be clumsy or refined in modeling and contour, its decoration crude or artistic. Its form and size will, however, normally conform to the shape and the dimensions which have been found suitable for a given purpose, storing oil, carrying water, or cooking meat. These standard forms, however, are not individually invented but represent the product of the ingenuity of generations of potters corrected by the practical trials and experiences of generations of pot-users. Similarly, any musical composition must reveal to some degree the character of its composer.

Yet this element of novelty, this individual contribution which each composer brings to his music, is small compared to the elements which have been determined by earlier musicians, performers, patrons, audiences, instrument makers, impresarios and the host of human beings whose activities have to some degree made music what it is. Even the development of a highly personal musical style is a product of social evolution. The modern musician was born out of that conception of personal liberty which was crystallized in the struggles of the French Revolution. The tremendous self-affirmation of a Beethoven would have been impossible at an earlier period. The perhaps exaggerated emphasis laid on personality and individual expression during the romantic period derives directly from this root. Individual expression could not be exalted until a society existed which freed the individual from at least some of the obligations and repressions of earlier systems. Thus, the fact that recent composers have discovered personal variants of the common musical language, a manner of expressing themselves which is intimately individual, is itself both a product and an expression of a freer society.

CHAPTER IV

MELODY AS EXPRESSIVE SPEECH

IN a shrewd and imaginative book, "The Maltese Cat," Leon Underwood has described the way in which the cat hero learned to understand human speech. The cat early discovered that the important factor in human speech was not the words used, but the inflection, the color of the voice. The clue to the real significance of what was said was to be found in the emotional undercurrent which was revealed (often against the speaker's will) by the quality of his voice, by the subtle melody of speech.

This fantasy has its solid kernel of truth. Speech is not merely a medium for the communication of facts. It also communicates emotion. This it does through vocal modulation, through the timbre of the voice, as well as many other factors, such as speed of delivery and facial expression. But since the voice does oscillate between sounds of varying pitch, we may truly say that speech is a vague and subtle kind of melody. The characteristic undulations of the voice from low to high are different for each language and constitute its peculiar music. This is a factor which helps us to identify a foreign language even when we do not know what is said. It is a matter of great concern to composers of opera who try to cast the music of their dramatic or narrative passages in intervals suggested by the natural declamation of the words.

Among the various purposes for which speech is employed there are some which call for a highly inflected manner which more closely approaches music. One of the simplest uses of speech is to call attention to oneself or to attract the attention of others. Here the sustained tone of the voice enables the speaker to make himself heard more clearly than would be the case were he to employ ordinary speech. When stereotyped as

[67]

a formula this gives us the street cry. We have already said that speech conveys emotion as well as ideas. When emotion becomes so powerful as to cause the speaker to use the full pitch range of the voice or even to break out into wordless exclamations, we tend to approach the boundaries of music. Thus, the formless wails and howls of the mourners for the dead may finally crystallize in the lament.

The association of the recitation of liturgical texts with traditional musical formulas is very ancient indeed. Here, too, one might surmise that this practice enabled a large group of worshippers to hear the sacred texts more distinctly. No doubt in favorable instances it might, indeed, have this effect. Hints that we may derive from a study of the customs of primitive peoples, however, suggest that the original object may have been to give the sacred texts an awe-inspiring, an other-worldly, and, in some instances at least, a magic character. However that may be, the practice of intoning or chanting the words of the ritual is both ancient and widespread.

Language, once crystallized in verse, communicated its own rhythmic movement to the melodies to which it was sung. Thus, in the hymns of the Catholic Church, as well as in the courtly verses of troubadours and minnesingers, we have melodies which borrowed a definite rhythm from the verses with which they were associated. Courtly melodies were often definite and lilting in rhythm. Liturgical chanting was other-worldly in character and moved in the freer rhythms of speech. When we reach the seventeenth century and the development of opera, we have still another association of music and speech. Here it was a question of translating the impassioned declamation of a skilled actor into musical terms. Thus, opera approached the problem from the point of view of good declamation as well as that of the simulation of the inflections of the human voice under the stress of passion. The result was a speech-melody differing from all other kinds previously mentioned, and one to which we give the name of recitative. It survives in its simple form in such an opera as Mozart's *"Don Giovanni,"* to choose an example in the current repertory. The general principles involved have influenced all opera up to the present day.

A mother wishing to communicate with her small son at a distance almost always approximates a musical call. A common pattern is a sustained tone followed by a drop to a note of lower pitch. A somewhat more elaborate cry has been cleverly introduced into the radio serial "Henry Aldrich." No doubt a similar purpose has inspired a similar procedure from the earliest times. The farmer calls his cows, "Co boss, Co boss," as he walks through the pasture. The farmer's wife calls her chickens. Such calls are frequently so definite in pitch that they might be written down in musical notation.

The musical call reached its highest development where it was most economically useful, in the cries of street merchants and venders. Thus the London housewife might have heard, "Will you buy my sweet lavender?" or "Cherry ripe" from the street outside and, hearing, might hasten outside to buy. This practice can be traced back to the fourteenth century by poetic references. Composers like Jannequin (active during the first half of the 16th century) in his "Cries of Paris," Orlando Gibbons (1583-1625) and Richard Deering (1580-1630) in their fantasias on English cries took the trouble to notate these brief calls and to weave them into compositions which reflect the picturesque street life of former days.

The itinerant street merchant has all but vanished in our own country, but once the streets of New York echoed to cries of "Mint water" or "East, east" ("Yeast, yeast") as is shown by a quaint old children's book picturing street merchants of old New York. On the streets of New Orleans and Charleston Negro venders still cry the merits of ripe strawberries and blackberries, and, no doubt, will continue to do so till the noise of traffic finally drowns them out. The purpose of the street cry is to attract the attention of prospective customers and to identify the goods to be sold. Musically, it consists of a characteristic group of notes which is persistently repeated.

At moments of overpowering joy or victory a human being no longer speaks. He jubilates, he cries out. Such, perhaps, were the shouts which welcomed hunters back to some far-off circle of primitive huts. Such were the cries of joy which greeted the return of ancient warriers successful in battle. But gradually the wordless cries assumed form, to an extent became song. The Israelites sang praises to David, "Saul slew his thousands, and David his ten thousands." So must many another returning warrior have been greeted. In general the welcome of guests among primitive peoples was ceremonial in character.

When Handel in his oratorio, "Solomon," made the arrival of the Queen of Sheba at Solomon's court the occasion for a brisk and rhythmic instrumental flourish, he revealed that the instincts of an opera composer and those of an ancient ruler had much in common. Two purposes seem to have been served by such ceremonies. On the one hand the visitors were made welcome. On the other the host displayed the numbers and the richness of his household in as visible (and audible) a fashion as was possible.

Among the Wabanaki Indians, who occupied the area which is now Maine, the symbol of the arrival of visitors was a canoe bearing a white flag. "Then we gathered on the shore, men, women, and children, like a great procession, waiting to welcome them. . . . The stranger first sprang to land and sang the N'Skawewintuagunui (song of greeting), stepping slowly towards our chief in time to the song, while all the people sang 'hega, hega.' At the end of the song the stranger had drawn close to the chief, and holding out his hand said, 'I greet you, chief of the Passamaquoddy.' Then the people gave a great shout and fired off their guns." Though the ceremony of greeting was more elaborate than can be completely indicated by this quotation, the text of the song consisted only of repetitions of the word "hega."

If we turn to the people of the Congo in Africa, we find their formula of welcome similar. André Gide describes such an occasion in the following words. "This morning's march was like a triumphal progress: when we got to the first village, we had an enthusiastic reception, accompanied by singing and shouting, in a wonderful rhythm; . . . we got out of our *tipoyes;* mine was ahead. And then it was no longer a march, but a sort of race, escorted by tamtams and a troupe of laughing children. . . . From this village onwards as far as Pakori, where we arrived at about eleven o'clock and camped, we were escorted; the singing (in alternating choruses) of our *tipoyeurs,* and the village people never ceased."

It is perhaps chastening to reflect that, although the people of New York still shout their greeting to popular heroes as they ride up Broadway, they would find it very difficult to shape their greetings in a song as successfully as the American Indian or the African tribesman. In both examples we can see that the song is the complement of the shout of greeting and that one probably developed from the other.

The human being abandons words in moments of intense pain or sorrow and moans, cries, or wails. It seems strange to imagine that an expression so painful, even for the spectator, could ever assume a more organized or more artistic form. Yet this seems to have been the case with many peoples, even in that most final of all ceremonies, the mourning for the dead. Among the many songs which the French folklorist Tiersot published are two which he presents as examples of the laments or *voceros* improvised by bereaved Corsican women on traditional motives. The printed examples of the *vocero* are a lament for a murdered husband and one for a dead son. Yet when one examines the musical notation, one suspects that the recorded version must be far indeed from the unmeasured and passionate declamation of the original.

One of the strangest evidences that even sorrow for the dead may be translated into ceremonial terms is the widespread employment of professional mourners in the Orient, in Greece, and elsewhere in Europe. Violet Alford writes of the survival of these ancient practices in the Pyrenees as follows: "Ritual weeping is carried on all along the Pyrenees also. *Pleureuses* on the French slope, *Ploraneras* on the Spanish slope, make the heavens ring with their forced-out cries and wails, until they work themselves into a veritable frenzy of artificial grief . . . In the . . . *Vallée d'Ossau* these wailings gradually work up to improvisation in verse concerning the qualities and virtues of the dead. This is the *Aurost* . . . I have often wished to reduce to musical notation one of these improvised *Aurosts,* but none practicable have so far come my way. The lamentations rise and fall with artificial spurts of energy, and one might as well seek to note the howls of a desert jackal."

The lovely Scotch folksong, "The Flowers of the Forest," is supposed to be a lament for the men of Scotland who fell on Flodden Field. But here the melody, at least in the form in which it has been notated, has a measured and balanced structure which is far from the plaintive cry of grief though the emotional germ is the same in both.

The association of religious ritual and music has been close from the most remote periods to the present. Moreover, the conservatism which is evident in most religious rites has in some cases resulted in the preservation of very ancient musical formulas together with those of more recent origin. A very ancient practice was the recitation of religious texts to simple musical formulas which were repeated as many times as necessary till the entire text had been intoned.

Idelsohn, in his scholarly book, "Jewish Music," points out that the Talmud prescribes that public readings of the Bible should be "made understood to the hearers in a musical, sweet tune." This usage is at least as ancient as the first century. Such a practice has a parallel in the ancient intonations to which the Psalms are chanted in the Catholic and Anglican churches. The first syllables are often sung to a traditional formula (intonation), and then the remaining syllables are recited on a single tone up to the pause which marks the end of the first part of the verse. This point is marked by a melodic inflection called the mediation. The second part is recited on the same tone as the first up to the end of the verse which is again marked by a group of notes called the close. Thus we have a recitation on one tone with the beginning, mid-point, and close of each verse marked by a simple melodic formula. This method of performance sets the text apart and makes it seem remote, other-worldly.

Yet the recitation of texts of considerable duration to melodic formulas of very restricted compass was not confined to religious ceremonies though the practice has been preserved in the music of church and synagogue. Hints derived from widely scattered sources suggest that epic poems must have been chanted in a fashion which would have a basic similarity to religious chants of the kind described above. A melody in Botsford's "Folksongs of Many Peoples" is described as a traditional Chinese reading tune.

In speaking of the itinerant minstrels of the Serbs, the *guzlari,* who sang to the accompaniment of the *guzla,* a bowed instrument with one string, Rodney Gallop says: "Today there are few *guzlari* left, and these are seldom seen outside Montenegro and Herzegovina, but in their improvised ballads they have chronicled every important episode in Serbian history . . . even so recent an event as the tragic assassination of King Alexander. All these ballads are half sung, half recited, to a monotonous chant on two or three notes." Here, too, we find the custom of reciting a long text to traditional melodic formulas of very limited compass.

Homer was a blind minstrel and poet, and if such long poems as the Iliad and the Odyssey were sung (as seems to have been the case), some such simple and adaptable chant must have been used. The harpers of the Anglo-Saxons must also have had a comparable practice. Finally, the burghers of Germany, the mastersingers, seem to have recited their poems to melodies which had much more of the simple chant about them than of modern melody.

The chant was hardly more than an accessory of poetry or of sacred texts. It could have no independent life of its own. When, however, such clearly metric forms as the hymn developed, when the troubadours appeared and sang their love songs, music responded with strains which had a more definite rhythmic movement. The rhythm of the music still was dependent on the declamation of a poem; but, since the text of a metric hymn had a very decided movement of its own, the music developed a more precise and symmetrical movement which matched that of the verse. The melody was organized into phrases which balanced each other as did the lines of poetry. Moreover, since such melodies frequently moved with more freedom over a more extended compass, they were enjoyable for their own sakes. That they did have a life independent of their texts is shown by the fact that a well-known tune might be used for another text, provided that the metric scheme of the new text was the same as that of the old.

The courtly singers of the Middle Ages, troubadours and trouvères in France, minnesingers in Germany, sang to their ladies in verses which are frequently crisp and piquant in rhythmic movement. The melodies are frequently notated in a fashion which makes the pitch of the note perfectly clear but gives no indication of the relative duration of the notes. The reader who understands that such a pattern as the trochee was to be interpreted by holding the first tone twice as long as the second would have no difficulty in this respect. Readers who are acquainted with the mysteries of music notation will realize that such a scheme might be expressed by the triple meter of the musician. Thus poetic meter is one of the two influences which led to rhythmic music of the present day. The other influence came from the dance which will be discussed in another chapter. Yet both influences might be present. *"Kalenda maya,"* for example, was a dance-tune as well as a troubadour song.

Frequently this early metric music pursues its uniformly rhythmic course as if its creator rejoiced in his freedom from the vague pattern of prose and was delighted with the prospect of an endless procession of uniform metric units. Some of the melodies of this period in spite of (or perhaps because of) their rhythmic uniformity have a primitive and naive charm. Such a melody as *"Puer natus in Bethlehem,"* though not a troubadour composition, shows very well how delightful a melody may be which moves in an absolutely uniform metrical fashion, since the trochaic pattern is unbroken throughout. The end of this particular line of development is the song in which the rhythm, instead of being generated by the song text, becomes the dominant factor. This is most clearly the case in songs where the refrain or even the whole text is composed of nonsense syllables, such as "fa la."

The development of opera is unique among musical forms because it seems to have been evolved as the result of a very definite search for a suitable style. A cultured circle in Florence, the *Camerata,* studied and admired the classics with their wonder tales of the effects produced by Greek music. They wished to revive these wonders for themselves. Their search was for a kind of music which would heighten the declamation of their text but which would also arouse in the audience the emotion appropriate to the words declaimed. They wished to reproduce in music the expressive modulation of the voice of the trained actor. The result was musical recitation as is indicated by its name of recitative or *recitativo.*

The English music historian Burney quotes a letter from the poet Grillo to Caccini, a famous singer and one of the most successful composers in this new style. "We are indebted to you for the invention of a new species of Music; for singing without air, or rather for a melodious kind of speech, called recitative, which is noble and elevated, neither mangling, torturing, nor destroying the life and sense of the words, but rather enforcing their energy and spirit."

In practice this musical speech was allotted to a solo voice. The accompaniment was only suggested by a bass melody played by instruments such as the viola da gamba or cello. With this melody as a foundation, an added accompaniment was improvised on one or more instruments of harmony such as the lute or harpsichord. Such an apparatus seems very inadequate for the purposes of musical drama, and it must have proven to be so in practice.

There is, indeed, a certain nobility about such passages as the prologue to Peri's setting of *"Euridice."* There is warmth of expression which still can be experienced as one turns certain pages in Caccini's *"Nuove Musiche."* Nevertheless, the monotony of an entire drama presented in this style must have been extreme. It is difficult to evaluate such a practical matter, since all the critics of the period were busily engaged in praising the superiority of recitative over the older music which had preceded it or, conversely, attacking the new style as the destruction of true musical art. The proof that the development of a more varied musical style was necessary lies in the fact that such a development did take place relatively soon after the initial experiments.

Some of the various elements in opera which soon assume an increased importance are significant in themselves, but are not related to the present topic. Great strides were made in the technical development of the stage and of scenic effects. The theatrical engineer of the 17th century was not given to evading difficulties in spectacular operatic performances. If Apollo was to descend to earth on a cloud, this was not managed by letting an eyewitness narrate the wonder. Lowered by ingenious machines Apollo actually did descend in full view of the spectators.

The primitive musical accompaniment described above was first elaborated by gathering the court musicians and employing them in groups suitable to the mood of particular scenes. By degrees the stringed instruments gained the ascendency. They were supplemented by a rather variable group of performers on wind instruments. The classic orchestra began to emerge when the wind instruments became regular constituents of the orchestra.

More directly related to our subject are the changes which affected the vocal portion of the performance. The music at the emotional climaxes of the drama tended to be more lyric, more song-like. Finally, a clear distinction was made between speech-music and song-music. The former retains in general its previous character; the latter becomes the aria. The former states the situation; the latter expresses its emotional significance in song. It will be clear that, if the earliest attempts at opera sacrificed the musical elements to the dramatic, this later development sacrifices drama to music. In the spoken drama emotional outpourings do not follow in regular succession after short bits of dialogue, nor would it be possible to develop emotional moments on the spoken stage to the extent which they assume on the operatic stage. A brief recitative followed by a very extended aria is the rule in the Handel operas. What spoken love scene could possibly have the duration of the second act of *"Tristan"* or the final scene of *"Siegfried"*?

The public welcomed the development of the aria with enthusiasm, and opera received a characteristic imprint which is still felt. Captious critics have pointed out that operatic figures do not always behave in an intelligent fashion. They must, in the nature of things, follow their emotions rather than the dictates of intellect, and the course of their adventures is normally planned to secure as many emotional moments as may conveniently be contrived. The magic of music gives life to the heroes and heroines of opera, and gives us life as we share emotional experiences which are both more ideal and more untrammelled by the restraints of reason and prudence than most episodes of actual life.

[77]

The vocal music of the sixteenth century in the form of the madrigal was composed for an unaccompanied group of singers. Towards the end of the century, however, such works were often so arranged that the most attractive musical line was in the upper part. Though madrigals were primarily vocal, it had always been a usual practice to substitute instruments for voices. When all the lower parts of a madrigal were performed on instruments, the singer who took the upper part assumed the role of soloist with instrumental accompaniment.

This development antedated opera, and prepared for it in the sense that it helped to develop the concept of dominant vocal soloist with subordinate accompaniment, as opposed to the earlier ideal of a group of vocalists singing melodies of equal interest. Once a singer assumed the role of soloist, it was both natural and desirable that he should sing with a perfection which was not always demanded of ensemble singers. One factor which led towards vocal virtuosity was the custom of improvising florid passages and ornaments on the basis of a simple madrigal part. Contemporary examples show the amazing lengths to which this practice might be carried.

Such a trend was naturally carried over into operatic music, opposed by composers who wished their works to be respected, and favored by singers who valued the applause they received more than they feared the anger of outraged composers. This is not to say that feats of agility were cultivated by the singer to the exclusion of emotional expression. The assumption of a dramatic role demanded that the singer should convey to the audience the passions inherent in the role. Thus, the cultivation of expressive nuance and the development of technical facility evolved hand in hand.

Caccini himself was a renowned singer and many of his works, with their indications of expression and their ornamental passages, show his interest in the details of performance. His successors were to carry the art of singing to incredible heights and were to establish a type: the vain, temperamental, and greatly gifted virtuoso, the opera singer.

Later composers of opera were able to build on the discoveries of their predecessors. The treatment of the aria and the recitative crystallized into a convention. Nevertheless, composers continued to search intensely for the best manner of representing the human voice in passionate speech in the recitative, for perfection of form and expressive melody in the aria. The gradual spread of opera from Italy, the land of its origin, over all Europe brought into sharp relief the fact that each language has its characteristic intonations, speech rhythms, and vocal color.

This is a problem that rears its head in our day whenever an opera text must be translated from a foreign language into English. It is necessary to search for words in English that have approximately the same rhythm and the same intonation as the word used in the foreign text. At the same time at least the general meaning of the original must be preserved together with any traits of style that can be successfully transplanted. It is not remarkable that translations of song and operatic texts into our own language have generally been of indifferent quality.

The consciousness of the difference in the declamation of different languages was perhaps brought into the sharpest relief in eighteenth century France. In the period of Louis XIV opera had been dominated by Lully, Italian by birth, French in musical culture. Lully reigned without dispute during his own day and, after an interim, was succeeded by Rameau. In 1752 Pergolesi's comic masterpiece *"La Serva Padrona"* was sung in Paris. It precipitated a bitter conflict between the supporters of the two national schools.

When we come to Rousseau, we can see how completely he bases music on language. "If we ask which of all the nations ought to have the best music, I would say that it is the one whose language is the most suitable. This is what I have established previously, and what I shall have occasion to confirm during the course of this letter. But, if there is in Europe a language suitable to music, it is certainly Italian, for this language is sweet, sonorous, harmonious, and accented more than any other, and these four qualities are precisely the most suitable for song."

Later in the same letter he devotes several pages to a detailed and severe criticism of one of the most famous scenes of ancient French opera, the scene from Lully's *"Armide"* in which the rage of the enchantress at the victory of the hero Rinaldo over her forces is turned to love, and the dagger drops from her hands. This analysis is both too long and too technical for our purposes. We turn immediately to Rousseau's summation. "I believe that I have shown that there is neither measure nor melody in French music, because our language is not capable of it; that French song is only a continual barking, intolerable to an inexperienced ear; that the harmony is brutal, without expression, displaying only the filling in of a student; that French arias are not arias, that French recitative is not recitative. From which I conclude that the French have no music and can have none, or, that if they ever develop it, so much the worse for them."

It is indeed hardly necessary to say that we are less concerned with Rousseau's conclusions than with the basis for his argument. Indeed he weakened the force of his words by composing a charming pastoral opera to a French text,— *"Le Devin du Village"* ("The Village Soothsayer"). Other authorities of equal competence reached a contrary conclusion on the basis of the same evidence. Rousseau's case, however, rests on the musical qualities of language, a point of view which is completely operatic.

It is quite exact to state that the recitative and the aria remained the central features of opera up to the reforms of Richard Wagner. The use of the orchestra was developed, and more important recitatives were accompanied by the full orchestra, the so-called *recitativo stromentato*. The chorus, which had been entirely absent from the earliest operas, was employed to voice the feelings of crowds or other large groups. Concerted numbers appeared where the movement of the plot justified it, and the love duet was an almost necessary ingredient. Nevertheless, dramatic declamation and lyrical song remained the basic factors which were the substance of opera.

It is difficult, indeed, impossible, to deal adequately with Wagner who is one of the few composers who have turned opera in a new direction. He, like the earliest composers of opera, aspired to write music which grew out of and expressed the text. The distinction between recitative and aria which, as has already been indicated, was indeed an artificial one was to disappear. Opera was no longer to consist of isolated numbers: arias, duets, choruses. The music was to flow continuously in an endless stream of melody. The orchestra was no longer merely to accompany the voices but was to stress and emphasize the action. The expressive intentions of the composer were to be made explicit by the employment of short pregnant melodic figures, each of which was associated with an important element of the drama. These themes were the leit-motives or leading-motives. As must always be the case, these intentions were not completely realized.

Our present interest is in Wagner's treatment of his texts. Recitative does not disappear. Such moments as the opening scene of "The Valkyrie" in which Siegmund falls exhausted by the hearth and is discovered by Sieglinde are expressed in music which is surely recitative. Later in the act (Scene II) the passage in which Siegmund narrates the adventures which finally led him to take refuge at a strange hearth is equivalent to the dramatic accompanied recitative of the older composers. The "Spring Song" and the duet which follows express the love of Siegmund for Sieglinde. The act rises to an emotional climax with music of overpowering intensity. Yet here we have the aria and the duet, freely treated and unconventional, but clearly displaying their relationship to the older forms.

A real characteristic of Wagner (though not one which he acknowledged) is his use of the orchestra to sing melodies at climactic points in his compositions. Ernest Newman has justly pointed out passages where it would appear that Wagner conceived a symphonic development and adapted the voice parts to an orchestral score which was already complete in itself. Wagner found the orchestra so potent, so magnificent an expressive instrument that he trusted it to carry his melodies to a supreme climax. The human voice was added, but it merely duplicated melodies which were already complete in themselves. Perhaps the most familiar example of this kind is the moving "Love-Death" from "Tristan and Isolda" which is so frequently performed in the concert hall without the voice part. However, such a development carries us, as it carried Wagner, away from music which has close relationships with speech to symphonic music.

Nevertheless, even instrumental music had a definite indebtedness to opera and especially to the operatic orchestra. If we turn back to the eighteenth century and to the operas of Handel, we find that the aria usually opened with an orchestral introduction. The singer then sang the first part of his aria, perhaps interrupted by shorter interludes, but surely followed by a closing instrumental passage. In most cases this was followed by a contrasting section for the singer which also was introduced and followed by orchestral passages. Since the themes played by the orchestra were usually shared by the vocalist, there was a constant transfer of musical ideas and motives from the voice to the instruments. Moreover, these musical ideas were associated with emotions which were made clear by the text. Thus the instrumental language developed and was enriched by the discoveries of operatic composers.

By long familiarity composers, and finally audiences as

well, learned to associate instrumental melodies with definite moods. For example, a quiet undulation (an alternation
of a tone with the tone above it) appears in the "Nightingale Chorus" from Handel's "Solomon" to suggest the gentle
magic of a summer evening. The same pattern appears in
the opening of the "Forest Murmurs" from Wagner's music
drama, "Siegfried." Melodies suggesting a heroic challenge
to battle will leap confidently along the notes of the major
chord in the manner of a trumpet call. Playful love songs
may move in the measure of a gay dance. Songs of deser-
tion, laments, move mournfully and slowly. Melodies of
rage leap from low to high. These patterns and many more
gained definiteness and emotional content from their association with opera and their partnership in the passions of
the actor on the stage. They were, in a real sense, a deriva-
tive of speech even when they were played on instruments.
They brought the breath of human feeling to instrumental
music.

This may require a word of explanation since almost all
the instrumental music which is commonly performed at
the present day does have a definite emotional tone. Yet
this is not true of all early instrumental music. The
familiar Prelude of Bach (No. 1 in C major from Vol. I of
the "Well Tempered Clavier") is a delightful tone pattern and so is the Two Part Invention in F major. Yet they
hardly convey emotion, save perhaps a certain serenity and
purity in the one case and a sort of musical wit in the other.
Many early dances simply suggest movement, but are otherwise not emotionally colored, except so far as the dance
rhythm itself establishes a conventional mood.

Even with Bach this is so. His sarabandes sing with inspired emotion, but elsewhere in his dance pieces he plays
serenely in an ideal world of tone. It was the contact with
human speech through the medium of the opera that made
music passionate, that prepared the way for music like the
"Romeo and Juliet" of Tschaikowsky or the *Pathétique*

Sonata" of Beethoven. Whether this change seems a loss or a gain will depend on the temperament of the listener. Fortunately, the world of music is sufficiently wide to include both types of music.

Other and more general traits derived from the characteristics of human speech have been carried over into the realm of music. Speech tendencies which are nearly universal in our Western civilization have not only had a profound effect on vocal music but have influenced instrumental music as well. These ideas have to do with the modulation or inflection of speech, the register of voices, vocal quality, and the articulation of speech. Under articulation we include manner of delivery, ponderous or voluble speech, oratorical gravity, or gay chattering.

We associate ideas of increased emotional intensity, excitement, struggle, with steadily rising pitch. When we listen to two people who are deeply concerned in an argument, we are likely to note that the pitch of their voices rises as the emotions of the debate reach a white heat. In a similar fashion, a melody is likely to rise to a high tone at the moment of climax. In a Tschaikowsky symphony, for example, a melodic fragment is often repeated, moving higher and higher till a climax is reached. Usually an increase in loudness accompanies and intensifies such a passage.

The characteristic inflection for sadness is a descending one. The reader who declaims the phrase, "Ah me!" with appropriate expression will perceive that the voice drops from a higher to a lower tone. We associate this pattern with decreasing energy, weariness, dejection, sadness. It is usually conventionalized in music by slipping from any tone to an adjacent lower tone or, in musicians' language, by a movement of a descending half step.

With Bach the use of this musical sigh is habitual wherever grief is to be expressed. He employs it simply but with telling effect in his "Capriccio on the Departure of his dearly beloved Brother" at the moment where the grief of the family at the prospect of the imminent departure is depicted. The poignant *"Crucifixus"* from his "B minor Mass" is constructed over a persistently repeated phrase in the bass which descends by half steps. In the late nineteenth century Wagner uses the musical sigh to suggest the painful servitude of the Nibelungs. The Prelude to "Siegfried" utilizes this motive with overwhelming effect.

Earlier composers of vocal music habitually illustrated ideas involving climbing or descending with musical passages which moved from low to high or from high to low. A frequent occasion for the employment of such a device occurs at the phrase "and ascended to heaven" in the *"Credo"* of the Mass. The works of the English and Continental madrigalists abound in naive imagery of this kind. Many similar examples may be found in the music of Bach, especially in the cantatas. The idea was still current at the time of Grétry. He remarked rather dubiously in his memoirs (pub. 1789) that certain composers had gone so far as to employ descending tones with words which conveyed the idea of an ascent. He believed that it was better to conform to the convention than to take pains to deviate from it.

It has been pointed out that there is no real similarity between a musical tone of high pitch and the idea of height or altitude. What is not so commonly realized is that the singing of an ascending passage involves an increasing expenditure of effort with a resulting feeling of successful struggle towards a goal. It is this idea of struggle which is the essence of an ascent whether physical or figurative. Conversely, the descent from a higher to a lower tone involves a diminution of effort on the part of the singer and thus conveys a feeling of relaxation. Thus, it is not the presence of a high or low tone but rather the feeling of an increase or decrease in effort as the voice moves up or down which is the true justification for this expressive device. One must grant, of course, that with the early composers such details were sometimes emphasized to the detriment of the general effect.

The Bach theme for the cantata *"Nun ist das Heil und die Kraft"* ("Now is Holiness and Strength") is a wonderfully simple yet powerful application of these ideas. Here the composer is concerned with a theme that expresses the boundless power of God. The theme is pivoted on a repeated tone which is quitted by leaps of increasing size to successively higher tones. The impression of irresistible power is striking and is obtained by the simplest means.

If we analyze quiet and soothing speech, we find that its inflections are slight, that the intervals through which the voice rises or falls are small. In a comparable fashion the melody of a cradle song is likely to move smoothly and gently from tone to tone. If we turn to Handel's opera *"Alcina,"* we find that the aria *"Ombre pallide"* ("Pale Spirits") sung by the infuriated enchantress, Alcina, moves by leaps. The aria *"Verdi prati"* ("Green Meadows"), the farewell of the hero Rinaldo to the delights of the fields and pleasant groves of Alcina's realm, is extremely smooth in melodic movement. The mood in the first example is frenzied rage, in the second, gentle regret.

We may find more recent examples from the Wagner music drama *"Siegfried."* We may contrast the Magic Slumber Motive with its gentle downward movement with the unrestrained upward leaps of the Valkyrie Motive. In both cases two different characteristics are combined to secure a desired effect. The Slumber Motive descends quietly and smoothly from a higher to a lower tone—(downward movement progressing smoothly rather than by leaps). It typifies the spell which lulls Brunhilda to sleep. The Valkyrie Motive moves upwards with wide leaps to suggest the warrior maidens, the Valkyries, riding through stormy skies.

It would not be difficult to find comparable themes in purely instrumental music. We might contrast the opening theme of Beethoven's "Appassionata Sonata" (Op. 57) which leaps upwards to build a mountain of sound, with the serene beauty of the second theme of the first movement of his *"Waldstein* Sonata" (Op. 53) which moves tranquilly along the adjacent notes of the scale.

The conventions of opera, if not the circumstances of daily life, have caused us to associate certain characteristics with voices of a given pitch or quality. It is difficult to separate the two factors in practice though they are largely distinct. Thus a child's voice is likely to be higher in range than that of a woman. A woman in turn has a voice which is higher in register than that of a man. The word "quality," on the other hand, expresses the difference in timbre or tone color between one voice and another. Thus the tones of a man's voice will differ from those of a woman, even if we assume that both are singing the same words to identical musical tones. Less obvious qualitative differences appear between the tenor and bass voices or between the soprano and alto.

The operatic stage of the nineteenth century furnishes us with the most elementary application of the conventions which express our associations with the various voice types. The soprano is the heroine, the alto is quite frequently a woman of evil intent. Elsa, the heroine of *"Lohengrin,"* is a soprano, Ortrud a contralto. The tenor is almost uniformly the operatic hero while the bass, if not the villain, is relegated to such ceremonial roles as those of generals, counsellors of state, high priests, and so on. Thus Faust, in Gounod's opera of the same title, is a tenor while Mephistopheles is a bass.

This persistent convention in recent opera is the result of the association of a high vocal register with youth and love, low register with villainy, or at best, with the gravity of the mature man. This convention is often unjust to contraltos and basses who, in actual life, may be fully as virtuous and estimable as sopranos and tenors. Nevertheless, our convention is based on simple and natural grounds. The shrill

[87]

voices of children are inextricably associated with ideas of early youth, of innocence. In the same fashion the tenor voice represents young manhood, love, and courtship. The bass voice represents the mature man with the alternatives of noble authority or villainy. If the assignment of the bass voice to ill deeds seems less well-supported than the dedication of the soprano to virtue, we may reflect that many of the most menacing sounds in nature are low in pitch: the rumbling of thunder, the bellowing of the bull, the roaring of the lion. The shout of an enemy would seem more formidable if it were uttered in the resonant tones of a mature man.

Comparable distinctions are made in instrumental music. Thus, *"Les Tuilleries,"* a movement from Moussorgsky's "Pictures at an Exhibition," which depicts children at play chatters away gaily in the upper register of the piano. Wagner in the Prelude to *"Lohengrin"* represents the descent of the Holy Grail from heaven to earth. Accordingly, the Prelude commences with an announcement of the theme which symbolizes the Grail in the highest tones of the flutes and violins. Gradually the music descends from the heights till it reaches its climax in a fortissimo restatement of the opening theme in a lower register. The serene gravity of the melody of the Andante from Beethoven's "Fifth Symphony" is enhanced by the bland sonorities of the violas and cellos, while the *"Menuet des Feux Follets"* ("Minuet of the Will o'-the-Wisps") by Berlioz glitters with the shrill tones of the piccolo.

Closely related to the pitch factor is the articulation, the volubility or gravity of enunciation which expresses the character of a melody. If we turn once more to a comparison with speech, we can establish the principle that in general voices of high pitch are likely to speak more rapidly than those of low pitch. In the orchestra the agility of the flute seems almost unlimited. The unwieldy tuba must produce its tones with a certain deliberation. We associate rapidity and volubility of enunciation with playfulness. The declama- tion of the soubrette as compared with the measured and portentous declamation of the tragedienne, the prattle of a child in contrast with the weighty delivery of an orator.

In a comparable fashion, music which is deeply moving, serious, or impressive is likely to move with measured delibe- ration (*adagio* or *largo*), as, for example, the slow move- ment of Beethoven's "Ninth Symphony"; while music char- acterized by a light and rapid movement might be a scherzo or (if the movement is uniform and persistent) a perpetual motion. Such pieces as the Liszt *"Waldesrauschen"* ("Forest Murmurs") or *"Gnomenreigen"* ("Dance of the Gnomes") and the "Flight of the Bumble Bee" by Rimsky Korsakoff belong here.

Thus, music has borrowed many of its characteristics from speech because early music was primarily vocal music. It re- produces the expressive associations connected with voice quality, pitch, and articulation. In a certain sense it is a sort of idealized language, not without meaning, but conveying only the emotional overtones, the mood of speech without being impeded by the factual content, the rigidly limited significance of words. But, if music gains in ideal quality, in poetic suggestiveness, it loses in definiteness and precision of meaning. We recognize a melody as a lament. We do not know who laments or what brought about the tragedy un- less the text comes to our aid.

Thus, in vocal music it is possible to substitute one text for another, provided the mood suggested by the second text harmonizes with the emotional content of the music. The practice of adapting his music to new texts and new pur- poses was frequent with Bach. Rossini utilized the opening of a chorus from his *"Aureliano in Palmira"* as the cavatina *"Ecco ridente"* in his masterpiece "The Barber of Seville." Verdi's opera *"I Vespri Siciliani,"* composed for Paris, was provided with a different text and was produced in Italy as *"Giovanna di Guzman."*

[89]

In a literary work or a series of paintings such adaptations would be unthinkable. Literature and painting may communicate a mood, but it is a mood defined and limited by the specific character of the medium. Nevertheless the language of music grows richer. Its subtleties increase. In spite of its essential vagueness when employed as an art of delineation music tends to achieve a greater definiteness of expression. Yet the degree of definiteness attainable or in prospect falls far short of that which is usual in literature or the graphic arts. The great power of music lies in its poetic and moving speech, speech which is the more eloquent because it does not convey factual detail, which is the more compelling because it expresses the deep emotional undercurrents which control life.

Chapter V

THE ROLE OF THE MUSICIAN IN SOCIETY

IT is through the early epic poems and sagas that we obtain our first clear view of the musician. It is true that we can still see the musicians of Egypt, of Babylonia, and Assyria as they were depicted by the sculptors of those ancient times. We cannot see how they lived, what they contributed to their society, and how they were rewarded. They must remain images for us, frozen in the one attitude which the artist chose to depict. The poet-musician as we see him in the verses of Homer, in the sagas of the northern peoples has a certain reality.

The fact that music and gymnastics were the chief elements in the education of the Greek boy led the Greek philosophers to make very thoughtful statements which specify just what results were to be expected from this musical training and what the nature of the instruction was to be. In general the poems and the scales to which they were to be sung were intended to produce virtue and harmony in the pupil. Obviously such a plan demanded teachers skilled in both poetry and music. But the general level of musical accomplishment had already been surpassed by professional musicians and poets of special gifts. Such singers are mentioned in the pages of Homer. In this earlier time outstanding skill was more highly regarded and rewarded than in Plato's ideal state. Indeed, both Plato and Aristotle show a certain fear of the professional musician. Excessive virtuosity was fit only to move vulgar crowds. It was not an attainment for the free-born youth.

In ancient times the ability to sing was assumed as a usual accomplishment. We learn this from accounts of banquets where the accompanying instrument, lyre or harp, was passed from hand to hand until each guest had sung. Quintilian in his *"Institutio Oratoria"* has a passage which shows how prevalent the custom was and how necessary such skill was considered to be. "From the importance thus given to music also originated the custom of taking a lyre round the company after dinner, and when on such an occasion Themistocles confessed that he could not play, his education was (to quote the words of Cicero) 'regarded as imperfect!' " Turning to the British Isles we read in the pages of Bede of Caedmon's shame when he also was unable to sing when it was his turn to take the harp. Yet Caedmon was a humble stable-boy in his monastery.

A general knowledge of poetry and music was only possible if every boy were taught the art. We know much about Greek ideas on this subject, much less concerning the theories of the peoples of the North. A Viking called Kali summarized his accomplishments in verse:

"I am ready to play chess,   I can slide on snow-shoes,
  I know nine *idrottir*,   I can shoot and row usefully,
  I shall scarcely forget the   I know too both
    runes,   Harp-playing and metres."
I am a book-reader and
  smith;

Here poetry and music take their place with more practical skills. At a banquet given by King Harald Fairhair we are told that "of all his *hirdmen* the king valued his scalds the most. They were placed on the second high-seat bench (*annat ondvegi*)." Among the Vikings the scald or bard might marry a king's daughter.

The scald not only praised individuals but served to keep brave deeds in mind. We turn once more to the sagas to note that they were sometimes posted (like reporters at a football game) in order that they might be able to give a faithful account of notable happenings.

"It is said that King Olaf arrayed his men, and then arranged the shieldburgh which was to protect him in battle, for which he selected the strongest and most valiant men. He then called his scalds and bid them go into the shield-burgh. 'You shall stay here,' said the king, 'and see what takes place, and then no Saga is needed to tell you afterwards what you shall make songs about.' "

The position of the bard was high not only among the Vikings, but in Ireland and Wales as well. Freemen only might join their ranks. Only priests and warriors were regarded as their superiors. Their function of unifying their countrymen and calling to mind the deeds of the past was long carried on by a race of blind harpers and wandering minstrels. A grim testimony to the importance of the Irish singers is provided by the diligence with which they were hunted down by the British during the subjugation of Ireland under Cromwell. A tendency toward social stratification, however, appeared early in England where the "scop" was higher in the social scale than the "gleeman." The former might be a noble and was frequently a court retainer. The latter was a professional musician who performed for pay, sometimes adding tricks or feats of skill to his repertory.

Another function of the early singer was of a more practical nature. He was sometimes a singer of magic songs. This coupling of magic and music was very ancient. The singer was sometimes a priest, sometimes a bard. The Orpheus legend, in which the musician "made trees, and the mountain tops that freeze, bow themselves when he did sing," was not merely a poetic idea but was based on an ancient and deep-seated belief. Success in healing, in war, in love were all to be obtained by compelling the controlling forces, gods, spirits of the dead, opposing magicians to obedience through the union of the correct magic formula coupled with a musical intonation.

In this way the son of Autolycus stopped the flow of blood from a wound in Ulysses' leg. Thus Joshua caused the walls of Jericho to fall at a blast from his trumpets. Thus in

Virgil and Theocritus we find love-poems which do not merely plead for but compel mutual love.

The old tribal life was gradually replaced by the stratified society of the Middle Ages. The epic poem was replaced by the chronicle which was intended to be read, not sung. The magic formulas for success in love, for the cure of diseases, survived into the Middle Ages (and indeed survive to the present day) but with an infinitely gradual loss of belief. They form part of the folk-lore of out-of-the-way places and sometimes reappear in children's games which have lost their original significance.

As the old bard vanishes to the wild bogs of Ireland, the evergreen forests of the North, the Welsh mountains, the monk and the priest appear, bringing with them the songs which had evolved with the Christian Church, bringing too the fragments of musical learning which had survived the dissolution of the Roman Empire.

Their mission was to convert and to teach, to codify and standardize. Finally the song of the Catholic Church spread all over Europe, and it was one song. This was not accomplished without many struggles with reluctant or unwilling musicians and with the custodians of usages which were stubbornly maintained. Indeed, while the tide of Gregorian song was slowly sweeping across Europe, much survived that was akin to the old customs.

The Abbot of Malmesbury, Aldhelm by name, played the part of a minstrel at the market-cross of that place in the seventh century. He first collected an audience by singing popular airs and then sang the sacred melodies which he wished the people to learn. In monasteries and churches singers were trained. The clergy erected organs in the churches. As the art of singing in a kind of harmony developed, they practised these methods and found ways of writing down what they sang.

When chapels, organized groups of singers, were formed in cathedrals and in royal courts, the ranks of these zealous music teachers furnished many of those who sang and those who played upon the organ. The church offered the only refuge for the scholarly musician in a time of never-ending war. The church trained singers, furnished an opportunity for musical service, and preserved the accumulated knowledge and skill of past generations.

Yet in the market-place and by the fireside the old popular music must have persisted. The minstrel continued to sing and the juggler and acrobat amused the gaping populace with their tricks. Yet this music could not survive, because only the clerks of the church had the skill to record music and verse, and they either avoided such songs or used them for their own ends.

When the first courtly songs appear in France in the eleventh and twelfth centuries, we find once more a distinction in rank between the noble singer, the troubadour, who was the poet-composer, and the jongleur, a professional performer who went about singing the compositions of the troubadour who employed him. The dominant theme of the songs which they sang was the adoration of a chosen lady. There are songs of May and *Jeux-parties* in which riddles or difficult questions propounded by one singer are answered (in the first instance extemporaneously) by another. In the *Tageslied*, a favorite type with the minnesingers, a watchful friend warns an enamoured couple of the approach of day. Wagner has utilized this traditional subject in Act II of his "Tristan and Isolda," where Brangaene interrupts the duet of the two lovers with warning phrases as she keeps watch on the castle tower.

The striking fact about all the courtly singers is their preoccupation with the detail and the ritual of courtship. Many of the debates concerning minute details of etiquette appear to have been conducted in a legal fashion which contrasts oddly with their subject matter. The ingredients which entered into the attitudes and feelings which inspired these love songs were strangely diverse. The special devotion in-

[95]

spired by the Virgin Mary tended to raise all women in status. The code of knighthood demanded that the knight swear allegiance to his feudal lord. A similar allegiance to a chosen lady on a somewhat less realistic plane was entirely in accordance with the habits of thought of the period. The motive of ideal and unrequited love existed side by side with the frank realism of the popular song. The refinement of manners which were practiced did not exclude deeds of even more refined cruelty. Nevertheless the motive of romantic love which still dominates modern song has its roots in this early literature. We must not, however, expect the music to be "expressive," to mirror the sentiment of the poem. That was reserved for a much later period. As in the performance of the earlier poems, the emotion was in the text and the manner of performance, not in the music.

The pastoral, however, frequently possesses a frank and sometimes humorous realism which seems to reveal traces of an earlier tradition. In these songs a knight meets and woos a shepherdess. Sometimes he wins her love, sometimes he is driven off by her husband or lover. Sometimes when he fails to win her with fine phrases, he takes her by force. This genre may reveal a popular vein surviving from an earlier time and appearing chiefly in the songs written by singers of lower birth towards the end of this period of gallant song (i. e. in the thirteenth century). Certain later poet-musicians do indeed belong to the middle class. One of the best known and one of the latest, Adam de la Halle, was a bourgeois. This movement, so fruitful in France, had no direct counterpart in Italy where, however, we find simple folk-hymns or *"Laudi"* sung by the Franciscan monks and by the populace.

Many musicians entered the service of some great lord and found protection and employment there. An indication of the scope of an early musical establishment is furnished by the "Liber Niger Dominus Regis" which gives us detailed information on the English royal chapel at the time of Edward IV. Here we find a dean, 24 chaplains and clerks (among whom were the singers and organists), two epistlers, eight children (who sang the upper parts of sacred compositions), a master of the grammar school, and a master of the children. This last named official was responsible for the musical education of the "children" and for their proper instruction in the music which was to be sung.

Employment in such an establishment conferred a certain security on the musician. His position was legalized. Once a member of His Majesty's Chapel Royal, he normally enjoyed life tenure in his position. Often he was able to introduce his son into the service as his successor. Complete dependence on the good-will of the ruler gradually gave way to a status with certain recognized rights and perquisites. This is not to say that the necessity of pleasing the king was less important or that any one of the musicians would for a moment have considered any action which might conceivably offend the monarch.

These groups of musicians which clustered about the seats of power in Europe were at first primarily establishments for the performance of religious music. To these were added performers on various instruments, composers, and whatever musicians there were who gave promise of adding lustre to the fame of the ruler.

This opened a new life to the musician. Serious musician and church musician no longer were identical terms. Though the church remained the great school for musicians, it now was possible to be a musician and a composer of secular music. This statement, so obvious and commonplace to us, marked the starting point of the modern musician. By far the larger number of early composers wrote both motets for the chapel and madrigals for the court.

A composer known chiefly for his courtly compositions like Guillaume de Machaut (c. 1300-1377) must have had a more substantial means of support than music. De Machaut was a secretary at the court of Burgundy. Richard Edwards (c. 1523-1566) was an English poet and dramatist as well as musician. Several of the great Elizabethan madrigalists wrote little or no religious music. Gesualdo (c. 1560-1613) was a nobleman for whom music was not a means of livelihood. Thus the demands of the court for musical entertainment not only stimulated the production of secular music. It also made possible a new kind of musician, the lute virtuoso, the court poet and arranger of songs for masques and ballets, the composer of madrigals and other artful and courtly compositions.

When the power of towns and of the middle class became sufficiently marked, they too employed musicians. This was particularly true in the Germanies. The town musician was often a solid and respected citizen who played on a variety of instruments and composed music for them. Perhaps his music possessed more solidity than imagination. Possibly it lacked the latest graces of the court, but it suited its purpose, and it gradually formed its own tradition. Performers on brass instruments played chorales from the towers of walled towns. Town musicians supplied table music for municipal banquets. They played in the orchestra which accompanied the cantatas which were sung in the church on Sundays. The conspicuously successful merchant might become a patron and establish a chapel of his own.

Following the example of the guilds of craftsmen and merchants of the Middle Ages musicians also associated themselves together in protective organizations. Frequently these organizations appear to have been formed more to assure an income to a favored individual than as a means of assuring a fair livelihood to the rank and file. In France we find the "Corporation of Saint Julian," in England the "Musicians' Company." Both possessed a power of licensing performers which gave them considerable influence over the lives of musicians. The French "King of the Violins," however, did not find it easy to maintain his rule, and his authority was diminished by unsuccessful attempts to maintain his prerogatives.

Thus, still another door was opened to the musician. He

might seek the shelter of a walled city. He played for civic officials, for merchants and tradesmen. It was a less brilliant career than that of a member of a royal chapel. Nevertheless, it marked the establishment of middle-class security just as the formation of chapels-royal was an indication of the growth of royal power and prestige.

It was in an atmosphere of middle-class activity, watched over by church, school, and civic authorities, that Bach grew up and worked. His orchestra at St. Thomas' Church in Leipzig was drawn in part from town musicians, in part from university students, as well as from the ranks of his own students in St. Thomas' School.

Few writers give a clear view of the town musician as his contemporaries saw him. For this reason Ned Ward's jeering account of the municipal musicians of London, the "waits," deserves quotation here. The "waits" were the originals of the little groups of out-of-door serenaders which decorate our Christmas cards. The author of the "London Spy" (which first appeared in collected form in 1703) gives quite a different picture.

"At last bolted out from the corner of the street, with an *ignis fatuus* dancing before them, a parcel of strange hobgoblins covered with long frieze rugs and blankets, hooped round with leather girdles from their cruppers to their shoulders, and their noddles buttoned up into caps of martial figure, like a knight-errant at tilt and tournament with his wooden head locked in an iron helmet.

"One was armed, as I thought, with a faggot-bat, and the rest with strange wooden weapons in their hands in the shape of clyster pipes, but as long, almost, as speaking-trumpets. Of a sudden they raised them to their mouths, and made such a frightful yelling, that I thought the world had been dissolving and the terrible sound of the last trumpet to be within an inch of my ears.

"Under these amazing apprehensions I asked my friend what was the meaning of this infernal outcry? 'Prithee.'

says he, 'what's the matter with thee? Why these are the City waits, who play every winter's night through the streets.'

'Lord bless me!' said I, 'I am very glad it's no worse. Prithee let us haste out of the hearing of them.'

"At this my friend laughed at me. 'Why, what,' says he, 'don't you love music? These are the topping tooters of the town, and have gowns, silver chains, and salaries, for playing *Lillabolaro* to my Lord Mayor's Horse through the City.' "

A considerable number of explanatory notes might be required to explain all the oddities of Ned Ward's account. It may be sufficient to note here that the "faggot-bat" was a *fagotto* or bassoon. The strange wooden weapons were shawms or, in modern terms, oboes. The waits therefore constituted a wind band of the kind that was usually used at the time for marches or out-of-door serenades and dances.

Middle-class influence was also manifest in the increasing tendency to treat music as a business or as an accessory of business. Where town musicians played in the square on market days, we can easily see that the town fathers hoped that those attracted by the music would also buy generously. On a more splendid scale were the famous "Evening Concerts," the *"Abendmusiken"* which Dietrich Buxtehude conducted (from 1673) for many years in the great commercial city of Lübeck. Though they took place in a church, they were religious concerts, not church services. The local merchants contributed to the expenses of these festivals. It is reasonable to suppose that they felt that they were a profitable advertisement of the wealth and power of their city and an added inducement for people to congregate there.

The development of opera shows with especial clarity the emergence of the business motive. The earliest operas were experiments made by cultivated circles of musicians and intellectuals and were directed towards the revival of ancient Greek tragedy. Opera passed from this restricted milieu and, fused with the ballet and the pageant, became the plaything of dukes and princes. It became pompous, inflated, spectacular, the vehicle of ponderous allegorical compliments directed toward the monarch whose birthday, wedding, or success in war or diplomacy was celebrated.

Such displays were financed in the simplest fashion. The agents of the ruler extracted taxes from the people. The ruler put both hands into the treasure chest and spent for his pleasure and that of the court circle. The musicians who were molded by these circumstances were polished, pliant, eager to ponder the implications of a casual phrase from the lips of their master and anxious to anticipate his every wish. Such performances continued, but they were paralleled by the development of the public opera house which in its turn was peopled by a whole series of musical types, the impresario, the professional opera composer and conductor, the travelling opera singer who performed this season in Naples and the next in London.

At first singers were paid little. As opera-houses sprang up all over Italy, then all over Europe, a competitive struggle to secure performers who had found favor with the public led to the establishment of a "star system." While other members of the company were poorly paid, the *virtuosa* was begged to accept huge sums. She was proud, capricious, overbearing. Noble heirs sought to marry her and were prevented from doing so only by such drastic measures as imprisonment for the heir or banishment for the singer. She, like certain singers of more recent date, had her circle of swooning admirers. In short, a pattern was early established which has persisted with appropriate modifications down to the present day.

In France at the period of Louis XIV, though a similar transition took place, it showed certain interesting divergences from the Italian pattern. The earlier ballets of the French court were part of the royal pleasures and were paid for out of the royal treasury. As the musical establishments grew in complexity, it seemed economical for the king and pro-

[101]

fitable for the music-director to grant a monopoly in the presentation of musical-dramatic performances. The king's influence over music and text was hardly lessened since he granted and could withdraw the privilege. The music-director, on the other hand, was free to open the doors of the opera-house to the public and to install money takers there to collect the price of admission. The first holder of the privilege in France was a minor dramatic poet called Perrin.

He, unfortunately, had been luckless or imprudent enough to contract debts and, imprisoned by his creditor, was forced to intrust his affairs to two agents. These gentlemen pocketed the box-office receipts, coolly ignored Perrin in his prison cell, and failed to pay the singers. It is clear that there was money to be made by the musical pastoral which was on the stage, for we can hardly suppose that Sourdéac and Champéron were motivated by love of art.

Perrin and the musician Cambert who wrote music to his verses are forgotten by all save the music historian. It was Lully who negotiated for the privilege which Perrin was unable to turn to his own advantage. He became master of the "*Académie Royale de Musique et de la Danse.*" With his musical triumphs we are not concerned at this point. Lully was, however, a good administrator as well as a supple and clever courtier and a musician of very great gifts. Whether he fulfilled Colbert's wish for him we do not know. Certainly the wish with its emphasis on material rewards was very characteristic of the comptroller general of finances of Louis XIV.

"I hope that Lully may gain a million in making operas in order that the example of a man who will have made such a fortune by composing music may encourage all other musicians to make every effort to accomplish as much as he."

We do know that Lully amassed a fortune. He remains the perfect example of the successful monopolist and business man who was also a great musician. It was a career which showed brilliantly that music had become a business and might be conducted as an eminently successful business enterprise.

Few composers could gain the precarious position of power which Lully finally achieved. For most composers the position of court servant or chapel-master was the best that they could hope for. They would then settle down at some country seat or city palace. They would form and direct an orchestra, rehearse and perform the music of their master's private chapel. If he were musically inclined, they would play duets with him or form a string quartet in which he might take part. If the establishment were a large one, there might well be a private theatre, and the music-director would then have private operatic performances to organize and conduct.

Nevertheless, a study of the careers of composers from Haydn to Schubert reveals a significant shift from the service of an individual patron to the service of a wider public. Haydn himself passed most of a long life in the service of the Esterházy family. He spent a short winter season in Vienna, the rest of the year at their remote Hungarian estate. His music was largely written for the diversions at the Esterházy palace: works for the prince's orchestra, quartets for less formal musicals, duets and trios for the prince's favorite instrument, the baryton. Finally the prince died. His successor dismissed the musicians. By this time Haydn had a lifetime of service behind him.

Salomon appeared abruptly. "I have come to fetch you to England." This impresario and business man came from the modern world to Haydn who had just been freed from the service of aristocratic feudalism. It is doubtful whether a musician ever made a more abrupt transition from the past to the present. It is doubtful, too, whether Haydn fully realized the width of the gap which he crossed when he set sail for England. His journals, full of amusing detail, are silent on this point. One thing was amply clear. In England concerts were not only conducted as a business. They were a profitable business and one which was so well supported by both nobility and gentry that a composer could sell his compositions, not himself.

Haydn had not sought the change. It had sought him out. But he had seen and experienced both worlds, the old one in which a musician was a feudal servant and the new world of commercial England in which a musician might sell his power to perform or his compositions without living as a servant, an honored and respected servant perhaps, but still a servant.

Mozart, like Haydn, had no real desire to release himself from the world of aristocratic patronage. Haydn served patiently and with gratitude to the end of his term. Mozart, goaded both by the consciousness of his musical powers and the keen realization of the arbitrary restrictions and the harsh treatment which he had to endure, finally rebelled and left the service of his master, the Archbishop of Salzburg.

"Twice already that—I don't know what to call him— has said to my face the greatest *sottises* and *impertinences* which I have not repeated to you, as I wished to spare your feelings, and for which I only refrained from taking my revenge on the spot because you, my most beloved father, were ever before my eyes." Finally, the Archbishop's steward kicked Mozart down stairs. Mozart's childhood tours had been undertaken not only in the hope of immediate gain but to win fame in order that he might ultimately secure a place to some degree commensurate with his own enormous gifts. This place he was never to find.

Perhaps his failure to obtain a permanent and more adequate post was caused by the fact that prospective patrons preferred music which was a little simpler, more obviously tuneful. Perhaps it was because those who had the power to bestow places considered that Mozart had displayed a little too much independence. These matters do not appear in the record. Mozart, on a later occasion, placed himself in the way of the Elector of Bavaria. He recited his qualifications.

"I have been three times to Italy already, I have written three operas, I am a member of the Bologna Academy, where I had to pass a test, at which many maestri have laboured and sweated for four or five hours, but which I finished in an hour. Let that be a proof that I am competent to serve at any court. My sole wish, however, is to serve your Highness, who himself is such a great—'Yes, my dear boy, but I have no vacancy. I am sorry. If only there were a vacancy—' I assure your Highness that I should not fail to do credit to Munich. 'I know. But it is no good, for there is no vacancy here.' This he said as he walked away. Whereupon I commended myself to his good graces."

The appointment which Mozart finally did receive from Joseph II of Austria paid, as Mozart bitterly said, "too much for what I do, too little for what I might do." Two resources were left him beyond the uncertain returns from his compositions. He could give piano lessons which he did with a somewhat unwilling spirit. He could give subscription concerts. In a letter to his father in which he obviously attempts to put his financial prospects in the best light he lists the concerts which he has in prospect. But all these sources of income were insufficient to relieve him from the necessity of writing letters to his more affluent friends asking for loans.

One of the most curious facts about the musicians of France during the French Revolution is that they seem to have had no complete idea of the vast importance of the movement to which they contributed their talents. The pure precise classicism of a Gossec, the pretty if naive pastorals of Grétry seem strange for an epoch which produced the Marseillaise. Yet it was not till the grandiose popular festivals of the French Revolution that music was employed to remind the people of their worth and dignity as citizens, of the value of agriculture and the arts to the state, of the equality and the brotherhood of man. The ceremonial music of this period produced an effect which we cannot renew since it was designed, not for the restricted confines of the concert hall, but for the wide spaces of the *Champs de Mars*.

Even if some of the musicians of the period were hardly conscious of the full import of the advent of a new conception of man, or were, like Grétry, quite willing to forget the part they had played, nevertheless, a new place had been prepared for all men and the musician among them. "Citizen musician" had been born who would make music for the common good, an equal among equals.

Perhaps some parallel to this period with its passion for pageantry may be found in the triumphal arches, the festival odes, the hymns and marches which welcomed the arrival of General Washington in the period which followed our own Revolution, popular tributes to the man who had made himself a national hero. Surely Beethoven's pride, his faith in human destiny, his longing for an era of universal brotherhood owed much to fundamental beliefs fostered by the French Revolution.

Beethoven's status was a result of his fiercely free and ungovernable disposition, of his ability to impose himself on those whom he met, and of the fact that he was able to attract to himself a circle of aristocratic, wealthy, and at the same time amazingly tactful and considerate patrons. Yet even if we grant that his victory was largely a personal triumph, won by qualities both on his part and on that of his patrons which were altogether exceptional, we must nevertheless applaud his triumph. He was a free man. Perhaps only Handel before him had won that fierce struggle for independence, had gone his way, and had made that way the way of his audiences.

Beethoven, helpless as he was in managing his household affairs, was nevertheless a keen business man. He fought his publishers for a fair price. He wrote them menacing letters. He received a pension from a group of patrons to assure his presence in Vienna, and he complained bitterly when it was not paid. He passionately refused to alter a note or a detail of his more important works, yet he was willing to undertake such commissions as the four-hand marches.

Critics tend to pass over these characteristics of Beethoven or to regard them as flaws. They are precisely the marks of the struggle of the artist to live, to live in his own way without compromising his freedom, to create works which will represent the composer, not primarily the society for which he worked. It was as heroic a battle as that other struggle which he had carried to a successful conclusion, the struggle for a personal mastery of his musical materials in the face of increasing deafness.

Schubert completes the transition to the new world. Beethoven still lived to a considerable extent on money given him by his patrons. But where Beethoven was overpowering and spectacular, Schubert was quietly gifted. Where Beethoven had multiple powers of conquest as virtuoso, pianist, conductor, composer, Schubert could only compose. Even his facile pen could not create fast enough to enable him to live, nor was he able to induce his publishers to pay him well. His life marks, not the end of the system of patronage (which, indeed, survives to the present day), but rather the point where a musician tried to live by working for a public, not for individual patrons.

His attempts failed. Nevertheless, Schubert marks the beginning of a period where the musician was responsible not to a given nobleman or a circle of patrons but to the public. The public bought tickets to hear artists sing his songs. Thus he faced the broader responsibility of working for many, not for a few. The musician faced at the same time the loss of the security which he had enjoyed as a member of a royal chapel or the chapel-master of some local ruler. Moreover the public demands a certain drama, showmanship, bravado. It rewards profusely or not at all. The artist tended to lose the precious privilege of making intimate music for a small and cultivated circle.

Courts gradually ceased to be centers of creative activity. At most they could share with a larger public on a privileged basis the artists whom all the world might hear. The virtuoso was typical of the new period, fabulous, brilliant, dramatic. He was no longer caged for the benefit of a single courtly circle. The opera composers and the opera singers of the eighteenth century had already shown the way. The audience for music had increased. Travel had become quicker and somewhat less of an ordeal. Liszt, Paganini, Jenny Lind moved restlessly from place to place, a concert, a reception, an ovation, and then on to another triumph.

Spectacular stage operas developed when the opera-house doors were opened to the public, and perhaps in part as an easy bid for public attention. In a similar fashion the virtuoso opened his box of tricks to gain and to hold the attention of his new audience. The satanic Paganini with his aura of the supernatural, the stories of his romantic love affairs, his imprisonment, could probably have attracted a public without playing at all. Add to this highly colored background his spectacular technical discoveries, and one is in a position to account for the enormous sensation which his playing caused.

Liszt was a musician of great creative gifts. He was, to an altogether exceptional degree, capable of appreciating the work of contemporary composers of varied gifts, Chopin, Wagner, Grieg, and many others. In spite of his real greatness of spirit, he assumed or embodied spectacular traits which certainly did not lessen his interest for the public. His numerous and well-publicized love affairs, his profile and leonine mane, his uneasy oscillation between mysticism and romance, the somewhat unhealthy atmosphere of adulation which he inspired and in which he lived, the superficial glitter and the bombast which were characteristic of certain of his performances, all these factors did not lessen his box-office appeal.

Perhaps equally characteristic of the late romantic period was the emergence of the virtuoso conductor. Excellent concert orchestras existed during the classic period at London, Mannheim, Paris. Orchestral music gradually created its public. Orchestras were enlarged, standardized, subjected to an increasingly severe discipline. To attract a large public to hear this expensive apparatus it was necessary to exploit personalities, hence the important role played by the soloist in orchestral concerts almost up to the present day. Eventually, however, the orchestra itself became a virtuoso instrument; and if a personality was needed to attract the public, it was furnished by the conductor. This, however, was a very recent development. The conductor in the modern sense was a product of the romantic period. Mendelssohn, Liszt, and Wagner were pioneers in this new art, but it was perhaps Berlioz who exploited most exclusively the possibilities of a new kind of career.

He was hardly a performer at all, save for a youthful interest in the flute and flageolet and some proficiency on the guitar. Nevertheless, he explored the possibilities of each orchestral instrument in great detail and published his findings in a treatise on orchestration, on the art of arranging music for the orchestra, which is a work of great historic importance. He wrote for the orchestra with a brilliance and effectiveness which, if it sparkles less for present-day audiences, does so because many of his successors have studied his methods to good advantage.

The step from composing works for orchestra to conducting them was a natural one. His tours through Germany demonstrated that the conductor could henceforth be numbered among the virtuosi. How novel this role still was is amusingly revealed by Berlioz' account of his difficulties in securing a concert-hall in Moscow on his Russian tour.

"The nobles' assembly-room was, as I have said, the only

one suitable for my concert. Wishing to obtain the use of it, I had myself introduced to the grand marshal, a venerable-looking old man of about eighty, and proceeded to unfold to him the object of my visit. The first thing he asked me was:

"What instrument do you play?"

"No instrument whatever."

"In that case, how do you propose to give a concert?"

"To have my compositions performed and to conduct the orchestra."

"Ha! that is an original idea. I never heard of a concert like that. I will willingly lend you our large hall, but, as you no doubt know, artists who make use of it are obliged, in return, to perform at one of the private gatherings of the nobility."

Berlioz protested feelingly that it would cost him three thousand francs to pay the musicians for such a concert. The marshal remained adamant. Berlioz offered to play on the flute, flageolet, or guitar for the nobility. "But as it is about five-and-twenty years since I have touched either of them, I must warn you that I shall play very badly. Or if you will be satisfied with a drum solo I shall probably acquit myself better." Finally, an exception was made for one concert only, and Berlioz had won his victory.

His dreams of a gigantic orchestra were on such a pro-digal scale as to defy practical realization. He had indeed been confronted by the dilemma which has plagued orchestras and their conductors ever since, the problem of finding a sound economic basis for large-scale orchestral performances.

Berlioz was as striking a figure on the stage as Paganini or Liszt. Unluckily for him his music baffled contemporary audiences. His sharp criticisms and his Gallic wit amuse us, but made him enemies where he most needed friends. In spite of his aureole of red hair, his fiery and impetuous conducting, the novelty of the huge music festivals which he organized, he won only a partial victory. The fact that his real fame came from Germany, while Paris to a considerable extent remained cool or indifferent, was one of many disappointments which made his later years overflow with bitterness. Nevertheless his was a career which was infinitely characteristic of the progressive tendencies of this period.

The nineteenth century witnessed the gradual emancipation of the musician. The period of the French Revolution was, however, followed by a period of conservative reaction. The old world of aristocratic patronage was gradually crumbling. The musical vistas opened by the musicians of the French Revolution had been obscured. The new commercial world of business, imperialism, power politics found no place for the musician save as a purveyor of luxuries or as a fellow business man. He had neither the assured standing of a court functionary nor the consciousness of being the voice of his people. The musician who could furnish gaudy entertainment and calculate shrewdly the tastes of his audience succeeded. More poetic natures shrank into isolation and revolt.

Meyerbeer, who repeatedly tested and altered his brilliant and pompous scores, met with enormous contemporary success. But, while his habit of constant revision suggests the conscience of a careful workman, his careful exploration and preparation of every means to success were more typical of the prudent entrepreneur. What Meyerbeer accomplished on the great stage of the grand opera, Offenbach equalled in miniature in the operetta. In a series of facile, sophisticated, and satirical musical sketches he pleased the frivolous audience which was willing to laugh at itself provided the thrusts at its own follies did not go beyond good-humored parody.

Wagner dreamed of the "folk," but the youthful revolutionist and exile gave place to the more cautious friend of a generous king. In spite of the militant attitudes which Siegfried assumes, he is in Wagner's version no true folk hero, but a mere puppet in a larger drama. The simple moral of the Ring Dramas is the fact that the Gods are helpless to save themselves from ultimate destruction once they have violated the laws of justice which they established. Wagner triumphed over apparently insuperable obstacles to obtain adequate hearings for his works. The works themselves, however, are works of frustration. Senta sacrifices herself to redeem the Dutchman. Tristan finds the only solution for his tragic love in self-sought death. The twilight of the Gods and the death of all their number save Loki are the consequences of their failure to abide by their own laws. Does not this conclusion reflect Wagner's own tragedy since he could only attain his ends by stultifying compromises and by a policy of expediency which he himself would have rejected as a young man?

Yet Wagner's music remains a magnificent exposition of human emotion. The gentler romantic poets of his period turned to their inner world and wrote music which reflected in characteristic fashion the moods, the sadness, and the ecstasy which only their art could faithfully reproduce. Their reality was a personal reality, and their world was an emotional world. Though their contemporaries found them much more difficult to understand than the brilliance of the operatic stage or the pyrotechnics of the virtuosi, their works have survived the rest because they portrayed a reality common to all humanity, the reality of human emotion.

Yet the romantic composer faced the danger of developing personal fantasy to a point where it not only ceases to have universal validity, but even general comprehensibility.

When Schumann draws his own characteristics and those of his circle in his "Carnival," is he not offering to the public what remains (in this particular respect) a personal whim? As the isolation of the composer from his society increased and his narcissistic introspection became more pronounced, we find the divergence in style between composer and composer increasing, the circle of his audience contracting. Richard Strauss is more unlike Debussy than Haydn is unlike Mozart or Schumann unlike Brahms. Technical experimentation increases, the music becomes more complex, more anxious to achieve "differentness." New compositions are studied for "fashion trends." When a limit in complexity has been reached it suddenly becomes the vogue to write with exaggerated simplicity, to write like Mozart, like Bach.

This retreat into the ego has been countered by composers who have sought to root themselves firmly in their native soil, to write music which will reach a national public, or works which will express the feelings of all their fellow-men and not those of a narrow circle. Thus, many composers, though they have utilized the technical findings of their predecessors, have been caught by the democratic upsurge which answered the fascist challenge before the second World War. American composers have rediscovered the folk music of their country and have found in it a new significance. They have found their roots after a period of spiritual if not actual expatriation. Soviet composers, too, after a period of modernist complexity have endeavored to write in a direct and understandable fashion in an attempt to reach their enormous new audience. These are the signs of the advent of composers who may write for all of us, of the growth of a true people's music. This is not the only kind of composer nor the only contemporary trend. It is only one strand in a vastly complicated pattern of human effort. Whether it will grow and broaden as our democracy grows, only the future can reveal. What is clear is that such a development depends not solely on the work our composers do nor on the growth of our society, but on the mutual growth and interaction of one with the other.

CHAPTER VI

GREAT PERIODS IN THE
DEVELOPMENT OF MUSIC

NOT only did the function of the musician vary, but the function of music itself changed with changing social conditions. The incredible flexibility which gave music the power to sing of green fields and to evoke the sound of the shepherd's pipe, to mirror the passion of love, and to unfold developments which are their own delight enabled it to serve various societies in varied ways. With the same facility it enriches and solemnizes the rites of religion, adorns court ceremonials, or regulates the entrance of a victorious army. Though music has served such purposes throughout recorded history, there was a characteristic style dominant in each period which makes it possible for the skilled listener to assign most unfamiliar compositions to their proper time.

It is impossible to understand music which we have not experienced in some measure ourselves. The present sketch, therefore, begins with the earliest music which survives as a living force, the Gregorian chant of the Catholic Church and the comparable melodies of the Eastern Church and of the Orthodox Synagogue. Such musical forms have developed in connection with religious ritual, and an experience of a given type of religious music has to a large extent been confined to the members of a particular sect.

All these early melodies have in common the fact that they employ a single melodic line sung either by an officiant or by a chorus. Such music is not performed for the sake of its aesthetic effect but as a part of the act of worship. That its purely musical effect might still be very intense is evident from a statement like that of St. Augustine which records his response to the music of the early Christian Church:

"The voices flowed in at my ears, truth was distilled in my heart; and the affection of piety over-flowed in sweet tears of joy." Church authorities insisted in general that music should be the servant of the text, that the clear enunciation of the text of the service was a primary consideration.

The ancient melodies, though they do not convey personal emotion, do represent the collective beliefs and aspirations of those who shaped the ritual texts and those who adapted and composed melodies for them. Yet, though it would appear that the role of the musician was narrowly circumscribed, an examination of a series of Gregorian melodies will reveal not only simple settings where the music is clearly the servant of the text but also others in which the music is more elaborate and florid. These ancient monodies, moving among a few tones with the free rhythms of speech, were in a real sense the generators of modern music. They resounded under the vaulted arches of church and monastery. They were echoed in the melodies of the most ancient popular songs. The church musician was able to make advances which were critical in the history of modern art. The task of tracing the infinitely cautious and gradual development of the art of creating melodies which could be added to and sung with the Gregorian chants must be left to the music historian. We are creatures of the Renaissance. We seek a new, a personal expression in music as in the other arts. Composers of the Middle Ages, however, tended to rear their tonal edifices on borrowed foundations. They began, not by inventing a melody, but by choosing one from the repertory of Gregorian song. To this they added melodies of their own invention.

Indeed, at one period they went beyond this and wrote compositions in which all the component melodies were borrowed. The labor of the composer was expended in so adjusting these melodies that they fitted each other as well as possible. In some cases each melody was provided with its own text. If this appears incredible as a way of making music, and admittedly it violates all our ideas of the creative process, we must grant that it demands a considerable discretion in the choice of melodies and some skill in their arrangement. It is even possible to point out some cases where a similar procedure has been followed in modern times.

Some ingenious person discovered that it was possible to combine the melody of Dvořák's "Humoresque" with that of Stephen Foster's "Old Folks at Home." The quodlibet (in one sense of this word) involved a similar practice. Members of the Bach family are said to have had a cheerful habit of combining extemporaneously as many different melodies as they could in a not unharmonious melange.

Readers who are familiar with Bach's "Goldberg Variations" will remember that the last variation superposes two merry folktunes over the bass in the manner of a quodlibet. These, however, were specialized practices. The use of one foundation melody, the so-called cantus firmus, around which other melodies were interwoven, was an established usage and one which has not yet entirely vanished.

What inner need led to this development of harmonious choral singing? Was it due, at least in part, to a desire to initiate a more elaborate and grandiose style of performance for church festivals? Was it in its earliest stages an adaptation for church purposes of a tradition of improvised popular part-singing, which, as we are told, existed in Britain and Wales at an early period?

However these questions may be answered, the art of composing for a vocal chorus flourished. The serene perfection of Palestrina (c. 1524-1594), the versatile art of Orlando di Lasso (c. 1530-1594), the warm emotion of Tomás Luis de Victoria (c. 1548-1611) are better known to modern audiences than the music of many of their predecessors and contemporaries. The sixteenth century was a period of great composers who are unknown because their works are not performed. These masters wrote music again and again to the liturgical texts. The mass, the service in which the worshipper received wine and bread as the blood and the body of Christ, provided the texts of the *Kyrie,* the *Gloria,* the *Credo,* the *Sanctus* and *Benedictus,* and the *Agnus Dei.* Such texts were invariable. Other texts, like those used for the motet, varied and were frequently designed for a particular season of the church year.

The connection of religious choral music with the traditional melodies of the church gradually became more tenuous. The composer, no longer obliged to adapt his own thoughts to a controlling traditional chant, was free to create his own melodies and to treat them in a more personal fashion. In a sense the process was symbolic of the gradual diminution of the authority of the church. Eventually the musician emerged from cathedral and from cloisters and found other possibilities and other rewards for his art.

As the feudal nobles left their grim fortresses and built palaces and pleasure gardens, they also learned to lead a life which was more courtly, more luxurious. Lovemaking was no longer a brief and primitive rite but an elaborate game. And it was largely the language of courtship and gallantry that the musicians and the poets of the Renaissance spoke. Though hunger gnawed at the poverty-stricken peasants, plenty reigned in the palace. Nature no longer was a grim and frightful force. But when the musicians sang of nature they devoted themselves to the praises of spring. Heating devices were still crude, and it was left for a later and more comfortable generation to praise the beauties of winter. The art of the troubadour and of the German minnesinger was an art of solo song. If the singer accompanied himself on the instruments which he holds in miniatures of the period, and it is reasonable to suppose that he did, these accompaniments have left only the slightest traces in the written record.

It is possible to draw a parallel between trends in art and literature at the time of the Renaissance and characteristics of secular music at the same period. The flowering of poetry in the vernacular, the rise of naturalism in the representative arts were powerful influences on the musician. It is clear that the efflorescence of poetry at this time stimulated the musician to create music which would reflect a similar mood. The beauty of nature is mirrored in songs of the May as well as in the landscapes which form backgrounds to paintings of the Madonna. Musical settings of verses describing the hunt, a merry country dance, bustling street scenes are so many genre pictures.

As the resources of harmony developed, musical form, though still faithful to the movement of the poem, gained a greater independence. The *frottola* and other light and gallant songs for several voices appeared. It was in the madrigal, however, and in the songs which led to it that we first find a detailed musical commentary on the changing moods of the trivial and courtly verses.

These courtly musicians sang of things which remain because they are of the stuff of human life. They uttered the eternal but vain protest against the shortness of life, the brief span of love. Yet these expressions existed at the Renaissance, as they exist at the present, at two levels, the level of trivial enjoyment and the level of passionate emotion. Then, as now, most patrons evidently preferred a trivial and frivolous expression to a deep and searching musical experience. Indeed most court music was, almost by definition, frivolous music.

It often avoided deeply moving expression even where poet and musician were capable of achieving it because profound expression was disturbing. Music which was clever, witty, and cheerful was preferred. Yet again and again through the maze of courtly trivialities one can hear the authentic note of passion, the bitter-sweet of Binchois in *"Tristre plaisir et douloreuse joie"* ("Sad pleasure and dolorous joy"), the exaltation of Lassus in his *"Je l'ayme bien"* ("I love her well"), the sweet and pastoral joy of Morley, the elegiac songs of Wilbye.

[119]

Opera dominated the music of the seventeenth century. It contained within itself elements which were the essence of later music. The actors on the stage declaimed and sang their parts to an accompaniment which was supplied by an ill-defined group of instruments which gradually took shape as the orchestra. Accompanied solo song, a single voice rising against a background of instrumental harmonies, the gradual ordering of that most complex and most beautiful of musical mediums, the orchestra: such were the contributions of opera to music. But of the great composers of the following century Bach did not write opera at all, though his religious music is deeply influenced by it; Handel, on the other hand, was to turn from opera to dramatize the stories of the Bible in his oratorios only in his later years.

The adulation and glorification of the ruling monarch in operatic prologue, in court ballet, and in the royal chapel (where the monarch shared in the praises of God) were enhanced by new musical means. The ancient pomp remained, but new musical luxuries were added to it.

Two musical styles existed in the first half of the eighteenth century. For one which may be symbolized by the music of Handel and Bach we shall borrow the term "baroque." For the other which was elegant, courtly we choose the word "rococo." At this period it is typified by the harpsichord works of Couperin (later by certain compositions of Mozart).

Playfulness is a sophisticated trait in music. The grim struggles of the early centuries of European history had been succeeded by an era which provided leisure and expensive toys for the few who were privileged to play. This musical playfulness was associated with an aristocracy which was ceasing to govern and had only the task of amusing itself. These traits were perhaps most characteristically displayed in the music of the court of Louis XIV and XV. Perhaps never before was music so carefully adapted to the taste of a group of courtiers.

The opera of Lully possessed the grand and pathetic emotion of classic French drama. Beside this an intimate music developed. It was charming, pleasing. Passion must be avoided, because extremes of emotion cease to be pleasurable. It was witty, neatly balanced, symmetrical. Rococo art dealt in miniatures, tiny harpsichord pieces, chamber music for two flutes. The sight of neatly trimmed formal gardens was matched by the music of pastoral instruments, bagpipe and musette, even the despised *vielle de la rue,* the hurdy-gurdy. Such music was perhaps capable of a certain grandeur, but a grandeur in miniature. The period appears in retrospect as a fairy garden, but a fairy garden for princesses and princes. It seems pallid and passionless, an art in which perfection of taste has outlawed the raw currents of life as too crude, too uncultivated. It presents a terrible contrast with the lives of the common people who lived outside the palace walls.

Amusing and gallant descriptive titles, songs exclusively devoted to the pleasures of drinking and the retreats, advances, and final consummation of courtship, the delight in refinements of harmony and finesse of execution, all these were characteristics of this beautiful, but shallow and frivolous art. Its surface character, its avoidance of heights and depths make it seem formal and cold to modern listeners. Yet among the ornamental debris of the period are pieces so perfect, so subtly expressive within their self-imposed limitations, that they transcend their period and retain their power to move us. Perhaps the greatest master in the style was François Couperin who wrote exquisite miniatures for harpsichord with titles as carefully chosen as his notes: "The Floating Scarf," "The Love-lorn Nightingale."

A typical aspect of baroque music was the expression of pomp and grandeur. Such an expression depended on a certain massive simplicity of movement as well as on the actual volume of sound for its effect. Music of this kind was not only employed to glorify God (as in the *Sanctus* of Bach's "B minor Mass"). It might also serve secular ends. We find this note of pomp in the choruses of occasional congratulatory cantatas and in the solemn introductory movements of Bach's overtures.

The growth and the importance of the commercial towns of Bach's day and the attainment of relative security and comfort by the more favored members of the middle class had its effect on music. Another very characteristic expression was in the broad, simple, sometimes clumsy open-air music which was played from the walls and church towers of towns by groups of brass instruments. It was music which was popular in somewhat the same sense that the modern band-concert is popular. This music is of great interest, not because the music written for such occasions was always of high quality, but because it was music for the market-place, the guild banquet, music for the townspeople, not for a royal court. The rude, simple, and good-humoured pomp of this music heralded a new field for music and a new audience.

Somewhat similar in spirit, and connected closely with another phase of town life was student music, which, however, was designed for stringed instruments rather than the more sonorous brass choir. Music for the recreation of university students was often composed by musicians who directed the groups of student singers and players who met as a "collegium musicum." But this musical activity on the part of university students was only one phase of the musical life of the seventeenth century.

Music entered the family circle as it entered the guild hall and the university. Nothing speaks more eloquently of the daily use and enjoyment of music than the paintings of the Dutch masters of the seventeenth century who never tire of painting a music lesson, a solitary violinist or cellist, or a musical party. The middle class had made music their own. At the same time the music of courts became more highly organized, more carefully differentiated according to occasion and use, more refined, ingratiating, and subtle. One can imagine the feelings of François Couperin, chamber musician of Louis XIV, if he were confronted by the scores of the worthy town musician, Pezel (1639-1694).

The world of Bach differed in many ways from that of Lassus, Palestrina, and the other great masters of the sixteenth century. The serene spirit of collective worship that is mirrored in the music of the older composers is replaced by a passionate personal affirmation in the music of Bach. This is due in part to the shift in emphasis from the acceptance of religious authority which was characteristic of the Catholic faith to the emphasis of the Protestants on an individual interpretation of the Bible. It is due in part to a change in the means employed in religious music.

The church-goers who were bewildered and shocked by a contemporary performance of Bach's "St. Matthew Passion" were undoubtedly correct when they compared it to an "opera-show." The employment of a dramatic musical style almost necessarily implied a heightened personal expression, an effect which was confirmed by the use of soloists in contrast with the choral expression of the earlier masters. The pathos of Bach's laments, the tremendous positiveness and conviction of his energetic choral fugues, the serenity of his songs of faith, all represent the culmination of a new order of expression in religious music.

Of crucial importance in the work of Bach was the chorale. In the church service of his day the chorale gave an opportunity for the active (though at first extremely limited) participation of the worshippers. Many of the chorale tunes, strong and simple, were drawn from popular and traditional sources. They serve in Bach's dramatic works to symbolize the collective feelings of the worshippers in contrast to the individual expressions of the solo singers. The chorale melodies formed a common musical possession for the members of Lutheran congregations. Bach assumes this when he quotes chorale tunes with the idea that the listeners will associate the tune with the words, or when he arranges chorale melodies in a fashion which is only explainable if we understand that the musical treatment is justified by the mood of the text. The chorale constituted a basis for this musical culture and was the foundation of a whole group of musical forms, such as the chorale prelude in which the tune sounded above a web of accompanying parts devised by the composer.

Yet if we are to complete the picture, we must turn from Bach's prodigious musical labors in a narrow circle of provincial German towns to Handel who wrote opera after opera for the brilliant stage of London, the focal city of a great commercial empire. He wrote arias with a magnificent and soaring melodic line for the greatest singers of the day (drawn to a common center by English gold), arias of melodic grandeur, of moving pathos, of robust good-humor, of musical splendor which still stir us in the fragments which survive in actual performance. When opera failed to attract the fickle aristocratic circles which had first supported him, he turned to a broader audience and wrote his oratorios, sacred dramas for soloists, chorus, and orchestra, which were destined for the concert hall, not the church.

In the second half of the eighteenth century the musical center of gravity shifted to Vienna where the living current of music still flowed in royal and princely courts. Society was stable and meticulously ordered according to rank. Southern Germany and Austria were still feudal as compared with London or Paris. A Pouplinière, a middle-class farmer-general, might maintain his private orchestra in France. The Duke of Chandos, no real member of the hereditary aristocracy but a successful adventurer, might build a luxurious mansion at Cannons and hire a Handel as chapel-master.

In Austria, however, music was still a princely prerogative. Not until Mozart do we find a great musician seeking middle-class patronage, and Mozart did so only because he was unable to gain more aristocratic support. Yet a considerable number of Austrian aristocrats were avid melomaniacs. We may admire the superb musical organization at the court of Louis XIV, but we must remember that the instrumental music performed there barely exceeded the modest dimensions of the dances of the suite.

The nobles of Vienna listened to music which had become a living and developing language with its own laws and with a gamut of expression which had won its independence from the poet or the dancer. Its masters bore names which have become household words, magic words, Haydn, Mozart, Beethoven.

The word classic is unsatisfactory because it suggests a calm perfection which hardly does justice to the variety, the vitality, the emotional intensity of this music. Where earlier rococo music succeeded most frequently in creating melodic grace in miniature, the classic composers achieved the balanced structure of the sonata, the symphony, and the concerto, retaining something of the grace of the melodic charms of the earlier composers, but adding to it the breadth and passion of the larger and more dramatic forms.

The emotional message of the masterworks of this period transcends the prettiness and grace of the minor works to attain an incomparable grandeur and elevation of style. The romantic spirit was by no means confined to the romantic period which followed. Personal emotion was not invented in the nineteenth century. Indeed, it is perhaps as much in their power to convey emotion as in their superb control of balance and proportion that the great classics distinguished themselves from their lesser contemporaries.

Much music was composed and performed, particularly by the earlier classic composers, which did no more than produce pleasant tonal arabesques as a background for salon conversation. The earlier music of Mozart expresses with almost careless mastery the graces, the elegance, and the limitations of the rococo style. It is not surprising that such pieces should lack the qualities which mark the master-works which we still hear. Yet it is quite possible that many listeners of the eighteenth century were unable to

[125]

distinguish between the pages of the mature Mozart and the cheerful emptiness of routine eighteenth century music.

Not only did these cultivated aristocrats listen to music which demanded a sustained act of attention. They were also in constant pursuit of new music. This demand for novelty was responsible for the enormous productivity of the great classic masters. It was still difficult to obtain music from distant centers. Much music still circulated in manuscript. The insatiable appetite of these melomaniacs for new music remained the chief stimulus to the composer.

Many of these music-lovers, however, were not only munificent music patrons who maintained their own domestic orchestras and chamber-music groups. They were amateur performers as well. Prince Esterházy played the baryton and was responsible for many compositions which Haydn wrote for that instrument. Prince Lobkowitz, Beethoven's patron, frequently played second violin in the group which first performed Beethoven's string quartets. The Archduke Rudolph, another patron of Beethoven and for a time his pupil, not only played the clarinet but composed for that instrument. To no small degree we owe the repertory of the modern chamber-music concert to the personal enthusiasms of these and other eighteenth century Viennese amateurs of music.

The romantic composers changed music from within. Composers continued to write symphonies, string quartets, operas. It was a new spirit which illuminated the usual forms. Yet much that we think of as typically romantic was not really new. We may say with some justice that the classic musician composed music which expressed his society, the romantic musician music which expressed himself. Yet as we turn back the pages of music history, it becomes abundantly clear that personal expressiveness and in particular the characteristic mood of melancholy yearning may be found in such earlier composers as Monteverdi, Gesualdo, Binchois, Machaut.

We may point to an interest in the remote, the "Gothic," the exotic as a characteristic of the romantic period. Yet we have only to turn back to the quaint exoticism of certain ancient dances for the lute, to picturesque entries of dancers in court ballets, to the barbarian heroines of certain of Handel's operas, to the "Turkish" music of Mozart and Beethoven, the gypsy movements of Haydn to see that the romantics were not the only musicians to display an interest in local color or in the remote epochs of the past.

The interest in the strange, the supernatural, and the exotic, evinced by the folk-lore of Weber's *"Freischütz"* or Schumann's music to Byron's "Manfred," was not peculiar to the nineteenth century, as has been pointed out, but it was highly characteristic of the period.

Though the usual statements concerning the romantic period contain their element of truth, the romantic period neither invented personal emotion nor exotic coloring. The changes which took place in music as in life were due to three basic causes considered not only in themselves but as agents which changed the character of human experience.

These influences were the French Revolution, the Industrial Revolution, and the development of modern business enterprise with all that it implies. It should not be forgotten, however, that the French Revolution never completely achieved its goals, while the forces of industry and business were to remake the world.

The revolutionary doctrine of the equality of man had profound effects on the musician. If a musician was to be free, his music must express his own convictions, not the commands of a master. Beethoven's profound insistence on the creator's right to his own musical thought without alteration or hindrance shows this belief at its greatest intensity. But if all men were to be regarded as important, then what common and untutored men had sung also assumed a new importance. That Haydn and (to a lesser degree) Mozart were sensitive to popular idioms is revealed by certain of their compositions. But it was not until the nineteenth century that folk song was sufficently valued to be systematically collected and studied. It was because of this new consciousness of a folk heritage that music of the late romantic period mirrored national and popular characteristics.

The conclusion that music belongs to all of the people was not attained then nor has it yet been completely attained. Certain leaders of a later period were to see this as an ideal, the realization of which is still in the future. Two further conclusions may be derived from the doctrine of the importance of the individual man. One is the emphasis on individual differences. Rousseau stated this in its simplest form when he declared in his "Confessions," "I am different from all men I have seen. If I am not better, at least I am different."

It is difficult to assess the levelling effect of time on the music of the past. Did certain movements of Mozart and Haydn seem as similar to their contemporaries as to us? It would seem inevitable that there should have been a certain evaporation of personality with time. Certainly musical allusions which may have been clear to contemporaries are apparent only to specialists (if to them) at the present day. Allowing for this factor as well as we may, it still appears that there has been a clear general gain in individual differences as revealed by musical compositions which becomes more apparent as we approach the end of the nineteenth century.

A further extension of the same idea is the emphasis not only on the moods but also on the precise means which may best express them. It would perhaps not be unfair to say that though the operatic music of Handel portrays joy, rage, love, reverence, the representations of a given mood have a considerable likeness. This is partly because the subsequent development of harmony was precisely in a direction which lent itself to a multitude of subtle shadings, but also because the Georgian musician regarded his characters as conventional types rather than well-characterized individuals. The wicked enchantress, the unhappy lover, the brave warrior, and many other stock characters peopled his stage.

By the end of the nineteenth century the pendulum had achieved a full swing in the other direction. The character-delineation of Wagner not only extends to his minor characters in the works of his maturity. It even humanizes the strange collection of mythological monsters which people the dramas of the Ring cycle. Verdi, who employed the usual operatic lay-figures in his earlier works, attained a high degree of psychological realism in the works of his mature old age, "Othello" and "Falstaff." The whole emphasis of the impressionist composers such as Debussy and Ravel was on the delineation of delicate shades of emotion.

In one respect, however, the example set by the musicians of the French Revolution was not followed, indeed could not be followed. The great popular festivals of the Revolution were performed in the open air. The people were not only spectators but also participants. The grandiose gesture survived in the *"Eroica"* (the "Third Symphony") of Beethoven, the gigantic tone-paintings of Berlioz. The concept of a music which should be for all of the people vanished in the period of reaction which followed.

During the romantic period another great revolution was accomplished with a brutality which defies description. The Industrial Revolution disrupted the ancient patterns of rural life, crowded the workers into factories in an exploitation so bitter and so complete that any popular intellectual or artistic life became impossible for them. Yet the great stream of romantic music seems to deny or ignore the dominant fact of its period. Wagner did indeed write scenes which revealed the bitterness of industrial slavery. Yet the very avoidance of this dominant theme was significant. The great composers turned away from the pervading pall of factory smoke and sang of immutable things. They expressed the pride and splendor of the human spirit in such a glorious fashion that they still dominate the music of the present day.

To name them is to recall their music: the gallant brilliance and the folk-like simplicities of Weber, the lyric sweetness of Schubert with his moments of vivid power and tragedy, the dainty fantasy and the broad melody of Mendelssohn, the poetic revery and dramatic fire of Schumann, the elegant melancholy or the fiery outbursts of Chopin.

The music of the great romantics was a proud affirmation. Many lesser figures fled from reality or became purveyors of musical luxuries for those who could afford them. That Haydn was a court servant was no shame to him, for no other way of life was open to a musician of his particular gifts. The romantic composer who chose such a path, however, did so after the possibility of a new world had been revealed, no matter how briefly.

The elegant emptiness of Thalberg's brilliant piano compositions is only too evident to us. This accomplished pianist, however, furnished precisely the fare which high society could most easily relish. The gaudiness of grand opera with its display of empty pomp and its search for sensational effect is typical of the music serving the masters of the Industrial Revolution. Meyerbeer calculated the spectacular elements in his operas for the level of taste of the aristocratic Jockey's Club and included in his scores such sensational novelties as a dance of nuns and a skating ballet. (The various "Ice Follies" of the present day show that this idea has not lacked imitators.) Rossini poured forth a brilliant flood of melody in a succession of momentary operatic successes with a cynical disregard of higher dramatic truth which is only heightened by the acknowledged merits of his surviving masterpieces. A composer like Jacques Offenbach reacted by mocking the corruption of the period and then collecting the price of admission from those he mocked.

Such composers and such works represent the surrender of the composer to the wealthy and corrupt society which flourished during the period of reaction which was the aftermath of the French Revolution. This was not the main stream of romantic music which followed other paths. Neither should one commit the easy error of supposing that all the works of Rossini, of Meyerbeer, of Offenbach represent a surrender of high artistic ideals. The "William Tell" of Rossini, the "Huguenots" of Meyerbeer, and Offenbach's "Tales of Hoffman" among others reveal that these composers were capable of better things.

At the same time that the Industrial Revolution degraded factory workers to the point of depriving them of any share in the intellectual life and the culture of the period, it prepared a tool of cultural diffusion in the modern printing press. It established music as a business or rather a whole series of enterprises. This phase of the musical life of the romantic period, however, belongs to another chapter than the present one, but it should be remembered (though it is rarely remembered) that these, too, were characteristic aspects of the romantic period.

Such were the great controlling forces of the period. Certain more specifically musical aspects of romantic music demand at least a passing mention. Composers of the period sometimes treated the elaborate and balanced repetitions of the sonata and the symphony with great freedom. Music tended to hybridize with literature. Thanks to the development of opera the various rhythms and melodic figures which characterize the usual moods and situations had become familiar to the audience. Music was therefore able to present a sequence of moods or episodes which were explained by a statement or a poem prefixed to the score. This was the symphonic poem. Yet the essential vagueness of music resulted in a discreet limitation of the scope of most program music. Thus we find that *"Les Préludes,"* "Death and Transfiguration," and "A Hero's Life" all represent the adventures, the loves, and the apotheosis of a hero.

Besides these trends in the larger forms, the smaller and more intimate compositions, short piano pieces, songs assumed an unwonted importance. The *lieder* of Schubert, Schumann, and Brahms and such intimate compositions for piano as the Schubert *"Moments Musicaux,"* the Mendelssohn "Songs Without Words," and the Chopin *"Préludes"* are among the most familiar examples of a very large literature. Here the composer must be brief, epigrammatic. His mood must be condensed into a melodic curve, an accompaniment figure. Yet what is lost in breadth, in opportunity for development, may be gained in pregnancy, in intensity of feeling.

Though the polyphonic forms were never without their adherents, Beethoven and later César Franck attempted to revitalize the fugue. Beethoven incorporated the fugue into the sonata (tentatively in Op. 101, more elaborately in Op. 106 and Op. 110). At a later period Franck (in his *"Prélude, Chorale et Fugue"*) treats the form in a free, colorful, and highly pianistic fashion. That Brahms was a master of the polyphonic style is shown by such movements as the fugues in the "Sonata No. 1" for piano and cello and the "24 Variations and Fugue on a Theme by Handel."

The musical language of romanticism became the musical language of all Europe and of our land. In its later phases romanticism was modified, if only superficially, by the rising tide of national feeling. This had a less perceptible effect in Italy where opera so dominated the taste of the people that a national idiom in any other style hardly was possible. (The *"Danze Piemontesi"* by Sinigaglia show us that the attempt was made.) The idiom of the Viennese classics had become a European rather than a purely German possession. The later romantics, Brahms, Wagner, Bruckner, Mahler, Richard Strauss had only to mold a style which was already in being, in accordance with their temperaments. It was Wagner who was to modify it most strikingly, pushing the iridescent color of romantic harmony to the limits of its possibilities in "Tristan," expanding the orchestra to gigantic proportions, imposing a new type of opera, the "music-drama," on the public. His was an art in which every element was seen as if in a magnifying glass, enormous, intense. Yet when we are about to condemn him for his excesses, we turn to the "Mastersingers" with its warm, wise, and subtle humanity.

The most passionate devotion to musical nationalism was found, not in the heart of Europe but rather around its margins, Czecho-Slovakia, Scandinavia, Hungary, Russia. This was due in part to the late awakening of national consciousness in those areas, in part to the fact that the artists of these regions were brought into contact with a vigorous and living folk life, a folk life which had been largely destroyed in the more highly industrialized nations. The initial impulse which led to musical nationalism might be generated by the attack of an invading force. Thus Napoleon's invasion of Russia caused a wave of patriotic feeling which was one of the forces leading to the formation of a nationalist school of composers there. It might be born of a gradual awakening, of a spirit of liberalism and reform. This was the case in Norway.

A nationalist composer must have distinctive material to work on. This could only be found in folksong and folk dance. But where folk life had lost its vigor or where its idiom had already been absorbed into art music, no striking developments could be expected. Thus French folksong plays a relatively restricted role in French symphonic music of the nineteenth century. One may cite Vincent d'Indy's "Symphony on a French Mountain Air," Bizet's familiar *"L'Arlésienne* Suite" as exceptions. It seems probable that the French predilection for Spanish rhythms may have been due to a certain extent to the fact that French com-

[133]

posers found them more salient, more provocative than the folk-art of their own land.

Mozart already utilized themes with an Austrian folk character in such movements as the trio of the minuet from the "Piano Sonata in B flat" (Köchel-Einstein 498a) and the theme of the variations in the "Clarinet Quintet." But it is only the specialist who examines his music and that of the German romantics for themes with local color.

Chopin and Liszt, one an expatriate, the other a cosmopolitan, were not able to forget the land of their birth. Grieg gradually found his way from a cultivated middle-class environment to the music of the peasants. Dvořák, born close to the people, was unable to forget the rhythms of Bohemian folk-dances even in compositions inspired by American folksong. The Russians of the nineteenth century, Borodine, Rimsky Korsakoff, Tschaikowsky, Moussorgsky; the Spanish composers Albeniz, Granados, De Falla; Vaughan Williams and other English composers, and a long list of our own composers have to a greater or lesser degree proclaimed their musical allegiance to a soil, to a people, in their scores.

The excesses of romanticism led to the denial of romanticism, yet it cannot be said that this reaction was complete or entirely successful. Romanticism in its latest phases tended towards a pompous musical rhetoric and an enormous expressive apparatus, the gigantic orchestra of Wagner's "Ring" cycle, of Richard Strauss, of the Schönberg *"Gurrelieder"* or the symphonies of Bruckner and Mahler. A melody played by eight horns needs to be abundantly inspired to justify such a heroic sonority. Worse still, the musical idiom of the period was watered down into a sort of universal musical language, which still serves for parlor music, dinner music, and for the inanities of light opera.

Debussy's early music is still romantic in flavor, perhaps displaying the influence of Massenet. He turned to the pagan subtleties of the "Afternoon of a Faun," the orientalism of "Pagodas," to a refinement of feeling and mood which diverges from the main current of romanticism without entirely forsaking it. His is a suggestive art, hinting at emotion without entirely revealing it, fragmentary, evocative.

The reaction to romanticism was varied. On the one hand, the exploration of strange moods reached the tortured extremes of such works as the Schönberg *"Pierrot Lunaire"* or Richard Strauss's "Electra." On the other, we note the denial of emotion in the Stravinsky "Symphonies for Wind Instruments," the turning back to classicism in his "Piano Sonata" (1922) and "Octet for Wind Instruments" (1923). The inflated orchestra gave place to the chamber ensemble as in Stravinsky's "History of a Soldier." The astringent anti-emotional atmosphere of this work with its ingenious rhythmic design displays an extreme of anti-romanticism.

The experimentalists and grammarians of the newer music evolved strange new scales, new and unwonted methods of combining different scales and complicated rhythms. They were enchanted with American jazz which, having conquered our country, invaded Europe in the years which followed the first World War.

A considerable number of highly colored and pungent scores have gained a somewhat precarious place in the repertory; but, as the years passed, it became evident that, though the vocabulary of music had profited by a period of experimentation, audiences in general demanded a warmth of feeling which was typical of romantic music. The new dissonances added spice and piquancy to the popular forms, but in general, the period of experimentation and innovation has merged into a new romanticism to which folksong and a simplification of the technical finds of the early twentieth century give a new character. This trend toward popular themes has been shown in such works as Virgil Thomson's "The Plow that Broke the Plains," Roy Harris' "When

Johnny Comes Marching Home" or his "Folksong Symphony," and Aaron Copland's "Rodeo" or "Appalachian Spring."

This increased interest in folk material in our own country has its parallel in the Soviet Union where a great and varied wealth of folksong has been collected and exploited by their composers. The use of Cossack themes in Derzinsky's opera "Quiet Flows the Don" is only one familiar example chosen from many.

CHAPTER VII

THE PATRON, THE STATE, AND THE MUSICIAN

THE striking fact about the musician up to very recent times has been his dependence on the good-will and the generosity of those who employed him. This is most clearly shown in the eighteenth century when the system of patronage had reached its highest development. In early societies a minstrel might follow his chieftain to battle. In the Middle Ages he might work within the sheltering walls of a monastery or entertain the lords and ladies in some royal castle. The gradual increase in wealth, in individual security, the general interest in the refinements of life and in the arts were reflected in an increased demand for music. The musician was no longer a tribal retainer, no longer a feudal vassal, but he was still dependent on the good-will of a patron or a circle of patrons. When, in more recent times, he turned from a narrow and aristocratic circle to a broader public, when he became freer and more independent, the system of patronage declined in importance although it survives to the present day. Actually the term involves not one but a whole series of relationships. In all of these it is assumed that the musician can only successfully practise his art with the approval of an individual or several individuals of a higher social class. The musician performed for his patrons in return for encouragement and support. The nature of the bond between patron and musician might range from actual servitude on the part of the musician to a voluntary exchange of artistic services for a reward. The system reaches the vanishing point when a wealthy individual supports a composer without receiving any stipulated return. In many countries the growth of nationalism and of a pride in the artistic achievements of nationals led to the support of musical institutions (and in some cases of individual musicians) by the state.

The system of patronage grew up in a society which concentrated wealth in the hands of a few favored and aristocratic individuals. Many of them lived on country estates for at least part of the year though they might go to Vienna or London for the winter season. Organized entertainment was entirely lacking in the country unless it was provided by the master of one of these rural retreats. In the city the opera and a few concert series were the only forms of public musical entertainment. Most concerts of the period were not open to the public in anything like our sense of the word but were sponsored by a circle of aristocratic patrons. The musician clearly could only live and practise his art by composing and performing for the pleasure of musical aristocrats, by enlivening the monotony of life in remote castle or country-seat, or by adding to the brilliance of the winter season in the great cities of Europe.

Musical patronage reached perhaps its most typical form in the eighteenth century under the "enlightened" rulers of the little states which occupied the area which we know as Germany and Austria. A general interest in the arts, a paternal attitude towards gifted young men who could entertain them or play with them led to a remarkable flowering of the art of music centering about Vienna and the great names of Haydn, Mozart, and Beethoven, but embracing as well a whole network of establishments where lesser musicians made music.

The specific acts which a musician might perform for a reward ranged from a single performance to a lifetime of musical service. Novelty was much in demand. Thus the violinist and composer Ditters von Dittersdorf, when he wrote of the musical establishment of his prince, added "Whenever any *virtuoso*, singer or player came to Vienna, and deservedly succeeded in winning the applause of the public, Bonno (the chapel-master) was ordered to arrange the terms, and to secure him for the Prince."

The reward for such performances was too frequently determined by caprice. The childhood tours of little Mozart and his sister, for example, resulted in the accumulation of many elegant snuff-boxes but in very little in the way of a more substantial reward. Mozart complained bitterly in his letters about the Parisians. "They arrange for me to come on such and such a day, I play, hear them exclaim: *'Oh c'est un prodige, c'est inconçevable, c'est étonnant!'* and then it is—*Adieu.* ' " Dittersdorf, who played for the coronation of Joseph II, calculated that he lost four hundred ducats (£180) by this appearance. His expenses included the purchase of two court costumes which cost 700 gulden (£70). His reward was fifty ducats (£22 5s). On the other hand the reward might be as extravagant as these were parsimonious.

The compositions of a performer were a precious part of his stock in trade. Frequently he tried to keep them for his own use. Since patrons who were amateur performers might wish to possess and play the music they had heard, certain musicians had their compositions engraved in order that they might present them to their patrons in the hope of a substantial gift. The musician, like the poet and author, could inscribe a work to a musically-minded nobleman and hope that this personage would make a suitable response to the compliment. Beethoven had the custom of selling the exclusive use of his works for a limited period. It seems strange that the great "Third Symphony," the *"Eroica,"* which now belongs to all the world, could have been the temporary property of Beethoven's patron Prince Lobkowitz at whose house it was performed during the winter of 1804.

The extent to which the musician owed fixed and regular duties to his patron varied according to circumstances as did the extent to which the freedom of the musician was curbed by the demands and exactions of his superiors. The musician might actually be a servant or even a serf. Thus

Montbrun, the inventor of the sedan chair, (according to an account of a visit to Paris in 1658) "had many servants to wait on him and he takes no one who does not know how to play the violin; he has them play every evening in the summer in the middle of the *'Place Royale'* to the assemblage till midnight and past; and with this following he usually takes a boat in the summer in which he is stretched at full length while all the servants divert him with the violin."

In our own country Thomas Jefferson, in a letter to an unnamed correspondent, discussed the possibilities of combining the practice of music with more useful arts. "The bounds of an American fortune will not admit the indulgence of a domestic band of musicians, yet I have thought that a passion for music might be reconciled with that economy which we are obliged to observe. I retain among my domestic servants a gardener . . . a weaver . . . a cabinetmaker . . . and a stone cutter . . . to which I would add a *vigneron*. In a country like yours (where) music is cultivated by every class of men I suppose there might be found persons of those trades who could perform on the French horn, clarinet or hautboy and bassoon, so that one might have a band of two French horns, two clarinets and hautboys and a bassoon without enlarging their domestic expenses."

A nineteenth century traveller records the enormous extent of the regions ruled by Russian ironmasters and the former luxury of their establishments:— "In the olden times the *'Barrin'* lived in almost princely style . . . in a palace surrounded by highly ornamental gardens and extensive parks, laid out with the most excellent taste. In his gardens were hot-houses, vineries, and orange-houses, erected at great expense. Frequently he had a private theatre of his own; a band of music in constant attendance; and I know of at least one of the iron-masters of the last generation, who supported a company of actors and actresses, collected from among his own mujiks, whom he sent to St. Petersburg and Moscow to be educated expressly for his own stage."

Even where the person of the composer was not completely at the disposal of his patron, his personal liberty was more or less limited. It seems incredible to us that a violin virtuoso could be enjoyed exclusively by a single patron, yet we read that Tomasini, the favorite violinist of the fabulous Prince Esterházy (the patron of Haydn) played at only one public concert. Most musical readers are familiar with the obstacles placed by the Archbishop of Salzburg in the way of young Mozart's development, his refusals to permit him to concertize, his determination to hold him within the walls of his little court. It was not easy to leave a patron. Bach was thrown into prison for demanding too persistently that he be granted permission to leave the service of the Duke of Weimar, a permission which was granted grudgingly after an interval which Bach is said to have improved in a characteristic fashion by sketching his "Little Organ Book."

Under such conditions artists became adept at utilizing the persuasive powers of music to insinuate requests which they could hardly urge openly upon their masters. It is said that Josquin des Prés (c. 1445-1521), who had been promised a favor by his patron but who had not received it, was able to call attention to this fact by writing a motet on the text *"Portio mea non est in terra viventium"* ("My portion is not in the land of the living"). We are told that the hint had the desired effect and that Josquin was able to express his thanks in a similar fashion, this time in a motet on the text *"Bonitatem fecisti cum servo tuo, Domine"* ("Lord, thou hast conferred benefits on thy servant.")

Palestrina, too, seems to have understood how to attract attention to himself in a fashion at once flattering and diplomatic. His first published volume of masses (1554) opens with *"Ecce sacerdos magnus"* ("Behold the high priest!") a mass based on a melody which was used to celebrate the memory of a pope. To make his intention more specific the coat of arms of Julius III was printed wherever this melody appears in the score. In 1555 Palestrina was made a member of the Pontifical Choir by direct order of the Pope, without the usual formalities, a procedure which the other singers seem to have resented.

These anecdotes of an earlier period might well be coupled with the well-known tale concerning the origin of Haydn's "Farewell Symphony." Haydn's master, Prince Esterházy, habitually spent most of the year at his country seat. For the winter season he went to Vienna. Haydn and his fellow musicians looked forward eagerly to this seasonal change. One year, however, the usual time for departure had passed, and the Prince still lingered at Esterház. Haydn therefore composed his "Farewell Symphony." In the last movement of this work the scoring was so arranged that one musician after another took his instrument, put out the candles which illuminated his music stand, and filed out of the hall. At the end only Haydn and Tomasini, the favorite violinist of the Prince, were left. "If all the others have gone," said the Prince, "we may as well go too."

In all these cases we see music used by the musician for the furthering of his own ends. We also see behind the amusing anecdote the lack of freedom which made it indiscreet or impossible for the musician to ask directly for what he wished. Since he was not free, he had to hint or insinuate what he might not say directly.

Such are some of the instances where the composer has utilized his art to beg a non-musical favor. If the artist speaks through his art to society to express his beliefs, society on the other hand limits and bounds his sphere of expression. The ruling monarch, the patron, the state, the public, the censor, all have their objectives and their preferences. In very many instances patrons were content to establish the time, the place, and the purpose for musical performances, leaving the question of the music to be performed to the chapel-master.

Thus Haydn appeared in the ante-chamber of Prince Esterházy before and after dinner to discover what music was to be performed. We have at least one small indication that the Prince did indeed leave purely musical matters in Haydn's hands if we can credit one reply attributed to him. The Prince had on one occasion criticized a rehearsal. To this Haydn replied politely but firmly, "Your Highness, all that is my business."

In other instances a patron made requests which resulted in activities on the composer's part which, in some instances, he surely would not have undertaken on his own volition. Haydn's many pieces for the baryton would hardly have been composed had not his patron played this instrument. It is said that Mozart wrote his two duets for violin and viola to help Michael Haydn who had been ordered to compose a set of six for the Archbishop of Salzburg, but had been prevented by illness from completing his task. Mozart disliked the flute, but nevertheless wrote his lovely concerto for flute and harp at the request of the Duc de Guines.

There are instances which show that the patron sometimes insisted that music should correspond with his wishes in specific details. Thus Haydn hoped that his depiction of frogs in "The Seasons" would be forgiven. He was too old to change the score. This touch of realism owed its origin to a whim of the Baron von Swieten. They may still be heard in the score. Louis XIV actually locked up his composer Lalande while the latter wrote and re-wrote some little songs until they exactly corresponded with the royal wishes.

One great weakness of individual patronage from the point of view of the welfare of the musician and the development of the art of music was the fact that a whim, a financial reverse, death might destroy an entire musical establishment and scatter the musicians. Thus the panic of the Bishop of Grosswardein because he had been reported to Maria Theresa as a sponsor of forbidden and unseemly performances was directly responsible for the dissolution of his musical establishment and the dismissal of his musicians and singers. Haydn's freedom from the Esterházy service was due to the death of Prince Nicolaus the Magnificent (in 1790) and the accession of his successor who promptly dismissed most of the musicians and pensioned off Haydn. The death of a single wealthy woman caused the immediate suspension of the concerts of the "Friends of Music" which Artur Bodansky conducted in New York and the disbanding of its orchestra and chorus.

Such abrupt changes were less likely to occur in royal chapels, at least in later periods when a sort of court bureaucracy had gradually been instituted. Here the prerogatives and the rewards of the musicians were established, and the chapel persisted though the monarch would in due course die and his successor take the throne. Even here the monarch might theoretically dismiss the musicians of his chapel, but precedent and custom had established usages that most monarchs respected. In more modern times an institution which has gained substantial public support has a certain presumption of continuity. Music-lovers individually may lose interest, may move away, may die, but the audience survives and renews itself. The very substantial response of the radio audience to the appeal of the Philharmonic Society for contributions in the form of "radio memberships" is an indication of the public support which it had gained.

It was the shift from the composer who was willing to use his art to flatter or to gain a personal advantage to the composer who not only had convictions but expressed them proudly that measured the extent to which the musician gained his freedom. The victory was not easily won or complete. Liszt, the conquering virtuoso, could still write bitterly in 1835 that "the principal, *dominant fact* which for two centuries past stands out in the history of music and musicians, is their social *inferiority*" . . . Mozart, whose early days were spent in the service of the Archbishop of Salzburg, has left a letter which expresses his status in that household by his position at table. He sat above the cooks but below the valets.

Beethoven was able to maintain a fierce independence,

yet he, too, lived largely by his patrons. His obligations to them were slight. The regular attendance which was part of the routine of court life was intolerable to him. He even found giving music lessons a burden as is shown by his polite but uneasy relationships with his pupil and patron, the Archduke Rudolph. The old system of patronage had stretched to the breaking point, and a new form had emerged in which the patron granted financial aid to the artist in return for a privileged share in his art. This share might assume the form of a dedication, performances for a select circle of listeners, the prestige that comes from association with a famous or a promising artist. In this form patronage persisted long; indeed it still persists.

Even so, it is with a sense of shock, of having wandered into the wrong century by mistake, that one reads of the private orchestra of the fabulous Baron Paul von Derwies for whom the composer Charles Martin Loeffler played in his younger days. The orchestra numbered seventy players. On occasion the Baron was their sole auditor, listening attentively or willing to shorten a performance, *"sans répétition, Messieurs, s'il vous plaît."* In addition he retained a choir of forty-eight Bohemians (in default of Russians) who were taught to sing the chants of the Orthodox Church for the devotions of the household. One of the three special trains which were required to move the Baron and his household from his castle in Italy (where he spent his summers) to Nice (where he wintered) was reserved for his musicians.

The music most typical of the period of patronage bears its peculiar stamp, the gaiety, elegance, and wit, the surface brilliance and charm which reached their perfection in the lesser compositions of Mozart. It is an art which deteriorates in the hands of a lesser artist into a kind of conventional cheerfulness like the fixed smile of a movie actress. Mozart transcended the style in the works of his maturity where a deeper feeling penetrates and transforms the graceful melodic curves, a new gravity and fervor replaces the pretty melodic gestures of his earlier works.

Beethoven, though his self-will and determined independence speak from his more dramatic pages, knew well how to turn a courtly musical phrase, how to be graceful and pleasing. The mood of his "Compliment Quartet" (Op. 18 No. 2) appears in a number of his other compositions. It is precisely this quality of elegant trifling from which modern audiences turn away. They demand an idiom which is more personal, a mode of performance which is more emphatic, more passionate. Only as one learns to enter into the spirit of the period do its lesser compositions gain a momentary life. Even then we cannot dwell too long in this world where all emotion is agreeable and all allegros are cheerful.

The period of patronage carried the seeds of decay within itself. The musician strove to be free, to have the right to possess convictions and to express them. It was safer not to have ideas during the period of patronage unless they coincided exactly with those of the patron, yet certain musicians did have them and resolutely retained them.

Even as early as the Elizabethan period, such a musician as Byrd clung stubbornly to his religious convictions and remained Catholic under a Protestant ruler. It is clear that Queen Elizabeth tolerated such a divergence of belief in certain of her musicians at a time when toleration was not a recognized virtue. Her motives are not equally clear. It is even probable that they were mixed. It has been suggested that Byrd escaped without serious trouble because Elizabeth was musical herself and because she was especially indulgent to musicians. Very probably the opinions of a musician were not regarded as important, especially if he took no active part in propagating his beliefs. Yet Byrd's convictions did have a definite effect on his work as a composer as is shown by such specifically Catholic works as the Latin masses and the motets to Latin texts.

Other musicians were of quite a different temper. Many, no doubt, held that fixed religious or political beliefs were a luxury which a musician could hardly afford. The career of Paisiello who is barely remembered now, save perhaps as the composer of a charming air to which Beethoven wrote variations (*"Nel cor più non mi sento"*), is a wonderful example of the suppleness which was characteristic of certain musicians.

In his own day, he was famous for his sparkling operas. His reputation was largely won in Naples, a city which he left in 1776 to enter the service of Catherine II of Russia. Here he was lavishly rewarded for conducting Italian opera in St. Petersburg. On his return to Naples he became court conductor to Ferdinand IV of Naples. Ferdinand fought against Napoleon ineffectually, fled precipitately back to Naples and finally took refuge on a ship of Admiral Nelson's fleet. Since Ferdinand had been compelled to sign a treaty in 1801 which permitted the occupation of Naples by French troops, he could hardly refuse the "loan" of Paisiello to Napoleon when the latter requested it in 1802. Napoleon, though unmusical, was nevertheless an admirer of Paisiello's music. Napoleon's favor caused Paisiello to be treated with marked distinction during his stay in Paris. This success was followed by a retreat to Naples and the shadowed close of a career in a troubled world where neither his brilliant musical gifts nor his talent for intrigue could bring him security.

If the French Revolution embodied an ideal of freedom for the musician as for other men, the growth of the "public" made a degree of economic freedom a possibility. Perhaps one should say rather that, in exchanging one master for many, a direct personal influence for a diffuse and divided control, the musician enlarged his power to mould his own destiny. Since the musician is by natural inclination an idealist, we usually find him on the side of human freedom and progress. Thus economic freedom and freedom of thought and feeling went hand in hand. This is in direct opposition to

[147]

the view of the sentimentalists who feel that an artist should deal only with ideal matters. On the contrary, it is only when the artist can embrace and accept the ideals of his society, when his work brings him economic security, that his mind is freed.

Such a result was not achieved overnight. In the eighteenth century the artist could indeed take advantage of the eagerness of the nobility for a new musical sensation to choose the better of two offers. Thus Dittersdorf was able to bargain with Count Spork more advantageously because he had been offered a higher salary by the Bishop of Grosswardein. Count Spork, who received Dittersdorf contemptuously at first, while reclining on a sofa, gradually raised his offer to seven hundred gulden, to eight hundred, finally to nine hundred and fifty. Dittersdorf, who had been promised a thousand, was able to refuse him and take the better offer. In a similar fashion the offer made Beethoven by Jerome Bonaparte was sufficient to induce three of his Viennese patrons to guarantee him a pension if he would only remain in that city. (The Archduke Rudolph, Prince Lobkowitz, and Prince Kinsky were the three. Prince Lichnowsky had already granted Beethoven an annual sum).

But if the musician gained a certain freedom in this way, the development of music in London and the capitals of Europe made it less necessary for individual noblemen to maintain an elaborate musical staff. The members of the nobility tended to lose their isolation, to gather in the great urban centers. A congenial circle of aristocrats could join to support a series of concerts which would be at once more brilliant and more economical than concerts given by a private band of musicians. Thus the aristocratic concert tended to replace court and domestic orchestras. The performing artist who played for such an audience was less subject to individual caprice than one who was dependent on a single master.

Precisely in England, where the middle class had gained the

most power, we find that musical performances assumed a more democratic character. Perhaps it was Handel who first learned from bitter experience that it was safer to depend on broad public support than on the whims of a limited aristocratic circle. Even in England, however, it was not till the middle of the nineteenth century that concerts with a really popular basis appear. The concert orchestra gradually reached a size, a perfection of execution, and a degree of permanence which would have been impossible under individual patronage. In the modern concert hall the wealthy seat themselves in the boxes while students, workers, housewives look down upon them from the balcony.

Wealth in modern America is probably as unequally divided as it was in the eighteenth century, yet the individual music-lover of great wealth plays a relatively small role. The reasons for this change are complex, and the data on which a fair comparison might be based is not of a kind which is readily available. A number of American composers have received aid from wealthy individuals. A much larger number of promising performers have been helped in a similar fashion. The development of chamber music in this country owed much to the Flonzaly Quartet. This group was in a very real sense the creation of Edward de Coppet, a discriminating and painstaking lover of chamber music, who formed the group only after a long search for players who were capable of developing a highly unified and harmonious manner of performance. This enterprise was similar to the eighteenth century pattern in the close personal supervision which de Coppet gave to his project and in the fact that the quartet played exclusively for de Coppet and his guests for some time. Indeed, they continued to give private performances together with an increasing number of public concerts.

Certain American donors have preferred to endow institutions or to set up foundations to administer their gifts. Thus a bequest by Augustus D. Juillard was used to establish the music school which bears his name. Mrs. Mary Louise

Curtis Bok provided funds which established the Curtis Institute. George Eastman of the Eastman Kodak Company, unmusical himself, was responsible for the creation of the Eastman School of Music which, under Howard Hanson, has assumed special importance because of the encouragement given there to American composers. These institutions were anticipated by the founding of the National Conservatory of Music by Mrs. Jeannette Thurber, who brought Dvořák (1892-95) here to become its head. The Guggenheim fellowships include a limited number of awards to composers. Mrs. Elizabeth Sprague Coolidge is responsible for the Coolidge Chamber Music Festivals which are held in Washington. These concerts, for which much modern chamber music has been commissioned, have the unique distinction of belonging to the nation by virtue of their acceptance by act of Congress.

It is quite possible to say that the intervention of the patrons of Beethoven was critical in making it possible for him to create works which are still the daily bread of musician and of music-lover. Beethoven was obviously incapable of the exact conformity to etiquette which was required of a court musician. Patronage was at the same time essential to him and repugnant to him. He rebelled at details, submitted in essentials, yet was still able by some miracle of character to preserve the fierce independence for which we honor him.

It is difficult to say that American patronage has played any such decisive role. It is quite clear that a very large number of wealthy Americans have little interest in music and no wish to support it. This is perhaps most clearly revealed by a study of our more typical tycoons and industrialists. Most of our American music patrons have developed in an atmosphere of European culture. The old aristocratic culture depended on a tradition which was substantial enough to maintain a certain cultural continuity in spite of the obtuseness, lack of intelligence, or lack of musical endowment of many individual nobles. An absolute monarch might theoretically dismiss every court musician. He was in fact rather unlikely to do so because he had become accustomed to their music and was likely to regard it as an element contributing to his prestige if not to his enjoyment. It was part of a traditional way of life.

A modern American store-owner or industrialist is bound by no such tradition. The entertainment which is offered to everyone on a commercial basis is likely to satisfy any musical longings which he may possess. Extreme ostentation in the form of a private orchestra is no longer necessary since numbers of excellent symphony orchestras are already in existence. There is little that he can buy in the form of musical experience which is not available to those of lesser wealth.

The musician has also changed in character. Though some musicians still possess a marked predilection for wealthy acquaintances and an amazing degree of suppleness and skill in developing these relationships in an advantageous fashion, others prefer a more independent life. Famous soloists are clearly able to earn more through commercial channels than any private patron would be likely to offer them. Many musicians whose earning capacity is smaller prefer to earn their living without the blessings of patronage. The greatest hardship falls on composers who are in general unable to earn a living by their special gifts and must therefore live by teaching or by performance with a consequent diversion of effort and diminution of productivity.

In a certain sense court music was a function of the state. In another sense it might be a personal prerogative of the monarch. The phrase which covered one category of expenses for music at the French court *"Les menus plaisirs du roi"* (royal expenses for amusement) expresses this fact in a delightful fashion. In one sense, therefore, state patronage of music goes back as far as the organization of court music. In another sense we must wait for the development of nationalism before we can really consider state patronage as representing more than the will of the ruler.

It requires a certain exertion of the imagination to realize that there was a time when European musical culture was largely French and Italian. In the eighteenth century certain Frenchmen were eagerly celebrating the virtues of Italian music at the same time that others were condemning it as extravagant. Burney, the music historian, praised an English composer by remarking that he had absorbed the Italian style so completely that one would hardly suspect that he was English. In short the growth of musical nationalism and the thought that the musician expresses his country grew with the modern national state.

A part of the same development was the recognition by the state that music created by its nationals was worthy of support. This differed from the patronage dispensed by a monarch, because a monarch might and sometimes did favor musicians of a different nationality than that of his own subjects. Thus Charles II imported French musicians like Monsieur Grabu, who became Master of the King's Music, while English musicians were valued to the extent that they catered to the foreign tastes which their monarch had acquired during his continental exile. Most modern states take the view that support ought to be granted to musical institutions and, in some instances, to outstanding musicians. The state, in short, has become a patron. This development parallels the development of national consciousness.

French musicians at the time of the Revolution played an active part in disseminating the ideas of the state and in organizing the great open-air festivals which were a characteristic expression of the period. The state, on the other hand, subsidized or created the musical institutions which seemed to be most necessary to the country and most characteristic of its culture. Thus, the French government has subsidized the Conservatory (the national school of music), two opera houses (the *Opéra* and the *Opéra-Comique*), and a number of symphony orchestras including the orchestra of the famous *"Concerts du Conservatoire."*

The English government supports the British Broadcasting Corporation Orchestra. Certain famous English musicians receive the distinction of knighthood as a recognition of their services to the nation. Edward Elgar, Ethel Smyth, Arnold Bax, and Henry Wood have all been honored in this way.

The Scandinavian nations have been pioneers in the support they have granted famous artists, literary men, and musicians. Niels Gade received financial support from the Danish government in 1843 which later was changed to a pension for life. In 1874 Norway granted a life pension to Edvard Grieg which enabled him to devote all his energies to composition. Sibelius received an annual grant from the government of Finland in 1897 at a time when Finland had not yet become an independent nation. This was altered to a life pension in 1925 after Finland had become a republic.

The Soviet government probably gives the largest measure of support to music and musicians of any modern nation. Not only does it maintain opera houses, symphony orchestras, music schools and schools of the ballet, but it also builds clubhouses, studios, and apartments for musicians and other workers in the fields of the arts. Musicians are educated and maintained at state expense. In no other country are the ideals of the artist and the objectives of the government so closely allied.

Our own country lags far behind the European powers in its official support of music. Indeed the divorce between the government and the musician is almost complete. Aside from the support granted to the Music Division of the Library of Congress and Congressional acceptance of the associated Chamber Music Foundation, the only other existing music enterprises closely associated with the government are the army and navy bands and particularly the Marine Band of Washington.

The greatest experiment in the government support of the arts in the United States grew out of the W.P.A. which was intended to alleviate the catastrophic unemployment which developed as a result of the depression of 1929. The Four Arts Project, which included the Federal Music Project, was initiated in 1935. Not the least of its accomplishments was the revelation of a widespread popular interest in music which existing organizations had not met. It undertook musical research, established symphony orchestras and bands, set up educational centers where free class instruction in music was given, and instituted Composers' Forum Laboratories where American composers had their works performed and where the audience had an opportunity to make criticisms. It opened vistas which expanded as they were explored, which revealed the great gap between the music and the music instruction offered by private agencies and the music which our people wanted and needed. The Federal Music Project was destroyed by a hostile Congress in 1941. It seems likely to remain without a successor until a decided change in the climate of public opinion takes place.

If governments have sometimes served as patrons of the arts, they have also served as regulating agencies in the interest of what they considered to be public morality and security. The censor had little to do with instrumental works though Schumann, who inserted a reference to the *Marseillaise* into his *Faschingsschwank aus Wien"* ("Viennese Carnival Jest"), was delighted when the work was performed in Vienna without interference at a time when performances of the *Marseillaise* were forbidden.

Theatrical productions such as operas on the other hand had to pass the closest scrutiny of the censor. Though this gentleman dealt with the text rather than the music, his activities affected the opera composer by forbidding the performance of works or by insisting on crippling alterations. This conflict between the artist and the censor was the sharpest where a people were in conflict with the ruling group or where the rulers were an alien group supported by military force. Thus Czarist Russia and Italy under Austrian rule were subjected to an especially severe censorship.

Censors were vigilant in matters of public morality, but they were infinitely more sensitive to anything which might cast ridicule upon members of the aristocracy or which might arouse opposition to them. Thus, Verdi chose a mosι unlucky subject in the opera which we know as the "Masked Ball" (*Un Ballo in Maschera*). In the original version Gustavus III of Sweden was a central figure and his assassination by a group of disaffected nobles the climactic moment of the opera. The King of Naples could hardly be expected to approve of such a plot, nor was he appeased when a Duke of Pomerania was substituted for the King. Finally, in despair, Verdi turned from Naples and tried to have his work staged in Rome. But there he met new difficulties. Only when the locale had been shifted to our side of the Atlantic was the assassination permitted, and the victim became a governor of Boston whose fate apparently disturbed no one. Ridiculous as such manoeuvres may appear to us, it must not be forgotten that this was a generation of Italians who, deprived of the opportunity of direct expression, seized on conventional patriotic phrases in Verdi's operas and made them slogans and bywords.

Many music-lovers, many musicians, have a deep-seated objection to the use of music to reinforce statements of national policy. The objection most frequently raised is the least reasonable. The state, these critics say, is taking away the right of the musician to compose as he feels. This is a result of the nineteenth century belief in music as an exclusively individual and personal revelation. The beauty of the masterpieces of nineteenth century music will clearly demonstrate that this was a fruitful concept.

We would probably be quite wrong if we were to assume that Sir Edward Elgar was violating any personal conviction in writing those of his works which have a nationalist and patriotic, even an imperialistic character. We would be equally at fault if we assumed that the government exerted any pressure on the composer to induce him to produce these works. The honors conferred on him undoubtedly caused him to respond by composing certain occasional works. He thus reinforced with his music a certain concept of British sovereignty as completely as if he had been required by his government to do so.

After all, is it worse for a musician to use his art to reinforce a tenet in which he believes in a conscious fashion than to respond to the implications of the belief in his music without deliberate intention? Yet occasional music does have a bad name. The real question then would seem to be twofold. Are the aims of the state good and are they capable of inspiring a wholehearted devotion? Is the musician capable of identifying himself with the fundamental concepts which he is to express?

The same critics who frown on such a possibility accept as a matter of course the fact that a composer can so identify himself with a religious creed that he can write great music in spite of the very strict limitations which may be imposed by custom and ecclesiastical law. The many masterpieces of religious music do, indeed, demonstrate that an acceptance of a system of belief with the accompanying practical limitations may result in the creation of compositions of real musical beauty. Possibly the religious frame of mind is inherently more musical in nature than political aspiration. But are the humanitarian and social ideals of a great state entirely unsuited for musical expression?

The risks of state-patronized music are great and obvious. The terrible example furnished by the fate of the arts in Nazi Germany shows only too clearly what state control of the arts can lead to: the reduction of all art to the level of a propaganda poster, the suppression of all music which did not correspond with Nazi views, the silencing of all musicians who did not support in every respect the doctrines of the fascists, all these were inevitable consequences. Music was set the task of arousing a lust for war and of creating an emotional allegiance to a corrupt and vicious state. Musical progress ceased, but great music of the past was made to serve as Nazi propaganda.

Yet in our own country musicians seem reluctant to celebrate the really profound and moving accomplishments of the state. The T.V.A. has been celebrated by the ballad singers but not by the symphonists. We are still bound by a convention which makes it easier to write music celebrating the victories of war than the victories of peace. (Perhaps Virgil Thomson's music to "The Plow that Broke the Plains" might be cited as one of a number of exceptions to the rule.)

The rise of the modern fascist dictatorships, accompanied as it was by a coordination of the arts into a machine for cultural propaganda, had the effect of making many artists realize that they must take sides, that they must choose between struggle or submission. The interval between the two world wars was a struggle of ideals of which World War II was the continuation. The government of the United States, unskilled in such matters, was able to mobilize and utilize only a fraction of the musical resources available. Our clumsiness was in startling contrast to the efficiency of the Nazi use of music. They lacked any true view of the power and influence of music but nevertheless were able to use it in a skillful and compelling way as propaganda, as a means of adding emotional conviction to Nazi doctrines. Yet our composers and our arts flourished during the war, perhaps in part because the threat to freedom gave individual artists an added desire to affirm their beliefs. Musical art stagnated in Italy. Nazi Germany destroyed its art and remained sterile throughout the war.

It is clear that our tradition does not readily visualize the use of music to reinforce national ideals save on a popular level. We applauded Irving Berlin's "Yip Yip Yaphank," and we applauded "This is the Army Mr. Jones" even more vigorously. We bought bonds to the accompaniment of "Any Bonds Today." In certain of our propaganda films music was used with great effect. The Philarmonic Society commissioned a series of compositions on patriotic themes. What was done in this direction is likely to leave no permanent impression, yet it is clear that music could be a powerful weapon in upholding and adding emotional conviction to what is great in our tradition.

Our backwardness in this matter is no doubt due in part to official and brass-hat philistinism. Then, too, Americans have a deep and sometimes abundantly justified suspicion of officially inspired sentiments. Even so, it is strange that a country saturated to a unique degree with advertising slogans of dubious veracity and undoubted bad taste should be so extremely suspicious of the use of music to reinforce national ideals. We praise the merits of tooth paste in music more frequently and fervently than the Gettysburg Address or the Bill of Rights.

Chapter VIII

MEANS AND METHODS FOR
GENERALIZING MUSIC

Music is a means of communication between human beings. It lends emotional force to the words with which it is associated. Early music, however, was limited in influence by the fact that it was transmitted by oral tradition. The boy heard his father sing and thus learned his songs. He grew to manhood. Eventually he sang them to his own sons. Jenness and Ballantyne studied the people of the Northern D'Entrecasteaux Islands which lie off the coast of British New Guinea. They found that the children "watch the dances too and learn the songs; they share the wailing over the dead, and listen to the incantations for the sick and the magic songs that hush the winds and stay the fury of the tempests."

Such a method was suited to cultures without written records. It required personal contact between singer and pupil. It was limited in general to people who spoke a single language. It had the advantage of dispensing with any system of music notation. We may think of the lives of English cottagers, of Russian *moujiks* of former days, of our own mountain folk of the south, as poor and bare. Yet how many "cultured" college graduates could sing a hundred songs by memory as certain folk singers have done? The folksong was indeed only a simple tune repeated for each successive stanza of the text, but the people possessed and used it as few musicians of the present day possess and enjoy our more complex musical heritage.

How precious such songs might be to those who sang them is revealed by an anecdote concerning the English folksong collector Cecil Sharp. "When the old woman heard Cecil Sharp's enquiry, she replied that she knew the song. 'Shall I sing it to you?' she said; and raising her old weather-worn face to his, taking the lapels of his coat in her hands, and closing her eyes, she sang 'The Lark in the Morn' in her wavering yet beautiful voice, while he rapidly made notes. When the song was finished, she gazed into his eyes in a sort of ecstasy, and, in perfect detachment from herself, exclaimed, 'Isn't it lovely?' "

It is the same method of oral transmission which is employed in modern times to give children their early musical impressions, the cradle song of the mother, the rote songs of the kindergarten and primary grades. It is clear that it was not a completely accurate method of preserving and transmitting music, and its accuracy necessarily varied with the sureness of memory of the singer and of those who listened to him and repeated his songs. When we understand that not only the folksong literature but also the sacred songs of the various religious rites were originally preserved by oral tradition, we realize the importance of the method.

To convince oneself that traditional melodies do vary, it is only necessary to compare several copies of such a familiar melody as "Auld Lang Syne." The differences observed will not be large, but they illustrate the occurrence of variants. But "Auld Lang Syne" has appeared in print for many years, and a written or printed copy of a tune furnishes a standard with which other versions may be compared. Among traditional songs which were not written down, differences between variants might be much greater. Such differences might be improvements or they might (in the case of an unmusical singer) result in a deterioration of the tune. There seems little doubt, however, that an accumulation of such changes might contribute to the molding of the tune in accordance with the character of a people and make it a true expression of their feelings.

Music notation is a marvellous accomplishment which is only kept from further changes to suit the requirements of modern music by the difficulties (indeed, so far the impossibility) of training a whole generation of musicians in a new system and (even more) the tremendous task of reprinting the existing literature.

It is undoubtedly true that many features of present day notation were designed to suit musical styles which have passed out of use. The sharps and flats collected at the beginning of a line of music as the scale signature are intended as a convenient way of indicating which black notes of the piano are employed in the scale of a composition. But where an unusual scale is used which consistently demands the use of other tones than those indicated by the signature, or where the composer shifts rapidly from one scale to another, the tones indicated by the sharps and flats of the signature may have to be so frequently altered that it ceases to be useful. For most music-minded people the development of the art of writing music includes only the evolution of signs which symbolize and call to mind the various sounds employed in music, which indicate their length and their softness or loudness. There is another aspect of the development of notation which has never been described, at least not in a complete and comprehensive form. The art of music notation has varied according to the use which was to be made of it in a given society. We in the United States are apt to consider that a certain ability to read music is a proper accomplishment of every child who attends our public schools. Early music notations were understood only by a given class, most commonly the priesthood.

It was perhaps safer to have no notation at all. That, however, involved the risk of a change due to a slip of memory. If a song with magic powers were changed, its effect might be lessened or altogether destroyed. Thus, when a chant had to be transmitted to many people, or when the risks of inaccurate oral transmission appeared to be great, music notation appeared. Early notations were not intended for general use. The fact that they could not be deciphered by the uninitiated was an advantage rather than a disadvantage. This enigmatic character was due to two facts. One was the imperfection of early notation which could not convey a song to anyone who had not already been familiarized with it. Secondly, since the earliest chants were believed to possess magic power, it was vital that they should not fall into alien or hostile hands. Thus, early notations had a double function, to preserve and keep secret.

Seldom has the belief in the power of music and the idea that its complete use is properly reserved to a dominant group been expressed more clearly than in a Chinese treatise, the *"Li-Ki."* "Music is intimately connected with the essential relations of being. Thus, to know sounds, but not airs, is peculiar to birds and brute beasts; to know airs, but not music, is peculiar to the common herd; to the wise alone it is reserved to understand music. That is why sounds are studied to know airs, airs in order to know music, and music in order to know how to *rule.*" Thus, in the Chinese view unrelated sounds belong to the animal world, folksong to the common people, but only to the initiates of the ruling class the music which possessed magic power.

Among the ancient Hebrews the Levites were the priest-musicians. The musical lore necessary for the prescribed rites was transmitted in temple schools. This was evidently true of ancient Mesopotamia. The scribe who transcribed a Sumerian hymn and its supposed musical notation added a direction: "The initiate may reveal it to the initiate." Wilkinson, who had studied the elaborate rites of the Egyptians, remarked that their notation, if they possessed one, would surely have been kept hidden from all except the priests. Villoteau, who entered Egypt as one of the scholars chosen by Napoleon to study that country, was able to obtain some information concerning a system of notation preserved by the Coptic priests. With the technical details of this system we are not concerned here. What is important to us is the fact that the system was a zealously guarded secret. The belief in music as a magic power gradually faded and, with the passing of this belief, the necessity for keeping it secret diminished.

Indeed, the rapid spread of Christianity over all of Europe and the difficulty of preserving the authentic form of the chant presented a problem of quite a different kind. The church desired to preserve a musical and ritual unity which was at first precarious, later more precisely regimented. Once the period of primitive Christianity had passed, the song of the church became the province of a fairly limited group of ecclesiastics and musicians. Nevertheless the conversion of the people of Europe and later of the New World presented enormous problems if any kind of ritual unity was to be obtained. It was necessary to collect, to select, and to arrange the songs of the church, to train musicians, to multiply copies of accepted versions of the songs of the church.

The work of collecting and arranging the songs of the church, accomplished by Pope Gregory and his predecessors, led to the establishment of a singing school. During his lifetime and that of his successors copies of the "Antiphonary" and trained singers were sent where the need or the opportunity seemed greatest. Pope Gregory himself sent a copy to the Lombards. Later Paul I sent a Gregorian antiphonary to Pepin the Short. We are told that the singers of this monarch had much trouble mastering the complexities of Gregorian song. Charlemagne pursued the same task with energy, and schools of singing were established at his request at Metz and Soissons.

Criticisms of singers who roar or bellow the sacred chants are in all probability not entirely called forth by lack of skill, although no doubt many did indeed lack skill. There was also a conflict between local traditions of performance and the manner of singing approved by the church. The need for a clear notation which would serve as a guide to singers wherever the church had made converts was obvious.

[163]

The first methods of writing music were aids to the memory rather than exact notations. In the pictographic notations of the American Indian, for example, the images incised on a sheet of birch bark suggest the basic idea of the song to the singer. This in turn is associated with the actual tune and with the words of the text. Even now we utilize no method of notation which is comprehensively exact.

Only as music was institutionalized, codified, did a definite system of notation appear to be necessary. Yet even here the accomplishment (as far as it has been preserved to us) lagged far behind the rites of which it formed a part. The Babylonian notation (if indeed it was a musical notation) has not yet been interpreted in a convincing fashion. Not till we reach the Greeks do we find a notation, not the first in all probability, but the first which has been preserved in an intelligible form. To the Greeks we owe the idea of identifying tones by letters, a device which is still employed at the present time.

Not until the Catholic church was faced with the problem of unifying and standardizing its musical ritual do we find the symbols which eventually developed into Western notation. At first, signs or accents were written above the texts of liturgical chants. These signs or neumes appear in manuscripts of the eighth and ninth centuries. The pitch was roughly pictured by the elevation of the signs above the words of the text. The idea of placing the signs on, above, or below a straight line drawn above the text made a more exact notation of the pitch element possible, and by the eleventh century this idea was elaborated into the musical staff. As the neumes were altered into notes and groups of notes, they were placed on or between the four lines which were eventually employed in notating the ancient chants. (The modern system of five parallel lines is a comparatively recent device.) Thus the notes were at last clearly defined as high or low.

For a long period the duration of each tone was gov-

erned only by the expressive declamation of the text or by
its metre where the text was in verse. The hymns of the
church and the songs of the troubadours derived their regular and rhythmic movement from the metre of the text.
Gradually music evolved its own metric system, a system
which necessarily became more exact as musicians experimented in the combination of melodies. Where singers performed different melodies at the same time, they needed a
common measure for the notes they sang if they were to ar-
rive simultaneously at a given point.

The final consequence of these changes was a notation
sufficiently precise to make it possible for a skilled musician
to sing from its notation a song which he did not previously
know.

With this development (as with the development of written language) came a new need for education, for systematic
and deliberate instruction in the new art. Anyone with an
ear for music could learn songs by rote, and many people
still do learn tunes in this way from the singing of a friend
or the repetitious radio. Music notation was not easily mastered without a teacher. It did not reveal itself to the uninitiated. Thus, there developed a distinction between those
who could and those who could not read music. Cultivated
amateurs and professional musicians alone could take part
in performances. Unskilled music-lovers were gradually reduced to the role of the listener, the audience. Nor has the
progress of democratic education yet succeeded in giving all
our people the power to read music.

In an earlier chapter the emergence of composers and of
performers specializing in secular music was sketched. The
earliest Western notation, as we have seen, was a church notation. The needs of the town and court musician were different, and this, together with the growing importance of instrumental music, were to cause profound changes in music
notation. The professional singer and even more the professional instrumentalist was likely to regard written music

as a sketch which he elaborated in ways which he had learned from his teachers or by listening to skilled contemporary performers.

Ornaments such as trills were often not indicated at all or were sparsely and sometimes vaguely marked. (The little sign +, for example, served for a long period as a hint that an ornament of some kind was desired at that point.) The accompaniment to a melody was often represented only by the bass part, and to this, aided perhaps by conventional symbols, the player added the necessary chords. It is clear that skill in elaborating the skeleton which the notation furnished could only be acquired after a long apprenticeship.

The amateur could share in this instrumental art only if he were especially gifted and had the opportunity of learning the tradition, or if he possessed wealth and leisure, or a sufficient balance of these various factors.

There was indeed a kind of notation which was explicit at a time when the usual staff notation required the kind of elaboration which has just been described. This was tablature. It was a picture notation based on the fingerboard of such instruments as the lute or the guitar. Though it utilized a series of parallel lines, these lines do not represent sounds as in modern staff notation but symbolized the strings of the instrument. Signs placed at given points on a printed line were directions to the player to place his finger at the corresponding location on a string of the actual instrument. In short, tablature was a set of ingenious and condensed directions for performance. It has survived to modern times in forms adapted to the banjo and the ukelele. Though the notation was employed by professional performers on such instruments as the lute, the guitar, and the viol, it was peculiarly adapted to the amateur musician. Once he understood the principles on which the notation was devised, he had merely to follow the directions, confident that the sounds which emerged from the instrument were those intended by the composer. This required much less training and skill than first imagining and then producing a sound written in our usual notation. Tablature required the player to make a given movement. Staff notation demands that the musician conceive a sound mentally and then produce it. To a certain degree, tablature was intended to serve the amateur who wished a quick and easy mastery of music.

This sketch notation for instrumental performers and notation by tablature lasted roughly through the time of Bach. The generations of composers who followed became by degrees more and more explicit in writing down their thoughts. This was due not only to the fact that composers were more anxious to secure a performance in correct style but also to the need of making music more accessible and easier for beginners and amateurs. By this time, the circulation of music was expanding, and there was therefore less certainty that a performer would elaborate a piece in accordance with the intentions of the composer.

Bach wrote much of his keyboard music for teaching purposes, but his pupils were largely promising youths who worked in close association with him or members of his own family. The pieces for beginners which he carefully fingered, the table of ornaments which he wrote out for his sons testify to his interest in teaching. These works remained in manuscript during his lifetime, largely, as we must suppose, because the demand for them was not great enough to warrant an engraved edition. Bach's own son, Johann Christian Bach, and Mozart also wrote pieces for beginners, but the demand had increased and the pieces were therefore published. In general the notation of Mozart leaves less to the discretion of the performer than Bach. His system of ornamentation is simpler. If a song accompaniment was required, he wrote it down, just as it was to be played. Rather sparsely scattered "expression marks," absent in Bach, now appear.

It was, however, not only music for beginners that was more carefully notated. Music for professional performers tended to be notated in a more explicit fashion. The elaborate ornamentation of such French harpsichordists as Chambonnières, the carefully worked out arabesques of the slow movement of Bach's "Italian Concerto," reveal the virtuoso who wished to explain, to fix and transmit his performance as far as that could be done by symbols.

The widening circle of those who wished to share in the knowledge of music finally reached a point where the usual staff notation as we know it seemed to require a further simplification. Some reformers wished to replace staff notation with a new system. Most of these systems were foredoomed to failure; but they are significant in any event, because they reveal the middle class, then the workers reaching out for their share in music. Many of these systems were doomed simply because they could express adequately only music of a very rudimentary kind.

Thus, Rousseau wished to replace our musical staff and the notes placed on it with numbers designating the different notes of the scale. Numbers are still used for this purpose but as a teaching device rather than as an independent notation. Miss Sara A. Glover adapted the ancient sol-fa syllables and used them in the early years of the nineteenth century to teach children easy melodies. The idea was taken up and improved by the Rev. John Curwen whose system was widely used in England and exerted a considerable influence on public school music in the United States. As C. F. Abdy Williams has said, "It was very energetically brought before the public by its founders at a time when there was little knowledge of music in England, and a growing desire to know more."

Nevertheless music notation gave music wings. A song might be admired and repeated by singers who had never heard it sung. It might cross frontiers and travel to new lands. The notation of music, unlike written language, gradually shook off its local peculiarities and became the same wherever Western civilization penetrated. It was international where the printed word was national, though the great region of the East pursued its own paths.

Important as were these discoveries, the knowledge of music was still restricted. Manuscript music required hours of painstaking work on the part of the scribe. Copies could only be multiplied by a repetition of the same process, and as copies were made, mistakes were multiplied. Mistakes appeared by inadvertence when a skilled musician made the copy, through ignorance or carelessness when the work was entrusted to a copyist. Thus, the diffusion of music was still hampered by the lack of a means of reproduction which should be both more accurate and cheaper than the manuscript copy. The answer to the problem was found in the application of the art of printing to music. Yet the practice of circulating music in manuscript persisted for long and, indeed, still serves for music which is in limited demand.

The concept that music is the property of the composer hardly existed before modern times. Only with the establishment of copyright laws did this idea find legal expression. In the sixteenth and seventeenth centuries, however, a musician could retain music for his exclusive use only by keeping it in manuscript. The ideal that music was to be shared hardly existed. The composer or performer often found it advantageous to retain works for his exclusive use. Again and again a musician who finally published his works protested that he had done so only because incorrect copies or unauthorized editions had been circulated. Sometimes this was in all probability a conventional gesture, but often it must indeed have represented the best way out of a bad situation. To such circumstances we owe the preservation of much music of real interest.

Many difficulties had to be overcome before music could be printed. Particularly troublesome was the fact that musical symbols are not printed on a single level but range up and down over the lines and spaces of the staff. The first books which contained music merely left blanks for musical illustrations which were afterwards filled in by hand. Other volumes utilized the art of the wood engraver to produce blocks from which musical examples could be printed. Such a block could only reproduce the one example engraved upon it and thus lacked the flexibility of type. Ottaviano Petrucci da Fossombrone finally succeeded (1501) in printing part-music from musical characters which could be disassembled and used again for other publications. Though the work he produced was beautiful in quality, it required two printings, one for the parallel lines of the staff, the other for the notes and the other symbols. (Some authorities believe that a third impression was required for the text.) Such music printing was expensive and the editions were small. In spite of this, the development marked a revolution of the greatest importance. It was now possible to multiply and diffuse musical compositions by mechanical means. It had the same significance for the musician that the original invention of printing from movable type had for the author and his readers. When we read the familiar story of the music which Bach copied by moonlight, we realize how true such a story is to its period, how different from our own situation.

Printing music from a woodblock was an adaptation of an artistic process to a practical end. The art of the copper engraver was utilized in a similar fashion. The musical staff and the symbols of notation were incised on a smooth copper plate. When the hollows thus formed were filled with printer's ink, the plate was brought into firm contact with a sheet of paper by means of a press. The paper absorbed the ink and was withdrawn as a sheet of music. Later the process was simplified by the use of stamps or punches which were tapped with a hammer in order to impress the symbols on the plate.

A totally new approach was the process of lithography. Here the musical notation was transcribed on the smooth surface of a stone with a grease-crayon. After the prepared stone was treated with an acid bath, only the crayon marks retained the printer's ink. This process was received with much reluctance by conservative music publishers as well as by musicians. Since it was cheaper than engraved music, lithographed music made its way in spite of opposition and was much used for the publication of popular songs.

The process which is employed at present utilizes the techniques of punching and engraving to prepare the original plate. Instead of printing directly from the engraved plate, however, an impression is transferred to a special copper lithographic plate. From this a large edition may be printed without wearing out the original.

Much study needs to be devoted to the gradually expanding circulation of music. We do not know very much about the size of the editions of early printed music nor about their cost. Yet these are two of the crucial points in the development of music, for a widespread knowledge of music depended to a very considerable degree on the possibility of producing large printed editions. If music was to be available to music-lovers of moderate means, the cost per copy must be low. The machinery of production has passed from the hands of the scribe and copyist to the worker at the hand press and from him to the automatic press of the present day. The number of copies produced in a given time has increased, and the cost of producing a single copy has diminished.

Even the fact that music is relatively cheap and abundant does not mean that it will reach the hands of all those who could use it and profit by it. Only in the United States has the next step been taken. Even here the public music library is an exceptional occurrence, though most libraries do include books on music, and many circulate music. The idea of a library where anyone may withdraw music and books on music for study or amusement, may listen to or withdraw phonograph records, is one of the brighter signs of musical democracy in our own country. It is in complete opposition to the principle followed in the famous music libraries of Europe where the conservator was, as the word implies, someone who preserved books but was under no obligations to make them available even to qualified students. It would be unfair not to mention here the pioneer work done by the Music Library at 58th Street, New York City as a branch of the public library devoted solely to music.

The diffusion of music could not be attained by printed copies alone. The development of music printing went hand in hand with important advances in the teaching of music. Music teaching of the sixteenth, seventeenth, and eighteenth centuries was largely concerned with the training of professional musicians. The exceptions to this rule were wealthy and titled dilettanti who played only for their own pleasure. But the development of the art of teaching music antedates the art of printing.

In the turmoil which accompanied the disintegration of the classic world music teaching survived, where it survived at all, in church and monastery. Choristers who sang the music of the service obviously needed to know the traditions of the chants they were to perform. Certain ecclesiastical establishments became nurseries of composers and of singers. Such centers as the Chapel Royal in England, Hainault in the Low Countries, are well known to every student of music history for this reason. Choirmasters were always in search of gifted boy sopranos. For a poor boy such centers offered the only means of obtaining musical instruction. The list of composers who commenced their careers as choir-boys would be a long one and would include the names of Lassus, Haydn, Purcell, and Grétry.

It was the demand for composers, singers, and instrumental performers created by the establishment of opera houses which caused the development of a new type of music school in Italy. Conservatories were originally connected with homes for foundlings or hospitals. The intention was to furnish a means of livelihood for the inmates as well as to adorn the church services of the institution.

They outgrew their original purpose, however, and became the nurseries of the multitude of singers, composers, and instrumentalists who made Italian opera world-famous. The most celebrated musicians of the time headed these institutions: Durante, Leo, Jomelli, Vivaldi. The musical traveller never failed to visit the conservatories and to record his impressions in his notebook. One of the most striking may be found in Rousseau's "Confessions."

"Music, the like of which is to be found nowhere else in Italy or in all the world, which to my thought is superior even to the opera—such is the music of the *scuole*. Every Sunday at the vesper services in each of these four *scuole,* motets are performed by a full chorus and large orchestra, composed and directed by the greatest masters in Italy. These are performed within grilled enclosures, solely by girls of whom the oldest is not 20 years of age. I can think of nothing more thrilling, more moving than this music. The church is always filled with admirers; even the singers from the Opera come to profit by those excellent examples of good style in singing."

Neither the choir school nor the conservatory envisaged anything as ambitious as the musical education of a whole people. For the most part the mere conception of such an idea was left for a later period. Yet here and there in the Europe of the eighteenth century music was taught to the common people, not to make professional musicians of them (though an occasional graduate of the common schools did attain that goal) but as a part of their basic schooling and as a means of self-support while they were in school. In certain German states and in Bohemia music was taught in the schools. Such music instruction never was general, never was regarded as the right of every child. Even in recent times effective music instruction has often been limited to favored localities or to schools which served a more privileged group than the common schools.

Music instruction in our country, as in Europe, rose originally from a desire to improve the performance of church music. The folk heritage which the early settlers brought with them from Europe survived in isolated communities to our own day without any formal aids. The effective performance of psalms and hymns required a somewhat more formal type of instruction which was furnished by the itinerant singing master who taught the rudiments of music and a repertory of familiar hymns to the boys and girls of the neighborhood. In the South "singings" and revival meetings kept the familiar tunes in the minds of the people.

The initiation of music as a subject in the public schools, however, dated only from the nineteenth century. Lowell Mason, who was widely known as a composer of hymns, taught music in 1837 in a Boston school. This was the beginning of a movement which aimed at bringing music to every American child. This aim, however imperfectly realized, is of definite historical importance. Music, at first introduced into the elementary schools, was gradually accepted as a high school and as a college subject.

The development of music education has not only brought music and some knowledge of music notation to many children; it has also raised the level of professional performance. It may seem strange that the art of performance which depends so greatly on physiological factors could be indefinitely improved. The same improvement is apparent in a more tangible form in the field of athletics. Runners have been competing for generations. One would suppose that a point would be reached which would represent the maximum possibilities of the human body. It may be true that such a point will ultimately be attained. Up to the present runners are still able to break the established speed records. This too is largely a matter of education. Trainers and coaches have studied and restudied each movement so as to gain every possible advantage. In a similar fashion each technical discovery made by a great performer or composer has been studied and taught by skilled teachers. It is said that when Liszt appeared he was the only person who could play his compositions. How many student pianists of today rattle off the Hungarian Rhapsody No. 2 with a considerable degree of success! Paganini's concert pieces for violin represented the utmost in violin technique when they were composed. Many concert-goers have heard the "Perpetual Motion" played by all the first violins of the Philharmonic under the direction of Arturo Toscanini. Thus, the technical accomplishments of a few highly gifted performers have become the common property of all well-equipped professional musicians.

In the earlier part of this chapter the development of musical notation was sketched as well as the successive advances which made the mass production of music possible. But music notation, even in its present state, is not perfect. The earliest notations were primarily records of the pitch, later of the duration of tones. Gradually signs for nuances from soft to loud, indications of conventional ornaments and other directions for performance were added. No matter how elaborately such matters were indicated, there were always traits of style, shades of interpretation too subtle to be captured by notation. There was always much which had to be learned from the actual performance of artists.

A printed page of music, therefore, is not enough. The actual sound is needed. This need was realized long before the technical means to carry it into effect were available. Automatic harpsichords date back to the sixteenth century. The keys of the instrument were actuated by appropriately spaced studs on a revolving drum. The motive power was furnished by turning a crank as in the hurdy-gurdy. Père Engramelle, in a volume which deals with the art of so spacing the studs on the barrel of such instruments that they might reproduce music accurately, speaks with regret of the loss music had suffered because there was no way of preserving the actual

[175]

performances of famous artists. "We would still enjoy at present the execution of Lully, of Marchand, and of all the great men who have filled their contemporaries with astonishment, if they had understood the system of pricking their pieces, which, transmitted by themselves to posterity on unalterable cylinders, would have preserved this form of expression of which we can only form an idea through history." The barrel organ and the automatic harmonium were sometimes employed in country churches in nineteenth century England. The remark by Rimbault, a well-known organist and scholar of the period, that "we need scarcely point out the superiority of an accurate mechanism over the imperfect manipulation of an inferior performer" throws light on the poverty of musical resources in small communities at the time.

The player-piano was to play an important though brief part in the spread of music. It was extremely popular in the early years of the twentieth century though the first instrument with a pneumatic mechanism is said to have been manufactured in France in 1863. The playing mechanism of the player-piano was controlled by a roll of paper perforated by dots and by slots of various lengths. When these openings coincided with holes in a fixed bar over which the paper passed, a puff of air was released which actuated the sounding mechanism for a given tone. The length of this tone depended on the length of the opening in the paper roll. These instruments found their way into parlors and into bars. A newspaper clipping of the time comments, "Almost every week it is announced that some piano-making firm is to put a new kind of self-player on the market . . . It is precisely in supplying this general lack of opportunity for the frequent hearing of good music that the self-player finds its field of utility."

The rolls for the more highly developed Ampico, Duo-Art, and Welte-Mignon instruments were cut by well-known performing artists, but these instruments, though capable of more nuance than the implacable early player-piano, were eventually displaced by the cheaper phonograph and radio.

It was not till the phonograph was invented that Engramelle's dream could be adequately realized. In the simple Edison phonograph of early days, the voice of the recording artist was directed into a horn. A thin diaphragm located in the soundbox, which communicated with the horn, moved in and out in response to the vibration produced by the voice. On the lower side of the diaphragm was a stylus which engraved on a revolving cylinder of soft wax a line which corresponded exactly with the vibration pattern of the song. If a reproducing stylus followed the grooves cut in the record, the vibrations of the diaphragm were repeated and communicated to the air and then to the ears of the audience. The performance of the singer had been duplicated.

It was the phonograph which first provided "canned music" for the people. It placed actual musical performances under the control of the purchaser to be heard, to be repeated, or stopped at will. The machine henceforth was part of the baggage of the explorer and anthropologist. It could record the music of remote tribes and of vanishing cultures. It could preserve and repeat the performances of great singers and performers for a later audience which would otherwise know them only as names. Recent as the invention is, its value to the music historian is already great. Such household words as Chaliapin, Caruso, Melba are not merely symbols of the transitory success of a great singer. We can still hear them sing and can reproduce the tones at which an earlier generation of opera-goers marvelled.

The early Edison machines were imperfect. Their tone had a characteristic twang which was hardly flattering to the performer. Yet these machines were eagerly bought and used. Successive improvements, notably electrical recording and amplification, brought better reproduction. Within recent years recordings of large works, symphonies, concertos, operas have been made. The resulting advance in musical understanding on the part of phonograph owners is difficult to estimate but clearly is very great. Neither the modern high fidelity phonograph nor a library of records is cheap. For those who can afford it, the phonograph brings music, not the notation but the living performance, to the home of the music-lover.

Repetition has been stressed as the basic prerequisite in developing an appreciation of great music. The phonograph is the most perfect instrument for producing repetitions. The radio stations which broadcast recorded music are also playing an important role in familiarizing the great public with symphonic music.

The final development which made it possible for music to reach wider and wider circles was the radio. The musician is hardly concerned with early experiments in the transmission of electrical impulses because the early transmitters were only capable of intermittent signals which could not be used in the reproduction of musical tones. It was not till 1900 that Duddell discovered that an electric arc could be used as a source of high frequency energy. This provided a sustained carrier wave which made the transmission of music possible. By 1908 German engineers had succeeded in transmitting music for a limited distance.

The "radio tube" invented by Dr. Lee de Forest replaced the unreliable electric arc. Pioneer radio stations like KDKA in Pittsburgh broadcast not only phonograph records but actual performances. In 1916 David Sarnoff advanced the idea of the mass production of "radio music boxes." The radio became a necessary piece of home furniture. By 1925 a nation-wide hook-up was an accomplished fact. A year later programs were received and rebroadcast from Europe. Such are some of the crucial steps in the development of the most potent instrument for the diffusion of music which the world has yet known.

This country has decided to utilize radio primarily as an

advertising medium. In spite of that fact the radio industry utilizes vast quantities of music, chiefly popular music, to a lesser degree classic music. Current radio broadcasts possess well-recognized defects: a preponderance of programs of poor quality from any imaginable standard, blatant and fatuous "commercials," an understandable inclination to remain innocuous by broadcasting mediocre music of known popularity. Nevertheless they must be recognized as the dominant influence in music education and in the diffusion of music at the present day.

The very ease of manipulation of the radio possesses corresponding disadvantages. It is employed as stimulant or distraction while the housewife does her dusting or the schoolboy his lessons. Often it is heeded only when some particularly strident or bizarre effect strikes the attention of the listener. Music is heard carelessly without a sense of its deep and abiding values. None of these difficulties and abuses are necessary, but they are frequent and persistent.

The radio, however, does not and cannot provide the listener with intelligence or with discrimination. It supplies him with music which is good, bad, and (most frequently) indifferent. In a sense it intensifies rather than satisfies the need for a kind of music education which will foster a discriminating musical judgment. Properly used the radio is capable of bringing an amazing variety of music to the auditor without requiring more of him in the way of physical skills than an ability to manipulate the very simple controls. It can bring to the listener a familiarity with the stand- and repertory although it does not permit the auditor to repeat at will as does the phonograph.

In 1926-28 the sound film still further complicated the pattern of musical life. Music for the silent films had furnished employment to many musicians. The only novel feature of early "movie-music" was the manner in which patchwork scores were assembled or utilized. The usual procedure was to furnish a cue-sheet to the conductor or organist listing appropriate selections and specifying the number of measures of each which were to be employed. Musicians became expert at weaving from sixteen measures of this selection and twelve measures of that something like a continuous score. Volumes of music were issued containing compositions appropriate to various typical dramatic situations, "Hurries," "Misteriosos," "Love Themes," and many others. With the advent of the sound film such makeshifts had to give way to a synchronized score, composed, adapted, or arranged as the case might be. A certain number of scores were commissioned from well-known composers without altering or greatly influencing the basic musical patterns of the industry.

These three great factors in music had enormous cultural implications. They also profoundly affected the business of producing music and the manner in which the public listens to music. The concert has been relegated to a very secondary place. The means by which most listeners hear music, listed in the order of their importance, would probably be radio, movies, phonograph, concert or other direct performance.

These then are the steps which have gone far towards bringing music to the people. In simpler cultures oral tradition sufficed. Then followed the long struggle to reduce impalpable sound to definite symbols. This development went hand in hand with the development of music teaching since formal instruction was necessary for an understanding of musical notation. Music printing multiplied the copies of music and lessened their cost. The finer nuances of style and expression never could be captured by notation. The actual reproduction of music itself was achieved imperfectly by the automatic instruments of the sixteenth and later centuries, but in relative perfection by the modern phonograph. Finally the radio, which, almost from the very beginning, employed the phonograph as a source of broadcast music, was able to make a single performance audible over a wide area. It could be heard in the home, in the barn, on the road in an automobile. Professionally performed music has really reached the people in their homes, and it is available to them without demanding any special skill on their part. At the same time that this medium discouraged some amateur performers, it stimulated a latent interest in music in other listeners.

CHAPTER **IX**

MUSIC AS A BUSINESS

MUSIC was first a medium for the expression of the individual's emotion or served as a communal expression in which he joined his fellows. It then became a service performed by a retainer or servant for his lord, or by a wandering minstrel for the people gathered in the market-place. The nordic bards or scalds were, at least to some degree, musicians by profession and lived by their performing skill. A Viking king might invite a bard to spend the long winter months in his hall and would provide for his support during this period. Rewards for individual performances were often generous.

A passage from Gunnlaug Ormstunga's Saga reveals vividly the hesitation of a monarch who was uncertain of the proper reward.

"Gunnlaug said: 'I have made a song about you, and I want to get a hearing.' The king answered: 'No man has before delivered a poem to me, and I shall certainly listen to it.' Gunnlaug then sang the *drapa*. . . . The king thanked him for the song and asked his treasurer with what it should be rewarded. He answered: 'With what will you reward it, lord?' The king said: 'How will it be rewarded, if I give him two *knerrir* (trading ships)?' The treasurer replied: 'That is too much, lord; other kings give costly things, good swords or good gold-rings, as rewards for a song.' The king gave him his own clothes of new scarlet, a lace-ornamented kirtle, a cloak with the finest furs on it, and a gold ring which weighed a mark."

Later monarchs were equally willing to be amused. The old account books give an idea of the kind of entertainment which musicians offered and the rewards they received. A

Scotch "High Treasurer's Record" (for the reigns of James III and IV) is amusingly explicit.

1491. Aug. 21.—Item to iiij Inglis pyparis viij unicorns vij.li. iiijs.

1497. Apr. 10.—Item, to the tua fithelaris that sang Graysteil to ze king, . . . ix.s.

1500. Mar. 1.—Item, to Jacob lutar, to lowse his lute that lay in wed, . . . xxxij.s.

In case a translation is necessary we may interpret the record as follows: four English pipers received eight unicorns (a gold coin), then (on another occasion) seven unicorns, four shillings. The abbreviation "li." stands for "*licorne*," the French word for unicorn. Two fiddlers that sang "Graysteil" to the king received nine shillings. Jacob the lutenist was given thirty-two shillings to redeem his lute which he had pawned. A scale of values is provided by the fact that a sheep could be bought for three shillings. These rewards and many others seem generous enough but they must be placed against other days when the royal bounty was not forthcoming. Such a situation was described in an anonymous French poem:

"Each lost his gift, it was not paid;
The menestrels are all dismayed
For on them none will aught bestow.
Since gifts are what they live upon
Now, seeing they are trampled on,
Elsewhere their tales to tell they go."

The separation between performer and audience becomes more clearly perceptible during the Renaissance. Cultured amateurs in Italy formed academies for the performance of vocal music. These circles included professional musicians. Ruffo, who composed some delightful vocal chamber music, was so employed. In the latter half of the sixteenth century, however, the function of the musician changed from that of a teacher and coach of amateur performers to that of a professional performer with a limited circle of hearers.

MUSIC AS A BUSINESS

In spectacular display performances there is a distinction, less apparent at an earlier period but more marked at a later date, between spectator and executant. The court balls of the Renaissance were in a real sense ceremonial displays in which the nobles of the court were the performers. The masques of the time of Henry VIII did not employ professional performers. The king and members of his court appeared in disguise and, having danced, doffed their masks to reveal their identity. At the court of Louis XIV the king not only played an important part in devising the court ballets, which were much more highly organized and artfully devised than those of earlier periods, but also took leading parts himself with ladies and gentlemen of the court. At the same time, however, other roles were taken by professional musicians and dancers. By the end of the Grand Monarch's life he had slipped back into the audience. The performer mounted the stage. The audience sat at its ease. The performer displayed his skill as a dancer or singer for his livelihood.

One other change was necessary to transform such a court entertainment into the modern opera house. The doors had to be opened to the public, to anyone who could buy the ticket which was his evidence of payment. This new development took place when opera became a business enterprise. Venice was first in this development. In 1637 the Theatre of San Cassiano opened there as the first public opera house. The director here was Benedetto Ferrari, one of the universal talents of the day, singer, lute player, poet, composer. At first the company operated on a cooperative basis. Members of the company accepted a share of the profits as their compensation. This was soon succeeded by a system which is essentially the modern one. The impresario appeared and assumed the responsibility for organizing the performances. He hired the performers who were paid a stipulated salary.

The vogue for opera in Venice was amazing. Other theatres opened till it was usual for four different operas to be presented at the same time during the season. According to Galvani, a nineteenth century authority, admission to the theatre cost two lire. Families with any pretensions to wealth or culture hired boxes. Music lovers saw an opera repeatedly, and they must have gained an intimate familiarity with this music which would be hard to match at the present time.

We have said that the doors were opened to the public. It was, however, a very limited public that attended such performances. Only the well-to-do and the well-dressed were admitted. The door-keeper kept out those without tickets and those of whom he disapproved. Nobles might, however, pass him with impunity. Indeed in France the manager of a theatre was murdered in cold blood when he tried to keep out a nobleman who wished to enter without payment. In eighteenth century England servants were crowded into a special gallery at the opera. Thus the English music historian Burney says of Arne (the composer of "Rule Britannia") that "such was his passion for Music, that he used to avail himself of the privilege of a servant, by borrowing a livery and going into the upper gallery of the opera which was appropriated to domestics." In Venice, according to the same authority, the gondoliers were permitted to take possession of an opera-box when its noble owners were not present. Burney quite reasonably ascribes the superior singing of the Venetian men to this custom. Gradually the audience took on a more middle-class atmosphere. Although this enlargement of the circle of the audience has been continuous, we are likely to forget the many who are still barred from our concert halls not so much by a social code as by poverty and a lack of the leisure necessary to develop a taste for such music.

One effect of the gradual process which brought music to larger and larger groups of people was the development of music teaching as a profession. One may frankly recognize that there were and are moments when the piano lesson degenerates into a weary gesture on the part of parents in the direction of "culture." It is necessary to look deeper, to see that thousands of children are able to penetrate to some degree into the kingdom of music as a result of these lessons in perhaps the best way, by actually playing music for themselves. The devotion of the viola player to the amateur quartet, the eagerness of the high school boy to attend band or orchestra rehearsals, the solace and pleasure gained by the amateur pianist who makes music by and for himself, all these are indications of the extent to which the pleasures of music have been brought to the people by perhaps the least appreciated of all workers in music, the music teacher.

We have seen that a small and privileged class of musical amateurs in earlier days received their instruction from court musicians who were sometimes especially appointed for that purpose. Thus Louis XIV was taught the lute by Germain Pinel. When the king turned from the lute to the guitar, Pinel retained his post, but another master, possibly Francesco Corbetta, was chosen to teach him the guitar. We are told that Louis as a young man would retire even from the council chamber to amuse himself by singing and playing. The great François Couperin taught the princes and princesses of Louis's household the art of harpsichord playing. Perhaps it was largely because of these forgotten pupils that he wrote and published a method for this instrument which is still a precious source of information. Thus the opportunities for the privileged few were superb.

As the middle-class gained wealth and security we find musical amateurs appearing in that group and even among the workers. Such music-lovers were numerous in England during the seventeenth and eighteenth centuries, as we might expect, since the people of that country enjoyed at least a small degree of security and leisure. Immyns, the self-taught lutenist, was a poor attorney's clerk. Britton, the musical small-coal man, was a street vendor. The musical amateur who will be familiar to most readers is Samuel Pepys.

A tailor's son who gradually rose to a position of some

[187]

importance as Clerk of the Acts to the Admiralty, Pepys played on various instruments, he sang, he read theoretical treatises on music and even composed melodies. His wife took singing lessons though her ear was not good and almost succeeded in learning to trill. Finally, perhaps defeated but still undaunted, she learned to play the flageolet. Pepys took more pleasure in teaching music to Mercer, his wife's pretty maid, whom he found more musical: "And after supper falling to singing with Mercer did however sit up with her, she pleasing me with her singing of 'Helpe, Helpe,' till past midnight."

If we assume a good ear and keen interest in music, the ornamental nobleman of the period had every musical resource at his control. A less privileged mortal like Thomas Britton would fill his bags with small-coal (charcoal) and sell it on the streets of London. Only when his day's work was done, when the maids of London would buy no more coal, could he turn to music. Yet in his scanty intervals of leisure he mastered the harpsichord and learned how to tune it. He collected an important musical library and organized the series of concerts for which he is chiefly remembered. Yet such skill in music was possible for workmen or petty tradesmen only if they were possessed by a great determination.

By the nineteenth century music was added to the ornamental accomplishments which a young lady should possess. When the great heritage of music reached the middle classes, one must admit that it was frequently much watered down, no doubt in deference to the limited capacity of the average student and the superficial and sentimental tastes which prevailed at the time. But music had at least become part of a complete feminine education, one of the graces of life in a civilization rich enough to afford them. The "teaching piece" designed to enable the beginner to make music of a sort, to impress the parent, to gladden the family circle with polkas and schottisches made its appearance.

MUSIC AS A BUSINESS

The humble music teacher began to tread the streets of the city from one overstuffed Victorian parlor to another, and the sound of the Czerny "School for Velocity" was heard in the land. The importance of the movement should not be lost sight of as we contemplate its more humorous aspects.

All this activity had a very mixed character, partaking at the same time of business enterprise, sales promotion, educational idealism, and musical ingenuity. The piano in the parlor was a symbol of success, a sign of a social as well as a musical triumph. Every family with a piano in the parlor and children in the nursery aspired to music lessons. These lessons were sometimes regarded as doubtful blessings by the recipients. Their effects were not always happy nor long lasting. But one more closed door had been unlocked, the door of the music room. Henceforth it was to stand open. Not all children were to learn to play the piano, but a very large number of them were to have the opportunity of trying.

There is nothing strange in the fact that the musician tended to make his living in a way characteristic of his period. It is equally understandable that in a period of great commercial enterprise he should behave as a business man. At the time of Queen Elizabeth we find two famous English composers, Tallis and Byrd, the recipients of a very typical concession, a monopoly on the printing and sale of music and of music paper. As the musician emerged as a man who controlled his own destiny, the business motive becomes more prominent. The lack of a sound financial position is reflected with tragic irony in the letters of Mozart in which he insists on the need of a good business system and represents as temporary a financial crisis which was in truth permanent and progressive.

Strangely enough, the growth of the romantic spirit with its scorn of the practical and monetary aspects of life coincided with the increasing urgency of the business motive.

[189]

Liszt, who was the very embodiment of the romantic virtuoso, comments shrewdly on this aspect of a musician's life in a letter to his friend and patron, Carl Alexander of Weimar. "At all times," he observes, "people have treated artists as imaginative beings and have even exerted their wits to explain our conduct by the exclusive preponderance of this faculty." He concludes with irony, "Rossini was of the timber from which the best bankers are made," . . . . "and certainly there are no tax collectors or public accountants so minutely exact in their account books as so and so among my honored colleagues."

But if music has become a business, its rewards are distributed in a most curious fashion. One does not need to insist on the meagre returns of the music teacher who creates the great audience without which opera and concert could hardly exist. It is even less necessary to contrast the pay of the music teacher with the sums earned by the favorite songster of the hour. The singer's manager is only too ready to furnish us with these facts. Musical fame has ceased to be a simple matter of performing and then awaiting the verdict of the public. The public is coaxed, not to say coerced, into rendering the desired verdict by every device which an ingenious publicity agent can conjure up. An initial success is pyramided into a fantastic triumph with recording sessions, concert engagements, guest appearances on the air, and contracts from Hollywood crowding one another as a host of camp followers strive to profit in every conceivable way by the fame they have helped to create.

The same inequality is revealed if we compare the rewards of the musical comedy composer with that of the musician who creates string quartets or symphonies. A single "hit" will suffice to place a man who puts together a show in a very comfortable financial position indeed. A "serious" composer will find that his receipts will equal his expenses only in very exceptional instances. Attempts have been made to meet the difficulties of the symphonic composer in a variety of ways, all of which assume that our society should continue to hear modern symphonies even if it is clearly unwilling to pay for them through any of the usual commercial channels.

The dominance of the business motive has shifted the role of judge and critic from the individual patron to the many-voiced audience. At the court of Mantua, at the opera-house of Frederick the Great, it was not necessary for the composer to please the audience. It was the ruler who had to be pleased, and it was the ruler who paid the bills. Moreover, the principle of court etiquette would insure that whatever was approved of by the king would be admired, at least in public, by the members of the court. That strenuous efforts would be made to induce the king to approve or to withhold approval goes without saying. But no matter how many polite suggestions were whispered in the royal ears, the verdict which decided the fate of a work was uttered by one man. At the court of Louis XIV, Lully, whose astuteness in practical matters was well known, found it advisable to consult the king concerning the choice of a plot for an opera as well as the treatment of the subject. Portions of the music were presented to court circles as they were completed. Thus, by cleverly following such hints and suggestions as the Grand Monarch vouchsafed, Lully could be reasonably sure in advance that his work would be well received. Even his enemies, who were numerous, would not openly or directly oppose the royal verdict. Lully, moreover, possessed a monopoly granted him by the king. He had no competitors, and he saw to it that the regulations governing the musical resources of other dramatic companies were so drastic that they could not rival him in this respect.

If we turn to the Royal Academy of Music of London in the days of George I and of Handel, the pattern which reveals itself is more familiar. The gentlemen-subscribers paid substantial sums into the cash box of the organization. Handel and other composers were engaged to compose operas. There is no evidence to show that the governing board endeavored to influence Handel in his choice of subjects or in the treatment of a subject once it had been chosen. What we know of Handel's fierce independence of spirit is completely opposed to the supposition that he could have been so influenced. What he did have to reckon with were the tastes and the whims of his audience and the strife of aristocratic cabals. His enemies went so far as to hire street arabs to tear down posters announcing his works. The victories of Handel over his public and his defeats were so interwoven with court intrigues, party feeling, and personal rivalries that we can hardly regard them as verdicts on the music at all, but merely as reflections of the relative power of opposing court factions for whom an opera was an opportunity for a test of strength.

Two facts are of special importance in this connection. One is the fact that the mode of organizing the production of operas was essentially modern since it resembled a joint-stock company. The second important point is the diminution of royal power in determining the destiny of music. George I was a sturdy champion of Handel's music, but his support was insufficient to save Handel from failure and bankruptcy. Chesterfield's witty remark that "he did not wish to intrude on the King's privacy" at a thinly-attended performance was at the same time an indication that royal taste and public taste were no longer the same thing. Handel's final success was won by appealing to the tastes of a broader public. Nevertheless the role of the privileged classes in determining public taste was to be very great long after the time of the Georges.

As the audience became large, less exclusively aristocratic, it also tended to demand music of a simpler and less sophisticated type. The composer found it expedient to write music for the "crowd" which was more direct, more immediately appealing. Thus, Handel wrote such melodies as "Hail the Conquering Hero." Such a concession to public taste has always led to protests that the art of music is being vulgarized and destroyed by popular influences. No doubt some composers will continue to write music which can appeaʌ only to a limited and specialized circle. If, however, the composer and his audience evolve in the direction of democracy, the composer must find his highest mission in writing music which embodies the aspirations of his people, music which is popular in the best sense. Beethoven's most familiar works with their broad humanity give us perhaps the best hint of what such a musician might achieve. In any case, the periods in which great masses of the people come into contact with sophisticated music are temporary and transitional in character. Once the new audience has acquired the necessary experience it is on an equal footing with earlier and more privileged music-lovers.

Just as opera responded in a variety of ways to the requirements of business, so the concert assumed a more commercial aspect. Opera and ballet had always been display pieces which were normally presented before a numerous audience. The concert, however, began as domestic music performed for a courtly circle. Three steps were necessary before the musical recreation of a court was transformed into the modern concert. One was the transference of the place of performance from a salon or drawing-room to a place of public resort. The second was the establishment of a fixed price of admission symbolized by a ticket, in place of the optional and variable gift with which an artist appearing at court was rewarded. The third was an extension of the first tendency. Since the artist wished to increase his profits, he sought to enlarge his audience. He could do this in two ways, by playing in larger auditoriums, or by travelling from one musical center to another so as to be heard by various groups of music-lovers.

Yet it is strange to see the slow and hesitating progress towards an institution which we take for granted. Thus Mace, in his quaint volume entitled "Musick's Monument,"

(1676) gives a plan for a music-room. The performers were to be seated in the center, the listeners in partly-enclosed galleries above and around the central space. The economic factor did not trouble Mace at all, for he has only provided for twelve of these listening rooms. *"Those* 12 *Galleries,* though but little, will (I believe) hold 200 *Persons* very well, without *Crowding."* His design and his text make it clear that he was approaching the problem from the point of view of some wealthy music-lover ("It may become any *Noble, or Gentleman's* House"), though he also praises it as an ideal music-room for his University (Cambridge). Yet, in the separation between audience and performer, he has anticipated one of the characteristics of the modern concert hall. He is equally anxious to prevent aristocratic members of his audience from being incommoded by contact with music-lovers of lower birth, and he speaks with feeling of their trials in ordinary concert rooms, "Persons of Quality, being sometimes *Crowded up, Squeez'd,* and *Sweated* among people of an *Inferior Rank."*

Equally interesting were the musicales organized by Thomas Britton, the "musical small-coal man." Handel, Pepusch, and other musical celebrities mingled with titled ladies and gentlemen who climbed the narrow outside staircase to Britton's upstairs music-room. The initial impulse here was simply the making and sharing of music. Later a shilling was charged, but this was, at least in part, a payment for the "dish of tea" which was served to members of the audience.

Historians have less to tell us about the early concerts of Paris than we might wish. Mersenne mentions concerts which he must have frequented (c. 1630). We know that Sainte Colombe and his two gifted daughters made music on three viols. Were these concerts chiefly designed to attract pupils? Was there an admission charge? They were perhaps select gatherings where a musician endeavored to attract a following.

MUSIC AS A BUSINESS

A halfway stage between court music and the public concert was the subscription concert. This plan, which is still practiced, obliged the performer or his agent to seek out and obtain the names (and the money) of the music-lovers who would attend the concert. For the performer this method had the merit of guaranteeing the receipts in advance of the performance. He could also use the names of his most influential patrons to induce others to follow their example. A letter from Mozart to his father lists the dates and the locations of his concerts. It is a long list. Most of the concerts were at the houses of members of the Viennese nobility, thus insuring a restricted and aristocratic audience.

The circle of the audience was somewhat enlarged when a society rather than an individual performer was the sponsor of a series of concerts. Concerts of this kind mark the transition from the naive early enterprises to the modern concert. Such societies existed in Rome and in London where groups like the "Academy of Ancient Music" were active in Handel's period. Sometimes an impresario rather than a governing board organized such series. Thus J. C. Bach (the son of the great J. S. Bach) organized concerts in London. Better known was the later series organized by Salomon who provided a special attraction for his subscribers by importing Joseph Haydn to London under an agreement which resulted in the composition of the famous "London Symphonies."

It is strange to find in a musical enterprise the same form of organization which might promote the manufacture of woolen goods or brass kettles. Yet it was no longer possible (at least in England) simply to take the money from the people in the form of taxes and spend them on an entertainment which was largely destined for the pleasure of one individual. The times had changed and, instead of the king and his pleasures, we have the board of directors, the stock holders (the subscribers), the purchasers of the product (members of the audience), and the workmen (singers and

musicians). This is esentially the modern pattern. It has however been modified in a number of significant respects.

The concert which developed into a business enterprise
has ceased to function effectively in many instances as a
means of making money. We have traced the early steps
which ultimately led to this dilemma. The artist, once he
gains the freedom to make contracts, plays to larger and
larger audiences, first in any available room, then in specially constructed auditoriums. Then he multiplies his audience by travelling from one musical center to another: he
goes on tour. Now, with the advent of radio, he has reached
a point where he can reach a nation-wide audience from a
single broadcasting studio.

In the meantime the costs of giving a recital in a large
city have increased. If he has multiplied his audience, he
has also multiplied the cost of hiring a hall. It is notorious
that, in large centers, the paying audience equals the size of
the hall only in the case of a few extremely popular artists.
Artists who cannot attract a paying audience send out
passes which admit their bearers for a nominal price. Nevertheless the concert halls in our large cities are in continuous
demand by artists who either hope eventually to attract an
audience of profitable size or plan to use favorable newspaper reviews to attract pupils and to secure paid engagements elsewhere. If they fail to secure favorable reviews,
they are at least richer in experience.

As the controlling power passed into the hands of the
public through the possession of a mere slip of cardboard,
this power was not only divided but diffused. It was relatively simple to muster the friends of the Prince of Wales
to hiss Handel's operas. It is much more difficult to mobilize the great public of the present day. It is even difficult
to know in any precise fashion what the public wants. It
seems quite certain, for example, that many radio programs
exist not because the public enjoys them but because it
tolerates them.

Yet this diffuse and unorganized group potentially controls the destinies of our music. It does so by purchasing concert tickets or by failing to do so, by applauding once it has reached the concert hall or by failing to do so. The radio artist has a still more tenuous link with his public. Members of the radio audience may send in postcards and letters indicating approval or disapproval. This fan mail testifies to the interest or lack of interest which the public displays in regard to an artist or a program. It is reasonably certain that this response is unrepresentative. The various ratings and surveys on the basis of telephone calls, popularity polls, and the like are studiously tabulated and assiduously studied by sponsors, artists, and executive officers of broadcasting companies. The interest is, however, considerably more intense in regard to comedians than musicians.

Since the survival of an artist may depend on his ability to attract attention, we have developed increasingly elaborate publicity mechanisms. It should be apparent that the verdict of an audience can be swayed by such devices only if they are unable or unwilling to discriminate for themselves. Outstanding excellence will no doubt continue to make its way once it manages to reach the public. Artists who display excellence of a novel or unusual kind together with performers whose merit is not overwhelming may easily fail for lack of support.

The need for a sure success on the part of conductor and concert artist alike has had a constricting effect on the concert repertory. Music in the eighteenth century was not a commodity. It was a luxury, and musicians had to be continuously productive to satisfy the demand for novelty on the part of their aristocratic patrons. Music was produced for use, not for profit. The musician's reward was his salary, and composition was undertaken as part of his official duties. Exceptions may of course be noted. Haydn's Salomon Symphonies were very well paid for. His long series of early symphonies were, however, composed in connection with his duties as chapel-master to the Esterházy family. Mozart composed many of his Salzburg works in connection with his duties as concertmaster. Under the system of patronage it was not of enormous importance that each work have a resounding success. If a work pleased, both patron and musician were better satisfied. If it did not please, there was always another day and another symphony. Variety was of great importance since the audience in a provincial court remained substantially the same. It was therefore not possible for the conductor, the orchestra, or the soloists to repeat to the extent that is usual today.

The situation of the modern musician is very different. The successful soloist, instead of remaining in one circle, plays for an audience which may be scattered all over America, Europe, and perhaps other parts of the world. His contact with an individual audience is fleeting. He must capture their attention at the outset. To this end he must employ works which have proven their power over audiences, works of known effectiveness, "battle horses," with perhaps a few novelties in his last group to attract the attention of any sophisticates who may be present. The orchestra conductor also tends to be cautious rather than bold. To be sure, his audience has a greater stability. But some of his subscribers do not like modern music. Novelties require special attention at rehearsal though they do not always get it. Though the subscribers have heard Beethoven's "Fifth Symphony" a hundred times, they still prefer it to a modern work. And there are always the youngsters (and older listeners who have discovered music later in life) to whom the most familiar work is fresh and novel.

Thus, both soloist and conductor are likely to restrict their repertory to pieces of known effect, to limit the number of novelties, and even here to give the preference to new pieces by well-known modern composers rather than to compositions from promising but unknown talents. In both fields the business motive is at work. The virtuoso must attract and win over his audience at once. Without a following he loses his career and his livelihood. The concert conductor is motivated by similar conditions. The result is a narrowing of the repertory, a tendency to play only works that can pay their own way, a further narrowing of the already narrow channels for creative expression. Thus novelties by modern composers are not welcomed unless they offer special advantages. A world première of a work which has received sufficient advance publicity may indeed even provoke spirited competition between rival conductors. Such was the case in the first American performance of Shostakovich's "Seventh Symphony." In general, however, a new work rouses little interest. As a result of this lack of a real demand, symphonic works represent a financial liability to the composer rather than an asset, since the expense of preparing the score and the parts is frequently greater than the performing fee plus any royalties that the composer is likely to receive in the event that the work is printed.

Yet symphonic works, piano concertos, and operas are written and offered for performance year after year. There are compelling drives which motivate the composer in his profitless but not unprofitable activity. The prestige which follows the performance of a work by a major symphony orchestra has a certain practical value. There are always individuals to whom the opportunity for personal expression, the joy of having one's say, outweighs the desire for financial reward. Very potent is that peculiarly American optimism which always assumes that the usual fate is reserved for others but a special and exceptional destiny for oneself.

The main concern of this chapter is with the musician and with the people who are in immediate contact with him, the members of his audience, his pupils, his publicity agent and manager. A whole group of businesses and industries developed as the practice of music became more and more widespread. Three industries, sketched in briefest outline, must serve to indicate the characteristic line of development.

[199]

These are the manufacture of musical instruments, the music printing trades, and the production of reproducing instruments. The last have had a most important influence on the musician in the immediate past and in the present.

The manufacture of musical instruments has passed through three stages. In the first, instruments were so simple and the demands of musical performance so limited that every man might make his own instrument. The shepherd in the fields might make a simple pipe and play upon it. As musical performance became more complicated, certain craftsmen became makers of musical instruments. This was a long development which reached a culmination in the work of the great Italian violin makers. The name Stradivarius is familiar to thousands of people who have never seen one of his instruments. Musical instruments made by an artist craftsman were necessarily expensive and could be produced only in limited quantities even where the master worker was aided by assistants and apprentices. As long as music itself was restricted to a limited circle of professional musicians and wealthy amateurs, this was sufficient. With the development of music teaching and the coordinate increase in the number of students it was necessary to produce cheaper instruments, and to do this they had to be produced in larger quantities. The principles of mass production were applied to violin making. Standardized parts were turned out, each by a different workman, to be assembled by still another man. Production was centralized where materials were abundant or easily accessible and labor was cheap: Mirecourt in France, Markneukirchen in Germany, Czecho-Slovakia, Japan. In America violins and double-basses were made in which the back and belly were machine-made aluminum stampings.

The professional musician is likely to regard this whole development with contempt and distaste. For him a violin is a beautiful example of skilled craftsmanship. He demands that the instrument should respond to his every demand as a player. From his point of view he is quite right. What is often not so clearly recognized is that without the cheap mass-produced violin, thousands of children would be unable to learn to play at all since they could not afford a better instrument. The ten dollar fiddle is a symbol of musical democracy. It is also frequently a symbol of the exploitation of labor.

This progress towards a cheaper product and a more abundant output may also be traced in the music publishing trades. Here, too, it is fair to say that most modern commercial editions are neither so durable nor so beautifully printed as the work of the early printers. What is abundantly clear is the fact that there has been an enormous increase in the size of printed editions and a marked, though by no means uniform, reduction in the price per unit. Unfortunately we know little about the sale price or the size of the editions of the earliest printed music.

Burney gives an interesting account of the Italian violinist Matteis which clearly reveals the limited circulation of certain imprints of the seventeenth century. "After this, he discovered a way of acquiring money, which was then perfectly new in this country. For observing how much his scholars admired the lessons he composed for them, which were all duos, and that most musical gentlemen who heard them, wished to have copies of them, he was at the expense of having them neatly engraved on copper-plates, in oblong octavo, which was the beginning of Engraving Music in England, and these he presented, well bound, to lovers of the art and admirers of his talents, for which he often received three, four, and five guineas."

The lists and title-pages of eighteenth century publishers sometimes indicate the prices charged for music. Thus an overture by Vanhal, published by Preston & Son, London, sold for two shillings sixpence. The same firm listed "Six Sonatas for the Harpsichord with Accompanyments" by

C. F. Abel (Op. 2) at ten shillings sixpence, "Six Solos for a German Flute with a Base" (Op. 6) at six shillings.

This elusive type of information is, however, abundantly available for our own song writer, Stephen Foster, whose successful activity spanned the years 1849-1860. A letter from Firth and Pond, who published many of his songs, shows that many of their pieces sold no more than a thousand copies and that a sale of three thousand copies was regarded as an excellent record. Yet in less than a year Foster's "Old Folks at Home" had already sold forty thousand copies. Two and sometimes three presses were kept busy without entirely meeting the demand. This, however, was a unique example of music circulation for the period. The usual price for the Foster songs appears to have been a quarter though a few were higher in price. This shows clearly the cheapening effect of mass production.

Foster's figure, however, has been far outstripped by certain later composers of popular songs (at least if we limit our figure to copies sold during Foster's own lifetime). The sale of "Yip I Addy I Ay" by John Flynn (which may be remembered by some readers) is said to have exceeded five hundred thousand copies. The "Prisoner's Song" of more recent memory attained a circulation of three million. (This figure, however, is a grand total which includes the sales of records as well as sheet music.) "The End of a Perfect Day" by Carrie Jacobs Bond exceeded this figure with a sale of over five million copies.

The introduction of the phonograph and the radio has had a tremendous influence on the diffusion of music. They were not only machines which could themselves be mass-produced but also potent agents for the distribution of music on a scale which would have been unimaginable at an earlier period.

The operation of machines for reproducing and transmitting music was described briefly in the last chapter. They have not only produced changes in our listening habits but have also basically altered the whole structure of the enterprises which supply us with music. This has involved a shift in domestic music from amateur performance to passive listening, and therefore from the purchase of sheet music and of instruments to the purchase of radios, phonographs, records. It has replaced the local theatre orchestra, the movie organist, the singing waiter, the saloon pianist, with the sound film and the juke box. It has correspondingly diminished the role of the music publisher.

A new business pattern has emerged in our own country and certain European nations. This change (heralded perhaps by the cries of street merchants and by musical performances which facilitated the sale of snake oil and other remedies at fairs and other gatherings) was brought about by the rise of the sponsored broadcast and the extensive use of music of all possible kinds as an aid in selling products.

The new pattern involves a free distribution of music to listeners in the hope that they would also listen to sales propaganda which is artfully woven into the program. In order to broadcast such a program a whole series of complicated arrangements are necessary: the hiring of the facilities of the broadcasting station or chain, the choice of the type of music to be broadcast, the selection of announcer and musicians. The exact character and content of the commercials are subject to elaborate calculations. The producer's recommendation of the product may even assume musical form as a "singing commercial."

This is a growth without precedent on its present scale, a growth for which only the merest hints can be found in the earlier development of music. It is money from the advertising budget of the manufacturer which provides us with most of our music today, which aids in balancing the budget of our symphony orchestras, of the Metropolitan Opera Association. The business man, in short, is the patron of the present-day musician. Instead of reserving music for his own use as did the aristocrat of the eighteenth century he distributes it to the public and hopes as a result to profit financially by an increased sale of his product. Music for him is a means, not an end in itself.

This is, in its most typical form, an American pattern built on the fact that we regard radio broadcasting as a field for private enterprise rather than a government monopoly. The pattern established by the B.B.C. in England may be placed in opposition to our system. Radio broadcasting in England is performed by a corporation which is an agency of the government. It is financed by a licensing fee which must be paid by each owner of a radio set. Instead of the weird patchwork of subject matter and taste levels presented by our own programs, three radio channels now operate simultaneously to satisfy listeners with serious intellectual interests as well as those who seek entertainment or distraction. A recent newspaper report will indicate the level of the "Third Program" focused on a sector of the public "that is not of one class, but that is perceptive and intelligent." Music occupies roughly a third of the allotted time. The intention is "to give the finest available performances of music of every style and epoch, with special emphasis on works of interest and beauty which are rarely heard in the concert hall or, hitherto, on the radio. Works already performed include Benjamin Britten's 'The Rape of Lucretia,' William Walton's 'First Symphony,' Purcell's 'Come Ye Sons of Art Away,' and Bach's 'Phoebus and Pan.' "

Our interest is, however, not only in the forms of business enterprise but in their effect on music and those who listen to it. Our system of radio broadcasting places the listener still farther from the performer, makes his control over the music which he hears still more tenuous, increases the probability that he will accept what he hears. We may distinguish three degrees of control in the performer-listener relationship. The listener may be the patron who chooses and compensates the musician and therefore may personally select or reject the music which he hears. The second stage is reached in the public concert hall. Here the performer depends, not on one nor on a few patrons, but on a large gathering of individuals each of whom contributes only a small fraction of his income. Not only is this relationship less personal, more indirect, but the verdict of the audience is reduced in the last analysis to a figure, the amount of money received at the box office. The artist has the same need to please his audience as before, but the individuals who compose it vary enormously in their tastes.

The link of the radio performer with his audience is still more tenuous. Fan mail, popularity surveys, the response of a studio audience give doubtful indications of a reaction which is infinitely complicated as a single performance may be shared by a multitude of listeners who vary in every conceivable way. The success of the program both from the point of view of sponsor and artist depends on audience response, but it is very difficult to estimate how the audience really does respond. It is even more difficult for the individual members of such an audience to express an opinion, to commend, or to protest save as one insignificant figure in a popularity poll or one postcard in a pile.

Moreover, as the participation of the audience in the making of music becomes slighter, the amount of active interest in the performance may decrease, the tendency to accept whatever is offered may become greater. An individual patron obviously must have desired music sufficiently to make the arrangements which were necessary in order to hear it. His approval or disapproval decided the fate of future musicales. The radio listener who does not leave his armchair, who does nothing to obtain his music, does not need to ponder deeply or select carefully. It is, moreover, manifestly unfair to blame the advertiser for securing his results as cheaply and as effectively as possible. On the other hand, where a large concentration of music-lovers exists in a given area, their potential purchasing power is likely to be considered in planning broadcasts at a level which will appeal to their special tastes. The success of such stations as WQXR and WNYC in the New York area, which depend so largely on the broadcasting of recorded symphonic music of high quality, shows that this may be so.

A huge new audience has been created for and by "canned music." Many words have been written on the effect of music on this new audience. Has reproduced music tended to stimulate or discourage individual amateur performance? Has it raised or lowered the general level of public taste? In the absence of a complete and objective study one can only answer that it has done all of these things and their opposites. Figures have less than their usual significance because we are not only dealing with a new audience but with one which is constantly expanding. There has been a tendency for "entertainment industries" to affiliate with a resulting diminution of free competition. Thus the name "Columbia" applies to a complex group of enterprises including a concert bureau, a broadcasting network, and the manufacture of phonograph records. The names of the few dominant producers in the movie field have become household words.

The musician, however, as a result of the increasing concentration of the production of music in a few focal centers, has suffered more and more keenly from technological unemployment. The early movie houses hired a pianist, an organist, or, if they had any pretensions at all, an orchestra. Thus, in the heyday of the silent films, there were hundreds of small theatre orchestras all over the United States. Now a single orchestra in a Hollywood studio records a score for a sound-film which will be shown at every cross-roads in the United States.

The radio has similarly made a single performance available over the entire country or the world. The virtuoso formerly travelled to play for audiences in different musical centers. Now he reaches an audience many times greater from a single room, a broadcasting studio. If he tours, and many artists still do this, he has a new motive, to allow the audience which has already heard his performances to see what he looks like. This is the era of the "personal appearance." Artists of an earlier era could only appear in person. There was no other way of performing for an audience. The advent of television on a commercial and national scale may remove this motive as well.

Fewer artists are required for performances. Standards of performance have risen not only because of the accumulation of technical knowledge but also because of intense and bitter competition. To some extent this decrease in the opportunities for public performance has been compensated for by an increased demand for music teachers, but the blow has, nevertheless, been a heavy one.

Such are the general characteristics of the music business and the interrelations of the business world with the musician and his music. It has been usual to ignore these factors or to assume that the development of music could be explained without reference to them. Music, however, is not only an ideal art. It is also a commodity which is bought and sold as are other commodities. A musician is not only an artist, he is also a business man who buys and sells.

CHAPTER X

THE MUSICAL LANGUAGE

THE earlier part of this book has dealt with the relations
of music to life, the part it plays in the experience of the
individual and in society. In this, the second part, the materials of the musician are to be discussed. The musician, like
any other worker, had to consider his resources in order to
make an effective and intelligent use of them. These resources were chiefly a knowledge of the capabilities of sounds
as earlier and contemporary musicians had learned to use
them and an understanding of the tools of the musician, the
musical instruments which translate the ideas of the composer
into actual sound. The characteristics of sound when organized as music are usually stated as rhythm, melody, harmony,
and form.

Rhythm includes all the characteristics of musical motion.
This expression may perhaps seem less clear than it should
since it is apparent that musical tones do not actually move
in the usual sense of the word. It is a comparison, an analogy,
rather than an exact statement. What does happen in music
is that various sounds follow one another in time. These tones
are short or long, and it is the "shortness" and "longness" of
successive tones, the patterns into which they are organized,
and the metric system which underlies them, which we consider under rhythm.

Meter plays an important part in Western music though it
is not a necessary ingredient in all music. Music, like poetry,
may move quite freely, or it may move in a manner which is
guided more or less by a regular pattern of stressed and unstressed tones. In Western music we have found that groups
of musicians can be synchronized by adopting a regular beat
or count and by grouping these counts in twos, threes, or fours

[209]

(less frequently in more complicated patterns). The listener expects that such a pattern, once established, will continue. Such a system of stressed time-units followed by unstressed units is especially characteristic of dance music and furnishes the 1-2-3, 1-2-3 of the waltz, the 1-2-3-4, 1-2-3-4 of the march.

If rhythm has to do with duration patterns, with stressed and unstressed tones, and with metric schemes, melody, though it inevitably involves the rhythmic factor, adds another element, that of pitch, of "highness" and "lowness." A melody consists of a series of related tones which follow one another in time. We think of a melody as moving up or down, but that also is merely a conventional expression. Nevertheless, the association of tones produced by rapid vibration frequencies with "highness" and those with slow vibration rates with "lowness" is so firmly established that one can only accept it as a convenient analogy.

A melody consists not of any tones but of a selected series which have evolved certain relationships through custom and use. In recent Western melodies, these tones are so related that the progress of a melody produces points of psychic tension and repose. The impression of repose or of activity is associated with definite tones in our major and minor scales. In certain other systems (the ancient pentatonic or five-tone scale, the modern twelve-tone system) the role of closing tone or point of repose may apparently be assumed by any tone of the scale. We learn that certain tones are followed by others by repeatedly experiencing melodies in which these tone sequences occur. A listener who, after hearing two or more tones, anticipates the next, is demonstrating the fact that he understands scale relationships.

A pitch pattern may be associated with a duration pattern, or a recurring pitch pattern may exist independently of a characteristic rhythm. A melody gains its effect through a movement of tones which increase and decrease psychic tension. This is partly because many tunes actually rise to a highest tone which forms a point of climax from which the melody then descends, partly because we have learned to associate certain tones of the scale with psychic tensions which are released when they are followed by tones associated with repose. A melody obtains unity by introducing and repeating a characteristic melodic pattern. A really complete statement of the reactions of a sensitive listener to even a brief melody would be of unimaginable complexity.

Harmony is really only another aspect of melody. There are indeed two ways of presenting tones. In melody the sounds follow each other. In harmony selected sounds are produced simultaneously, or, if produced successively, are nevertheless recognized as the constituents of a tone-group. Such a group is followed by other groups. Here too the composer utilizes the fact that certain groups or harmonies leave the hearer in an expectant, anticipatory frame of mind. Others produce relaxation, a feeling of repose. It would be too great a simplification to say that there are only two basic harmonies in recent Western music, but such a simplification would possess an element of truth.

The composer may combine the points of repose in his scale to form a harmony of repose, the active tones to form a restless group which nevertheless strives to move towards rest and finality. One may say that the passions, the strivings of Tristan, of Pagliacci, of Faust are summed up in an active sound group, restless, but seeking repose. Like human life, music passes from repose to activity, then to repose once more.

When a composer writes music which is longer than a simple melody, he faces the same problems on a large scale which confront him in miniature in composing a melody. In a melody he must secure unity by the repetition of characteristic tone and duration groups. He must attain a satisfactory balance between the different parts of his melody. He must attain a point of climax towards which the melody climbs and from which it recedes.

In a larger composition these problems of variety and unity, of balance and climax are problems of form. Instead of gaining unity through the repeated appearance of a group of a few notes, the composer plans recurrences of themes, often of some length. He attains his climaxes after a prolonged preparation. A song composer balances a short musical phrase against another. A symphonic composer achieves a balance of long and complicated musical developments.

The music-lover must have quite a different attitude towards the materials of music than the student of music or the professional musician. His business is to be emotionally stirred by music. If he is able to follow the manner in which the composer presents and develops his themes, he will listen with greater clarity. But relatively few do possess such an understanding of music though many are stirred by it. It might be useful to outline three levels of listening.

In the first, the auditor does not focus his attention sharply on the music, nor is he deeply stirred. The music remains a vague though agreeable background. At a somewhat more advanced level, the auditor does listen attentively though with rather frequent lapses of interest. He is pleasurably moved by the music. Perhaps he remembers the opening of one of the themes and finds himself humming it some hours later. The music, however, is not sharply perceived. Recurrences of themes are sometimes vaguely recognized, sometimes not noticed at all. Finally, there is the listener who is capable of complete absorption and self-identification in the music. The recurrences of themes are so sharply noted that the auditor could, if necessary, list the order in which they appear. In addition to this he is able to see that the composer has introduced passages which, while not restatements of the theme, have definite and intentional resemblances to it.

Such listeners are rare, and they must possess both a superior musical endowment and a rich experience in listening to music. Their approach to music, while not necessarily less emotional, is more intellectual. They are able to think music as well as feel it.

Composers are well aware of these gradations in the capacities of the individuals who form their audiences and for each level they have written suitable music. For the first group there is "parlor music," "dinner music," or "movie music." These repeat formulas so familiar that intellectual effort is hardly necessary. Every melodic contour, every harmonic sequence is so chosen as not to arouse the least audience resistance. This may happen when the composer's musical endowment and background is such that he naturally expresses himself in these terms. A composer of popular songs or show-music is likely to possess this particular kind of talent. Music in a popular vein may also be composed as the result of deliberate calculation as in the popular songs of Kurt Weill or Shostakovich, so different from their other music. Irving Berlin is perhaps the most striking example of a composer whose enormous popularity is due not so much to any quality of originality as to the fact that he was able to write songs which had a direct and immediate appeal. This is said in no carping spirit. It has been stated that Berlin's formal musical education was (and still is) of the slightest and that he completely lacks the equipment of the trained composer. Nevertheless it is in its way as difficult, perhaps more difficult, to attain complete success in a simple and limited medium than in a complex and varied expression like the symphony. Such a success is the more remarkable since any song hit is immediately followed by a crowd of imitations which endeavor to approach plagiarism as closely as possible without actually committing it. Yet what they chiefly do is to establish an unfavorable comparison between themselves and their model.

The second stage of development is the one in which most music-lovers find themselves. They like music. They are moved by it. Their response is very largely sensory and emotional. They do not distinguish sharply between styles. They may hear very well indeed, but they are not conscious in any definite fashion of what they hear. They are likely to recoil in an instinctive manner from any music which differs from the types which they have already experienced. Their musical fare consist of the light classics and the familiar pieces of the standard concert repertoire. They do not hear many of the relationships which give interest and unity to music partly because it has never occurred to them to listen for them, partly because they are likely to lack the capabilities which make it easier to recognize them. These are a musical memory so accurate that comparisons between what has been heard and what is heard become relatively easy and a knowledge of music notation which will permit the study of a musical score and the comparison of related passages. It is the possession of precisely these two factors which distinguish the relatively few listeners who are really able to grasp the relationships not only of the standard works of the concert repertory but also new works and unfamiliar works of earlier periods. But an adequate grasp of music notation is still largely limited to the privileged or the especially eager and gifted amateur.

Repeated hearings of a work will often clarify passages which at first seemed obscure or puzzling, but this is possible only in cases where repeated performances occur, where a composition has become part of the standard repertory, or where it has been recorded. In extreme cases it might be claimed that only the composer (and perhaps a few members of his circle) are really able to follow and completely understand certain compositions which are of a peculiarly complicated and intellectual type.

Thus, especially in a country where it has been recognized that music is one of the subjects which every child should experience, the problem of how essential intellectual understanding is to an enjoyment of music assumes great importance. It poses fundamental questions to which no simple answer can be given because composers differ basically in their attitudes and their objectives. The central issue can be stated very simply. To what extent does intellectual clarity add to musical enjoyment? To what extent can the relationships in music produce their effects without a conscious recognition on the part of the listener that they do exist?

It is clear that we cannot increase the musical endowment of a member of the audience. What could be done, as a matter of possibility, is to repeat musical experiences for the members of our future audiences, to educate them to a point where they would possess a satisfactory control of music notation. This in turn would be conditioned by the amount of leisure and of economic security which the great new audience for music can secure. We have brought music to everyone who possesses a radio. Yet this advance can be fruitful only if this new audience can acquire sufficient discrimination to select musical programs with taste and intelligence. This, however, does not in any way imply a distinction between a cultured few and a great mass who are incapable of responding to fine music. At present we do not know how large the audience for such music may be. Any thoughtful observer knows that the relationship in the United States between native ability and exceptional educational opportunities is haphazard and accidental. This is doubly true of the education of the music-lover which must of course remain secondary to those basic needs on which survival depends. The great new audience for music should be limited, however, not by present boundaries but by the extent to which these boundaries can be extended and enlarged.

The question of the balance of the intellectual versus the sensory and emotional elements in music can also be met in another way. The composer may adjust his style to correspond with the level of his audience. He even may be so fortunate as to possess the suppleness and the kind of endowment which enable him to please himself and his audiences at the same time. Such an adjustment of the style of the composer to the audience is most necessary at periods when there is a sudden expansion in the size of the audience.

The simplification which reduced the many competing voices of a Wilbye madrigal or a Bach fugue to the accompanied melody of later composers was surely not due exclusively to a single factor. One cause of the change, however, was the simple fact that secular music had become something to which one listened rather than something in which one took part. It was clear that it was easier, and from certain points of view more satisfactory, to listen to accompanied melody than to music in which the progress of several different melodies had to be followed.

It was during this period of transition that the modern concert appeared, and its very appearance was an indication that more people had the leisure and the inclination to listen to music. Music's emergence from the salon to the public hall is both a symptom and a result of a great expansion of the listening audience. It is then also reasonable to ascribe the simplification of music to the need for pleasing a new audience.

The romantic period died with Wagner and Brahms, with Bruckner and Mahler and Strauss, leaving only such belated figures as Sibelius and Rachmaninoff behind. Many of the musicians of the early twentieth century who followed were experimentalists writing for restricted circles of like-minded musicians and their friends. During this period, however, a second great expansion of the audience took place, due partly to the development of more symphony orchestras (notably in the United States), partly to the efforts of music educators, but chiefly to the advent of the phonograph and the radio. It is generally admitted that the radical experimentation of the 1920's has given place to a style which is simpler, more directly melodious, more popular. A comparison of Copland's "First Symphony" with his "Appalachian Spring," of Harris's "Symphony 1933" with his "Folksong Symphony," of Antheil's "Second" or "Airplane Sonata" with his recent "Symphony No. 4" will make the change evident. This change might of course be explained as merely one of those shifts in taste which occur when an audience is sated with music of a given kind and is ready to welcome a new music. It seems reasonable to assume that this particular change is also, at least in part, an adjustment to the demands of a new audience which responds more readily to music which is simpler, more directly melodious, more folk-like, without entirely discarding the dissonant discoveries of the "bad boys" of the 1920's.

The Soviet Union is another striking example of a country where an enormous and sudden expansion in the size of the audience has taken place. Here, too, a simplification of style is obvious in the recent works of the Soviet composers who are best known in this country. The "Seventh Symphony" of Shostakovich with its short simple motives is typical of his later manner and quite at variance with the satire and dissonance of many of his early works. Prokofieff's later piano sonatas, in spite of the technical difficulties which confront the executant, utilize themes which are clear, sharply defined, and melodious. This change is due in part to the fact that the Soviet government has given official encouragement to a simpler and more folk-like idiom. In all probability it was also due to an adjustment to audience response.

In the case of popular music no such adjustment was necessary, since a composer, if he wished to be popular at all, necessarily calculated his effects for the largest possible audience. Irving Berlin put the matter in its simplest terms when he said that "music must appeal to the mob," continuing "the mob is always right." What the future will bring in symphonic as well as popular music must be left for the future to decide. It is clear that the adjustment between the manner of the composer and the tastes of his audience can be made either by improving the musical understanding of the members of the audience and enriching their experience or by an adjustment on the part of the composer. In actual practice the adjustment is usually made from both sides. Not only have the opportunities for musical experience been multiplied but, except in the rarest cases, composers (whether they admit it or not) have always been infinitely sensitive to audience response.

One more point should be made by way of introduction to the second part of this book. Musical understanding depends on one of two approaches, the intuitive and the analytic. Many of the elements of music are understood, not by an intellectual analysis, but by an intuitive experience. Thus the effects of harmony, the balance of forms, can be analyzed only by a student with a sufficient control of musical notation to read a score, with the power to auralize the effects of music from its notation, and the theoretical knowledge and understanding which make it possible to associate a given effect with its cause. These effects may be felt in terms of their emotional product by a sensitive listener who has a sufficient experience in a given idiom to know which procedures are normal, which are exceptional, who is conscious of the emotional responses and the psychic tensions and relaxations which the music is calculated to produce.

Yet there are limitations which even a sensitive listener may find it hard to exceed. He may be conscious of the tone color of the various instruments, yet the usual check by an inspection of the orchestral score is denied him. Thus his continued progress in this direction depends either on learning to read music, or on the friendly aid of a musical friend or teacher. An aspect of music which can hardly be understood without a conscious intellectual effort is the formal design which a composer has constructed by the repetitions and the recurrences of his themes. Most listeners remain blithely unconscious of this factor to an extent that raises the question as to whether musical design should be consciously apprehended or whether, like the various joints of the cabinetmaker, its results should be enjoyed without understanding the factors which produce them. In the case of a symphony, the very repetition of a standard work will impress the themes which the composer has employed on the listener, at least to the degree which will make it possible to recognize them when they recur. Nevertheless this aspect of music, which usually remains vague and uncharted, becomes relatively sharp and clear when the traditional formal patterns of music are once recognized.

Novelties which are played only infrequently, or perhaps only once, must present special difficulties. The intuitive listener cannot gain familiarity with the work through repeated hearings. The student cannot consult a score which exists only in manuscript. Both are at a disadvantage, as is the composer who is seeking an audience for his works.

It would appear from the foregoing analysis that the great majority of the auditors in our concert halls are confronted with difficulties. That is indeed the case. Listening to music of any complexity is a task which demands more than the average listener possesses in terms of endowment and experience. Yet the great and vital role of music in human experience continues in spite of such limitations. It is useless to proclaim, as so many musical optimists have done, that great music is for everyone. It is so to the same degree that Shakespeare is available to everyone,—indeed to a lesser degree since many of our citizens could read the plays of Shakespeare if they were so inclined. But how many can really comprehend a Beethoven symphony, to say nothing of reading it from a score?

One may raise the question as to whether symphonic music is not too complex, too demanding from an intellectual point of view for its audience. In the long run a more or less stable equilibrium will no doubt be established by simplification on the part of the composer or by a rise in the cultural level of the audience. But in the future music must no longer belong to a privileged class but a whole people.

A book is no substitute for actual musical experience. At best it can only outline the factors which constitute music. It can call the attention of the listener to elements in musical effect and in this way may direct and guide the reader's attention to aspects which might otherwise pass unnoticed. In the final analysis, however, musical understanding, where it is to be developed at all, must be based on musical experience. All else remains secondary in importance.

Chapter XI

THE LANGUAGE OF INSTRUMENTS

A COMPOSER in the early days of instrumental music was concerned chiefly with the selection of instruments which were capable of playing the notes of a given melody or part. Even some of the scores of Bach suggest that the master might well have hesitated after copying a part as to the best designation. Should it be "flute," or perhaps "oboe," or simply "violin"? This was not true of the instrumental accompaniment of his vocal works. In Bach's cantatas he is infinitely susceptible to subtle tonal distinctions. The sentiment of a text immediately stimulates him to search for precisely the right instrument to suggest the distant chime of bells, the apocalyptic splendors of celestial triumphs, the sombre terrors of remorse. This was a search pursued by many early composers who tried to match the mood of a text with a quality of sound which suited it perfectly. In part the composer was moved by simple association. Royal music or music in a mood of splendor demanded the blare of trumpets, instruments which had, indeed, been reserved exclusively for the service of the nobility at an early period. Thus, trumpets introduce the "Festival March" from *"Tannhäuser"* while the heroic theme which opens Richard Strauss's *"Don Juan"* also owes much to the regal splendor of the trumpets.

To composers of the eighteenth century music with an Eastern character demanded the shrill piccolo, the crash of the cymbals, the thunder of the bass drum. These instruments are employed in the choruses of janissaries from Mozart's "Abduction from the Seraglio," in Beethoven's "Turkish March" from the "Ruins of Athens." The flutes and the reed pipes which shepherds have played from time immemorial while watching their flocks still have the power to arouse faint echoes of rural solitudes where distant music sounds across some quiet valley. It is from this store of associations that Gluck has drawn the inspiration for the marvellous solo for flute during the scene in the Elysian Fields from his opera, "Orpheus." Two pastoral recorders pipe interludes to Bach's shepherd aria, "Sheep may safely pasture." The song of the woodwind instruments rises above the quiet undulations of the strings in the movement, "At the Brook" from Beethoven's "Pastoral Symphony." Oboe and English horn respond one to the other in Berlioz' "Scene in the Fields" from the *"Symphonie Fantastique."*

The sound of the oboe, however, may convey associations which are altogether different, the snarl of a snake charmer's pipe or the skirl of Scotch bagpipes. The melodies and rhythms employed by the composer serve to complete the impression and make it more definite. The trombones in the scores of the great masters, on the other hand, have an inherent solemnity of tone. They chant with the voices of archangels the great chorale in the finale of the Brahms' "Fourth Symphony." This is a heritage from a past in which the trombones supported the voices of the choir in great cathedrals or played chorales from the towers of German churches.

One must not assume, however, that a composer merely reached into his orchestral color-box to select instruments with the proper historical associations. Many uses of orchestral instruments were happy discoveries by performers and composers based on the special qualities of the instrument, its technical possibilities, or out of a new perception of the psychological effects of certain tone-colors. Thus the facile brilliance of the flute suggested the sparkling of water, the glitter of jewels. The unexpected agility of the bassoon has a musical incongruity comparable to the visual humor of an agile caper performed by a very portly person. It is this quality which gives lively staccato passages on the bassoon their amusing effect. The plaintive effect of a legato solo in the upper register of this instrument was, however, based solely on the appropriateness of this tone quality to a given mood.

Thus, performers have discovered effects, possibilities, technical tricks, each on his own instrument. These, in turn, have been rediscovered by composers who through their imaginative and inventive power have seen how they might be utilized. In arranging orchestral music a composer thus has many considerations to weigh. There are practical matters: whether the range of the music is suited to the instrument; whether the part is so written that it can be played without undue difficulty and with good effect. There are considerations of suitable tone-color and mood.

Not only are the capabilities of the instrument important but also the style of the music. The shrill and incisive clarinet passages in Stravinsky's *"Oedipus Rex"* speak in an idiom very remote from the gentle clarinets of Mendelssohn's "Fingal's Cave Overture" (second theme). The stately trumpets of the classic orchestra are far indeed from the trumpet which screams with rage and despair in Stravinsky's *"Petrouchka."* The difference is not solely a difference in technical skill. It is also a difference in the musical language which in itself stimulates a novel treatment of the instruments.

Before proceeding to a more detailed view of the instruments of the modern symphony orchestra it may be well to point out certain difficulties which the amateur must face. Most music-lovers have a marked curiosity concerning the instruments of the archestra. The problem is to be sure that the instrument and the sound are clearly associated. At a symphony concert one can see a player pick up his instrument at the beginning of a solo and put it down at the end. Symphonic music over the radio does not offer this help. One is presented with the sound and with the sound alone. The only final solution for the student is a sufficient knowledge of musical notation to follow an orchestral score. The musical notation will then show exactly which instruments are active, when they enter, and when they cease playing. This is a high requirement. Music-lovers who do not understand notation would do well to study the following chapter, to listen to recorded solos on the various instruments, then orchestral solos and concerted works. A moderate period of study will enable a student with a ready ear to recognize the various instruments in solo passages. Less gifted listeners will require a longer period of initiation.

Man is a singing animal. Yet he has not been satisfied to make music with his vocal chords alone. From the most remote periods he has sought to adorn or replace vocal melody with the sound of musical instruments. One may say with some truth that there have always been two basic types of composers: those who are moved to music by words and images (the Wagner type) and those whose music never reaches such heights as when their melodies are sung by instruments (the Beethoven type). It is instrumental song that is the ideal language, the purest joy of the music-lover.

Yet the ways of music-making have remained simple. Up to the age of electricity man had learned to produce sounds in a rather limited number of ways. Most primitive of all were the resonant substances which produced sounds when struck, instruments of percussion. Then there were the instruments sounded by the breath of man or by an artificial wind source. At first these were mere megaphones which amplified and distorted the human voice till it lost its human quality and became an ancestral voice. Man learned to blow through pursed lips in such a way that they vibrated and thus could set the air enclosed in a conch shell or elephant tusk into vibration. In this fashion he prepared for the advent of the trumpets, the horns, the trombones, and the tuba of the modern orchestra.

A hole in a bone or a hollow reed produced a piercing

[224]

whistle when blown across. A series of holes in a tube stopped by the fingers or left open produced tones, lower or higher as the sounding tube is thus shortened or lengthened. Thus the herdsman's flute appeared. A short straw pinched between the fingers and slit into two opposite tongues can be made to squeak in an indeterminate fashion. Once inserted in a tube the squeak assumes the natural pitch of the tube and becomes a definite tone, an oboe tone. The transition from primitive squeaker to singing double reed may be observed before the concert by any member of an audience as the oboe players try their reeds before fitting them to their instruments.

In a similar fashion a single vibrating tongue cut from a cane is the prototype for the modern clarinet or saxophone reed. The modern reed is thinned to a feather edge at one end and is clamped at the other by a metal ligature against the opening in the mouthpiece.

Yet modern wind instruments, for all of their bewildering mechanisms of levers, pivots, and pads, have never strayed far from the shepherd's pipe, the whistle, and the trumpet of elephant ivory. We demand more notes of our instruments and have devised elaborate mechanisms to obtain them. The manner of producing sound from them, however, has not changed save in details.

The gap between the early stringed instruments (which employed a flexible vine for the string and a bark-covered hole in the ground for a resonating chamber) and the violins and guitars of more recent times is enormous. The creation of a supple and uniform string of gut was in itself a complicated achievement. Once made, it could be pulled or plucked by the fingers or struck with a stick or hammer. Later the more complicated method of sounding the string with a bow appeared, an invention of which the complete history will, perhaps, never be written. The musical bow, by means of a rosined ribbon of horse hair fastened to the flexible stick, alternately pulls and releases the string, and so sets it into vibration. Gradually the viols and violins emerged as the dominant bowed instruments in Western Europe. Stringed instruments sounded by a blow with a hammer lack the sustained song of the bowed instruments. It is a method of tone production which has only been conspicuously successful in the case of the piano where the hammers are operated indirectly by a keyboard. Such are the ways of producing sound which man has devised.

The grouping of instruments into families, their standardization, the partial solution to questions of proportion and balance, required a long historic evolution. An initial stage was completed by the end of the sixteenth century. The period of Bach witnessed the formation of the stringed orchestra, though the employment of wind instruments was varied and dependent on the available talent. By the classic period the orchestra had evolved as an exquisite and perfect instrument. The modern symphony orchestra hardly existed before Wagner had exerted his overwhelming power to create a vehicle for his own ideas.

The instruments of the modern symphony orchestra are arranged on the concert stage, as in the conductor's score, as instrumental groups or choirs. This is a practice which dates back to a time when choirs of voices and instruments sang alternately or joined in powerful harmony in the churches of Venice. In the modern orchestra the participating groups are the strings, the woodwinds, the brasses, and the instruments of percussion. The latter hardly form a truly self-sufficient unit but rather underscore the rhythms played by the other instruments. Only in certain modern compositions where great stress is laid on rhythm does the percussion section really function independently.

The conventional names for the various choirs are admittedly not entirely adequate. The brass group derives its name from the material of which the instruments are made. The percussion section is named from the manner of sounding these instruments. The woodwind instruments, which were at one time made of wood, are no longer exclusively made of that material with the advent of silver flutes and brass saxophones. Nevertheless, these terms are so much a part of the musician's vocabulary that they are retained here.

The strings were the foundation of the orchestra at the period of Bach and Handel. Indeed, works like the Handel "Twelve Grand Concertos" and the Bach "Double Concerto" are scored only for stringed instruments. (To be entirely accurate one would have to note that a keyboard instrument was also employed.) It remained the most important factor of the orchestra up to the time when a reaction to romanticism set in. Composers, tiring of the sensuous sweetness of string tone, emphasized the less personal tone of the wind instruments, introduced the piano, not as a solo instrument but as a new orchestral color, and experimented with the possibilities of the percussion instruments. This seems to have been a passing fashion only, because string tone still retains its dominant place in the symphony orchestra. In the dance orchestra the violins have been replaced by instruments of more penetrating and louder tone, the trumpet and saxophone.

The string orchestra is divided by convention into five sections. The sopranos of the group are the violins which in turn are divided into first and second violins. The violin is the favorite soloist, both in the symphony orchestra and in solo recital, rivalled only by the piano. The violin has four strings, each tuned five notes from the next. The tone varies from the rich and reedy sonority of the lowest string (G string) to the silvery brilliance of the highest E string. Higher tones are produced on each string by pressing the string against the fingerboard with the appropriate fingers of the left hand. The scale produced by thus playing successive notes on each of the four strings gives us the range employed by the early violinists. The art of shifting or moving the hand up the fingerboard towards the bridge made it eventually possible for violinists to reach the extreme high register which has been so frequently exploited in modern orchestral works.

The emotional warmth of string tone is chiefly due to the effect called the vibrato which is caused by a back and forth movement of the playing finger together with the player's hand and wrist. This apparently simple movement results in a slight wavering away from the pitch and back which lends warmth to the violin tone. No doubt it is to be regarded as analogous to the tremulous quality of the human voice under emotional stress. If the violinist's finger instead of pressing the string down to the fingerboard rests lightly upon it, the sound produced is small and flute-like. Such tones are called flageolet tones or harmonics. When the violinist plucks the string with his fingers, the tone produced is short and dry (*pizzicato*).

The right hand of the violinist is the bow hand. The varied use of the bow enables the violinist to connect the notes of a melody smoothly (*legato*) or to play each in a short and detached manner (*staccato*). The bow hair may move smoothly over the string or may be made to bounce off after a brief contact, thus producing a dainty staccato tone. In addition to suiting the manner of bowing to the music played the violinist can vary the color of the tone by bowing the string at points closer to or more distant from the bridge. If he plays over the end of the fingerboard, the tone is quiet, subdued. If he bows closer to the bridge, the tone has a peculiar glassy quality that has been used by modern composers for special effects (*sul ponticello*). In music of a gentle or dreamy character the composer may call for the use of the mute. This is a little comb-like device of hard wood or metal with coarse teeth slotted to slip over the top of the bridge. When it is employed, the tone not only loses in volume but takes on a subdued and characteristic color.

The viola is essentially an alto violin, with four strings tuned five notes lower than those of the violin. It is supposed that the disproportion between the size of the body, which is only slightly larger than that of a violin, and the relatively low pitch of the strings causes the characteristic timbre. Its tone may be described as veiled and melancholy. Composers rarely use the instrument for extended solos except in music of a dreamy, mournful, or elegiac quality. It shares with the cello the solo passages of Richard Strauss's "Don Quixote" and plays the role of the romantic and melancholy hero in Berlioz' "Harold in Italy." Its habitual use, however, is to complete the harmony of the strings. No doubt many concertgoers have never noticed it in any other role.

The cello is tuned eight notes (an octave) lower than the viola. It is so large that it is played in an upright position, leaning against the player's knees and supported by an adjustable pin. In older music the cello was almost exclusively a bass. In more recent music it has also taken over the role of a romantic tenor and has learned to sing sensuous inner melodies on its highest or A string. This lyric and passionate voice is one of the characteristic features of romantic orchestration.

As the double-bass is larger than the cello, the player stands or rests against a high stool while playing the instrument. It has, moreover, never been completely absorbed into the violin family. It still retains in many examples the flat back and sloping shoulders that characterized the ancient viols. Its strings are tuned four (rather than five) notes apart, an older tuning, retained here, no doubt, because of the large stretches required in fingering the instrument. The manner of bowing is also various, since some players grasp the bow more or less like a saw while others hold it like a large cello bow. The double-bass in older scores was the faithful companion of the cello. Indeed, the older composers wrote the same part for both instruments. The double-bass, however, sounded the octave below the written tones with the result that it gave enormous gravity and depth to the bass part. The bass is an infrequent soloist since its tone tends to be some-

[229]

what indefinite and vague without the cello. Together with the cello it plays such eloquent passages as the recitative in the last movement of Beethoven's "Ninth Symphony" or the ascending arpeggio at the beginning of the scherzo of the "Fifth Symphony."

The woodwind instruments are played by setting the air in a tube into vibration. The effective sounding length of the tube is adjusted by opening or closing fingerholes pierced in the tube. Modern instruments possess in addition a complicated mechanism of keys which serve to complete the scale. In the modern flute, indeed, all the holes are stopped by padded covers. In all these instruments the player can continue the scale upwards by blowing in such a way as to cause the instrument to speak in a higher register. This is roughly analogous to a male singer who continues an upward passage in falsetto. In tone production, however, these instruments are diverse, utilizing (as has been indicated earlier) three different methods of tone production. In the flutes the players blow across a sharp-edged hole in the mouthpiece. In the oboe group the sound is produced by a double reed, in the clarinets by a single reed.

The flutes of the orchestra are sopranos, coloratura sopranos if you will. Unlike the oboe and clarinet the flute is held horizontally and hence was formerly called the "transverse flute." The pure and limpid tone and incredible facility of the modern instrument are its most striking characteristics. The lower tones have a sonorous reedy quality which has been notably exploited by the French impressionists. The most familiar example is perhaps the solo which opens Debussy's "Afternoon of a Faun." The upper register is somewhat piercing, a characteristic which becomes more marked in the piccolo, the "little flute" pitched an octave higher than the normal flute. The lower register of the piccolo is not especially important, but the intensely brilliant and piercing upper tones add glitter to the most sonorous passages for full orchestra. It embellishes with scales and arpeggios the trios of military marches. It suggests the flash of lightning, the whistling of the wind during orchestral storms. It adds incisiveness to the great chords of the last movement of Beethoven's "Fifth Symphony."

The oboes are less numerous in the modern orchestra than in Handel's day. Nevertheless, the pair of oboes in the orchestra have a penetrating tone quality which can be felt even against the giant sonorities of modern scores. A modern oboe reed is made of two slips of cane, bevelled at the top, and fitted into a little tube of cork. Reed-making is a highly skilled art, and many players are only satisfied with reeds which they adjust to their personal requirement. The oboe, unlike the flute, is held vertically or rather at a small angle to the body of the player. Its tone has a nasal bittersweet quality, very reedy in the low register, shrill but sweet above. It lacks the facile brilliance of the flute and is elegiac and melancholy in mood. Its solo in the "Funeral March" from Beethoven's "Third Symphony" (the *"Eroica"*) shows this phase of its character. When the oboe is gay, it has a sort of rustic quality which has been so happily employed by Beethoven in the Scherzo of his "Sixth Symphony" (the "Pastoral"). When it is amorous, there is a touch of sadness under the surface. See, for example, the Dulcinea theme from Richard Strauss's "Don Quixote." It suggests the shepherd's pipe, the florid reed melodies of the East, pastoral and oriental moods.

The English horn, which is employed only in more recent scores, is neither English nor a horn. It is actually an alto oboe with a melancholy and veiled quality of tone due, in part at least, to the bulbous bell at the lower end of the instrument. It is gently reflective in what is, perhaps, its best known solo, the Largo from Dvořák's "New World Symphony," bitterly mournful in the "Swan of Tuonela" by Sibelius. The modern oboe family has no regularly employed tenor though the heckelphone was designed to fill this vacant place.

[231]

The basses of the double reed family, the bassoons, are quite different from the oboes in form. The bassoon is a large wooden tube, obliquely held, with the double reed mounted on the end of a gooseneck of brass tubing. The Italian name *"fagotto"* (a bundle of sticks) is not inappropriate. When closely examined, the tube of the instrument is found to be double. The breath of the player passes from the reed and brass gooseneck into the body of the instrument which contains two parallel tubes connected with each other by the U-shaped foot joint. In this manner the very long tube necessary to produce tones of low pitch is made manageable. The range of the bassoon is wide. It is sometimes difficult to associate the lyric passages in the upper register with the powerful and reedy bass tones. The considerable facility of the instrument in staccato passages is surprising and has been happily used in passages of a playful character. The melancholy opening of Tschaikowsky's *"Pathétique* Symphony" owes much of its effect to the brooding passages for bassoon in its lowest register. For the most part, however, the bassoon adds sonority to the basses of the orchestra or enriches inner parts without being individually conspicuous.

The contrabassoon, with a still lower range than the bassoon, is a more recent addition to the symphony orchestra. We may date it roughly from Beethoven (though Haydn used it in "The Creation"). Its heavy and unwieldy low tones were employed with remarkable effect in the grave-digging scene in "Fidelio." A unique(?) humorous cadenza for this instrument depicts the death of the Jabberwocky in Deems Taylor's suite, "Through the Looking Glass."

The clarinet family is even less completely represented. In addition to the normal instrument, only the bass clarinet is a regular member of the modern orchestra. The single reed of the clarinet family vibrates in an opening of the beak-shaped mouthpiece. In tone the clarinet is intermediate between the flute and the oboe, less limpid than the former, less intensely reedy than the latter. Its registers,

however, are very distinct: the lowest (*chalumeau*) register tremendously reedy and powerful, the middle rather neu-
tral and somewhat flute-like, the acute penetrating and shrill.
It is an instrument which tends under present broadcasting
and recording conditions to lose its reedy quality so that it
frequently approaches flute tone. Its facility is great without approaching that of the flute. Most early solos for the
instrument employ chiefly the upper and middle registers,
but later composers devised special uses for the sonorous low
register and valued the instrument for its expressive qualities.
Weber's use of the instrument to suggest the cry of Max in
the Overture to *"Der Freischütz"* is a classic and wonderfully
poetic use of the instrument. The bass clarinet is a cavernous
and sombre voice. Its phrases punctuate the monologue of
King Mark near the close of Act II of Wagner's "Tristan and
Isolda." Liszt wrote an important solo for the instrument
in his symphonic poem, *"Tasso."*

The brass instruments all possess great volume and sonority compared with the smaller and more delicate instrumental voices. In a climax the blasts of the trumpets and
the great voices of the trombones dominate the orchestra.
Earlier composers were, however, hampered in their use of
the horns and trumpets by the fact that the scale of these
instruments was incomplete. They were simple tubes of
brass, expanding to a bell at one end, and with a mouthpiece at the other which was cup-shaped in the case of the
trumpet, funnel-shaped for the French horn. In both instruments the length of brass tubing would have been difficult to handle and subject to damage if left straight. It was
therefore coiled though long straight trumpets are sometimes used for ceremonial purposes, like the stage trumpets employed in the procession in *"Aida."* Though the
scale was incomplete in the lower registers, the available
notes did merge into a continuous series in the acute register.
As a consequence of this fact, certain players of the period of
Bach and Handel concentrated on the mastery of the upper

register with the result that the trumpet parts in the scores of these masters have a florid brilliance which is rarely realized in performance by modern players whose training has been of quite a different kind. By the time of Haydn and Mozart the horns and trumpets were instruments of the full orchestra which reinforced sonorous passages· with robust sustained tones or incisive repetitions of a few simple rhythms.

Attempts to bridge the gaps in the scales of these instruments culminated in the system which, in its final form, is largely due to the inventor Sax. He contrived supplementary tubes which could be connected at will to the main tube to add new series of tones to the instrument. All the series combined formed a complete scale. The visible sign of this transformation is the set of three pistons operated by the right hand of the trumpet player. The valves of the French horn, with control levers shaped like teaspoon handles, operate with a similar effect.

The trombone, the third member of the brass choir, was in no need of this improvement since it varied its effective sounding length by a slide which could be extended or retracted so as to produce any possible tone within its compass in a simple, perfect, and unique fashion.

The trumpet is the soprano of the brass group. Originally it was employed to sound military signals and to add pomp and brilliance to a royal entrance. Many passages in the works of the earlier classic composers testify to its use in adding point and vigor to the orchestral tutti and to its persistent and traditional association with the kettle-drums. Only after valves had been added to the trumpet was it capable of song-like passages in the middle register. Even so, many of its most telling uses in recent scores are in accordance with its martial and heroic character. The classic composers contented themselves with a pair of trumpets. In the modern orchestra the number may be increased to three or more.

The horn, like the trumpet, served a practical purpose

and one that affected its orchestral use to a considerable degree. It was originally a hunting horn which signalled the diverse events of the hunt. The most conspicuous orchestral embodiment of the horn as a forest instrument is of course the horn motive of young Siegfried in Wagner's music drama of the same title. A famous theme for four horns appears in Richard Strauss's *"Don Juan."* Equally well suited to the instrument but quite different in mood is the theme of Till from Strauss's *"Till Eulenspiegel."* In a more mellow vein is the lovely horn trio from the middle section of the Scherzo of Beethoven's *"Eroica* Symphony" which finds a later echo in the exquisite passage (for two horns and two bassoons) similarly placed in Mendelssohn's "Italian Symphony." The opening of the Overture to *"Der Freischütz"* shows a typical romantic use of the horns while the three opening horn tones of the "Oberon Overture" are both simpler and more magic in their effect. The marvellous opening of Schubert's great "C major Symphony" for horn solo is another unforgettable moment. More sensuous is the romantic cantilena for horn which dominates the slow movement of Tschaikowsky's "Fifth Symphony."

The classic orchestra had only two horns, and less important scores of that period sometimes call for two horns or two trumpets. The number was increased to four, and for special works even higher demands are made. The horns add greatly to the richness of the orchestral texture when they support and double inner parts in a score, and they have the great merit of blending well with the brass choir, the woodwinds, and the strings.

The trombone, which had existed as an instrument long before its incorporation into the symphony orchestra, had been employed to support or even replace the voices of the singing men in the cathedrals. From this use comes our association of its tone with majesty, with solemn pomp and magnificence. It is this association which Schumann has so effectively exploited in the "Cathedral Movement" of

[235]

his "Rhenish Symphony." The trombone was originally built as a complete family but in modern orchestral practice is reduced to a trio consisting of two tenor trombones and a bass. They add richness and depth to the tone of the full orchestra or play the lower parts in passages for the brass choir. Solos for trombone are infrequent though a fine example occurs in the last movement of Schubert's "C major Symphony." The trombone in a popular mood is conspicuous in Chabrier's *"España."* Its powerful sonorities repeat the melody of the "Pilgrim's Chorus" in the Overture to Wagner's *"Tannhäuser."*

The tuba is also a creation of Sax. It serves as a great supporting bass voice for the brass choir or joins the string basses in an orchestral tutti. Its heavy and unwieldy tones were employed by Wagner to represent the dragon in *"Siegfried."* Wagner saw in the harmonies of these deep voices a tone-color appropriate for Siegfried's "Funeral March." Earlier scores sometimes call for a strange instrument called the ophicleide, the "keyed serpent," which played a role similar to that of the tuba. The fact that parts for this instrument occur in early scores by Mendelssohn ("Midsummer Night's Dream Overture") and Wagner (Overture to "Rienzi") will show how recently it was employed.

The percussion instruments are few in classic scores but become progressively more numerous in more recent works. Only the kettle-drums, hemispheres of copper with a membrane stretched tightly over the tops, were regularly employed at the earlier period. They were used in pairs and were often tuned to "do" and "sol" of the scale of the composition which was performed. They were used to emphasize rhythms. By alternating the blows of the two sticks rapidly a roll could be obtained which almost gave the illusion of a continuous tone.

Almost all the other percussion instruments had exotic suggestions when they were introduced. The cymbals, which came from the Mohammedan East, were first employed in stirring military music inspired by that of the Turkish soldiers, the janissaries. Later its brazen clash was used to mark the peak of climaxes of supreme importance. The triangle, a steel rod bent in the shape suggested by its name and struck by another rod, was employed to accompany a dance of Scythians by Gluck ("Iphigenia in Tauris"). It was used to give a silvery and piquant accent to more modern scores and even reaches the dignity of a solo in Liszt's "Piano Concerto No. 1 in E flat." The snare drum, played by two hardwood sticks with rounded ends, has a sharp and rattling tone due to the tightly stretched gut strands or steel springs (snares) beneath the lower of the two heads. It was originally employed to unify the steps of soldiers on the march and still remains preeminently an instrument for music with a dance character.

One group of instruments possesses bars graduated in size and arranged like the keys of a piano. If the instrument is small with bars of steel, it is a glockenspiel. If the bars are of wood, it is a xylophone. A larger instrument with wooden bars and with tubular resonators suspended under the bars is a marimba. In the celesta the hammers which sound the steel bars are actuated by a keyboard. This instrument in its present form dates only from the late nineteenth century, and the well-known passage in the "Dance of the Sugar-plum Fairy" from Tschaikowsky's "Nutcracker Suite" was one of the first and remains one of the best-known solos for it.

The mere listing of all the percussion instruments would demand a substantial section. There is the ominous tam-tam or gong, the tambourine with its jingles, the Spanish castanets, the Basque drum which has no snares, the large tenor drum, the *maracas,* which we borrowed from Latin-American dance music, and the wooden block from China. They are all occasionally employed, as are many more which have not been listed.

THE HUMAN SIDE OF MUSIC

Such are the instruments of the symphony orchestra. It is surely one of the most complex and most magnificent means of expression which the mind of man has conceived, and the music written for it is one of the most impressive human achievements.

Chapter XII

RHYTHM AND MUSIC

THE motion of some music owes its characteristics to the fact that we speak rhythmically. Operatic recitative, Gregorian chant, troubadour songs are all of this kind. We also move, breathe, and live in rhythm. Though in a broad sense this is true of all human movement, it is most obvious in the bodily movements of men engaged in repetitive work and in the dance. The relation of bodily rhythm to music is most obvious where men actually move to music, as in the military march, in social dancing, and in physical exercises performed to music. But much music which has no actual connection with bodily movement owes certain elements in its effect to this historical association.

The Finale of the "Fifth Symphony" of Beethoven, though not formally designated as a march, nevertheless has the regular and emphatic movement which suggests a jubilant procession. Other march-like compositions carry emotional implications of quite a different kind: the ostentation of Elgar's "Pomp and Circumstance March No. 1," the majestic grief of the "Funeral March" from Beethoven's "Third Symphony," the mocking irony of the March from Prokofieff's "The Love of Three Oranges."

Our object in the present chapter is not so much an analysis of the historical interrelationship of physical motion and music as a study of the actual associations of physical motion and music as they are reflected in music. Moreover, as we have seen, the rhythms of music carry emotional suggestions which may develop into a kind of musical imagery which plays so important a part in program music.

Music moves in tones of longer or shorter duration, but the fundamental measure of music, the count or beat con-

[239]

tinues unchanged, regulating and systematizing the varied movement of the melody. In an earlier chapter the relationship between poetic and musical metre was discussed. Bodily movement was the other determining force in the development of musical rhythm. Walking is perhaps the most basic movement for our present purpose.

The moment when the foot strikes the ground marks the accent. The time when the foot is raised, ready to descend again, is the unaccented part of the cycle. Thus, walking consists of alternate moments of stress and of preparation,— "hay-foot, straw-foot, hay-foot, straw-foot." The movement is duple, like the music which we count 1-2, 1-2, or 1-2-3-4, 1-2-3-4. Though walking is the basic movement, there are many other simple steps. In a series of leaps three stages are necessary. The moment of descent, of impact, again marks the accent. But it is not possible to jump again immediately. The knees must be more or less flexed in preparation for the next leap. Then the legs straighten and the body leaves the ground only to descend at the next stress. There are thus two stages preceding the actual impact of the feet with the ground, the preparation and the leap. Skipping is similar in rhythm except that the step forward is made first with one foot, then with the other. Such movements are ternary and would be expressed by music which is counted 1-2-3, 1-2-3. Thus the nature of the movement determines the grouping of accents and the stages of preparation which lead to the accent.

Only the most primitive dances, however, consist of a repetition of a single type of step. Where some special change of movement lends character to the dance, it is likely to be reflected in a corresponding alteration of the melody. Not infrequently the rhythm survives in music long after the dance which generated it has been forgotten. Thus, the lively galliard of the sixteenth century consisted of four equal steps followed by a leap. The steps were represented by four notes of equal value, the leap by a silence (rest) and the attitude which the dancer assumed after the leap by a final note. The pattern step, step, step, step, leap, attitude was literally reflected in early melodies for the dance. Later tunes respect the rhythms of the dance, but follow a somewhat freer course.

Not only were the rhythms of dance tunes and the movements of the dance closely related; the formal organization of the tune was frequently a direct outcome of the various figures of the dance. Many early dances might be said to have no form since the same step was repeated to the end of the dance. When, in a circular dance, a movement to the center is balanced by a movement away from the center, a certain number of steps to the left by a corresponding number to the right, the dance presents a feature which is the equivalent of two balanced musical phrases.

An early example is preserved by Attilius Fortunatianus, a grammarian who wrote during the decline of the Roman Empire, "Formerly the songs composed in honor of the gods were in three parts. There was first, turning to the right, a procession round the altar (strophe); then the same, turning to the left (antistrophe); finally the song came to an end before the altar in the presence of the god (epode)." It is easy to see that the movements the celebrants made were one with the text which they chanted as they moved and the music which gave life and solemnity to the text. In a similar fashion, each section of the charming tunes printed in Playford's "The English Dancing Master" (1650) is associated in the printed directions with a corresponding figure of the dance.

In addition to these relationships, each dance possessed a character, a mood, which could be conveyed by the movements of the dancer, but which was also imprinted on the music of the dance. In the case of the older dances this is, indeed, all that is left to us, a rhythm, a characteristic mood. The dance has given the composer a repertory of rhythms which he can use to suggest a mood.

Thus, the sarabande is grave and noble, the bourrée rough

and gay, the polonaise proud and spirited, the waltz graceful. Dance rhythms have passed from the village green to the
ballroom and finally to the realm of instrumental music from
the sixteenth century to the present day.

The pavane was already out of use in the lifetime of that
most diligent historian of the dance, Thoinot Arbeau (1519-
1595), for he tells us: "It has not been abolished and put out
of use, and I believe that it never will be, though true it is that
it is not so much practised as in the past. Our instrumental
performers play them when they lead a girl of good family to
a marriage in the holy church, and when they herald the entrance of the priests, the maceman, and the fellows of some
notable brotherhood. They also use pavanes when they play
for the entrance of a mascarade, triumphal chariots of gods
and goddesses, Emperors and Kings full of majesty."

Again, at a later date the learned writer Mersenne (1588-
1648) says "the Allemande is a dance of Germany . . . one
is satisfied today to play it on instruments without dancing
it, except at ballets." The minuet was preserved in string
quartet and symphony after it was no longer danced in the
ballroom. The waltz, which in the days of Johann Strauss
was the favored dance of society, an international sensation,
has now become a concert piece. In our own day we have
seen Whiteman and many others demonstrate that jazz will
attract audiences who come to listen, not to dance. In this
fashion actual dance music was transformed into the "idealized dance," and dance rhythms became a vital element in
our instrumental music.

A mere catalogue of dances would require a large volume.
Certain ancient dance rhythms, however, appear so frequently in modern concerts that they form part of our common
musical heritage. The dances of the sixteenth century are
either proud and courtly or popular and folk-like. They represent on the one hand the physical pride of the noble, his
naive delight in his own bearing and in his costly and elaborate costume, on the other the frank good-humor and animal

spirits of the peasant dance. The art of the dancing master was closely allied to that of the fencing master. Sometimes, indeed, one man functioned in both capacities. Both were valued arts of self-display. Among the many dances of the period two must suffice as examples, the pavane and the galliard.

The pavane required hardly more than a simple walking step. It had the movement of a grave and stately procession. Most of the older tunes for the dance are written in those ancient scales which, perhaps, had an effect of ceremonial pomp for the dancers of three centuries ago, but for us an air of melancholy regret which certain modern composers have been quick to exploit.

It was usual at this time to distinguish between the "low" and the "high" dances, that is: those which could be danced without losing contact with the dance floor and those which required leaps during which the feet of the dancer left the floor. The pavane was, as one would expect from its slow and measured movement, one of the "low" dances. It was composed of three contrasting strains. One of the most famous examples is the "Earl of Salisbury's Pavane" from the "Fitzwilliam Virginal Book." The French composers, and particularly the impressionist composers, liked to recall the music of an earlier period. In this spirit Ravel wrote his well-known "Pavane for a Dead Infanta" and the "Pavane of the Sleeping Beauty" (the latter from his "Mother Goose Suite"), and Debussy the Pavane from *"Pour le Piano."* It is the melancholy of the past which they have rediscovered in this ancient dance.

The foil to the pavane was the galliard. Where the pavane was stately, the galliard was alert and lively. The dancer of the galliard leaped and struck an attitude. Frequently the pavane and galliard were connected as a sequence of two dances. Sometimes, indeed, the galliard was merely a lively rhythmic variation of the tune which had been previously utilized for the pavane.

[243]

The list of dances of the sixteenth century might easily be extended. Most of them are rarely heard at the present time, though now and again some enthusiast for old music plays some of them on the lute or the harpsichord. Respighi arranged two sets of these old dances for orchestra, and in this form they have gone the round of the concert halls. Inevitably, in such a garb, they take on a more varied coloring, a somewhat more pompous atmosphere, which prevent us from hearing in them the characteristically dry and somewhat nasal quality of the lute with its crisp chords and discrete ornaments.

The dance succession which is hinted at in the pavane-galliard sequence or in the "dance" and "after-dance" of the German composers was further developed in the suite. The suite was a thing of infinite variety, a sequence of dances, all composed in the same scale. Early composers sometimes composed suites in which the number of dances was so great as to exceed the patience of most listeners. In some cases the performer was evidently expected to make a selection from the dances on the printed page.

Nevertheless, a fairly stable order did eventually emerge from this variety though composers (for example Bach in the "French Suites") always felt free to add other dances. This order may be stated as allemande, courante, sarabande, and gigue (jig). From the point of view of rhythmic variety it was an admirable choice. The pattern of movement might be stated as moderate, fast, slow, and very fast. The slow dance, the sarabande, occupied a central position just as the slow movement did in the later concerto and symphony. The rapid final movement had the same culminating effect as the sparkling finales of certain symphonies by Haydn. Each dance also possessed a highly characteristic movement and mood of it own.

The allemande has completely lost its dance character as we find it in the suites of Bach and Handel. Earlier it had the movement of a simple march which progressed in moderate fours. Thus we find it in the tower music of Pezel and in the early German organ books. In the hands of later composers its movement changed. The simple folk-like melody flowered into continuous passages and finally, with Bach, the movement has the aspect of a graceful prelude which moves in rapid and uniform tones.

A similar fate befell the courante. Its early development was varied, and a number of specialized types appeared which we need not consider here. It was an "elevated" dance which, in its fully developed form, moves in rapid threes. But where the early melodies move in tones of uneven value, the later composers veil this characteristic in a steady flow of passage-work. As a dance it combined a gay and lively character with a certain courtly pride. As a keyboard composition it moves with a crisp gaity which half obscures, half reveals the character of the dance.

Some writers have insisted that the sarabande developed from the courante. If this is true, the dance as we find it in the suites of Couperin and the great German masters is far removed from its origins. It moves in a stately ternary measure, and is frequently characterized by a rhythm which hesitates before the last count of the measure after two emphatic opening chords. Handel's familiar air *"Lascia ch'io pianga,"* which was originally a sarabande from his early opera *"Almira,"* reveals the pattern in its simplest form. Bach, however, transforms the courtly gravity of this dance into a supple and richly ornamented melody. The sarabande in his hands is transformed from dance to florid and ecstatic song.

The jig is of later date than the other dances of the suite. It appears in English manuscripts of Queen Elizabeth's day, and may quite possibly be English in origin. It is a lively and vigorous dance which is notated in an astounding variety of forms. The typical number of counts is two, though there are examples with one, three, and four counts. The number of counts is, however, less important than the fact that each of these counts is subdivided in three. Thus, in a two-beat measure there might actually be six notes in two groups of three each (the six-eight time of the musician). The jig survived as a folk-dance, but even the specimens incorporated into the suite have a fresh country vigor which preserves more of the dance spirit than any of the other usual dances of the classic suite.

Yet this merry and rhythmic dance received at the hands of certain composers (and perhaps most notably in many of the suites of Bach) a special and complicated treatment. Here the subject is first announced successively by each of the voices as in the opening of a fugue. The first part of the dance is continued in free fugal style. At the beginning of the second section the subject is again announced successively in each of the voices, but so altered that each upward progression of the melody appears as a downward movement, each downward move as an ascent. The transformation of the theme (the "contrary motion" of the musician) dominates the second part of the movement as the simple form dominated the opening section.

Such were the dances of the classic suite, and such were their characters as far as they can be caught in words. The suite was, however, a fluctuating form. Gavottes, bourrées, minuets, passepieds, loures, forlanes, and many other dances were often added to the normal sequence. It is interesting to note that these newcomers tended to retain their dance character better than the dances described above. It is almost as if the musician had not yet decided how to transform them and so set them down in a frank vigorous form, just as they were danced. This seems particularly true of Bach's gavottes and bourrées.

If the dances of the classic suite dominated the seventeenth and the early eighteenth century, the minuet was the dance of the later eighteenth century. For most listeners it is typified by such well-known examples as Mozart's Minuet from *"Don Giovanni"* and the Beethoven "Minuet in G." Actually the minuet varied greatly. It moved in moderate ternary metre. It symbolizes the spirit of the classic period and remains an epitome of courtly grace and elegance. Not only were sets of minuets composed for social dancing, but it was admitted to more serious company as a movement of the symphony and the string quartet. If we consider the thousands of such pieces which were composed, we can better understand Haydn's remark, "If anyone wishes to contribute to the art of music, let him compose a new minuet." The other dances such as the German dance and the contra-dance (sometimes corrupted to country dance as in the title of Beethoven's well-known examples) played a relatively secondary role.

Already, in certain melodies of Mozart we catch a hint, not of the fiery and capricious waltz, but rather of the good-humored Viennese Ländler which preceded it. Indeed, even before Mozart, an occasional melody anticipates the character of this, the most popular of the nineteenth century dances. Of the great classic composers Schubert was perhaps the first to compose true waltzes. (Beethoven did indeed write waltzes but they do not have the true Viennese character.) Schubert's compositions in this form have the appearance of chance improvisations which he happened to write down. Commonplace tunes and tender poetic melodies follow one another just as they occurred to the composer. They mark the beginning of the era of the waltz.

The waltz was a social as well as a musical sensation. The steps were simple. The intimacy of dancing in couples and the intoxicating character of the music caused more than the usual cries of immorality. The appealing sentiment of the tunes, the elasticity of rhythm, and a certain freedom in performance became characteristic of the fully developed waltz of Lanner and of the Strausses, father and son. The success of the Strauss waltzes was incredible, and they became national and then international figures. Perhaps the first famous "name band" to tour Europe, then the United

States, was the orchestra of the younger Strauss. All Europe danced to the Strauss waltzes.

The waltz has vanished, or is just about to vanish from our dance floors. But the Strauss waltzes still maintain their public as concert pieces. Our "Pops" concerts find them a necessary ingredient. One can hardly dismiss the waltz without naming some of the most memorable compositions in this form: the elegant and half-melancholy piano compositions of Chopin, the rich and varied Brahms' waltzes for piano (Op. 39) and his *"Liebeslieder"* for piano duet and vocal quartet (Op. 52). Though the minuet or the scherzo maintains its accustomed place in the symphony, it has occasionally been displaced by the waltz, notably in the "Fifth Symphony" of Tschaikowsky. It plays its part in *"Un Bal,"* the third movement of Berlioz's *"Symphonie Fantastique."* But long before this Schubert had written a trio for the scherzo of his great "C major Symphony" which is in true waltz style.

The waltz was not alone in its period though it overshadowed all other dance forms. The galop, the écossaise, the cotillion, were all favorite dances of society. Perhaps the most interesting rival of the waltz was the polka which rose on a wave of popularity which reached impressive dimensions. Contemporary caricatures emphasize the position in which the knee was bent at a right angle. The waltz was gradually evolved from popular dances of South Germany. The polka, however, seems to have been rather abruptly transplanted from the village to the ballroom. Indeed the dance is supposed to have been noted from the performance of a peasant girl by a Czech schoolmaster. As the polka became popular it was modified so as to exchange its native vigor for politer and more circumspect movements and, in this form, made the rounds of all the ballrooms of Europe. Whether the account of the origin of the dance is literally true or not, it does suggest the folk origin of the polka. Many of the most brilliant concert polkas were composed by Czech musicians, the polka from the "Bartered Bride" by Smetana, the more recent example from *"Schwanda"* by Weinberger.

This transfer of national popular dances from the village to the concert hall is not new. It is a development which is apparent in earlier times in the dances of the suite where the allemande came from Germany, the gigue perhaps from England, the sarabande purportedly from Spain, the courante from France. The two influences which modified such dances came from the musician and the dancing master. The former tended to elaborate and idealize the dance forms (the more recent arrivals in the classic suite were conspicuously more popular and more danceable than the earlier forms). The court dancing master and the other arbiters of etiquette were likely to prettify and restrain the movements of the dance to make it suitable for "politer" circles.

The social dances of the twentieth century provide two conspicuous examples of this transfer of dance idioms. One is the rise of American popular dances, their introduction into Europe in the period following World War I, and their eventual spread over most of the urban regions of the world. The other is the transference of Cuban and Latin-American dance idioms to North America together with many of the folk-instruments employed in this music.

No musical subject of recent times has been treated in so positive a fashion and at the same time with such a paucity of really factual data as the rise of "ragtime" with its later developments as "jazz," "boogie-woogie," "swing." It has developed its own highly specialized erudition which suffers from two deficiencies. The first is the fact that many of its early developments seemed so unimportant to contemporaries that no one bothered to record them in any exact fashion. The second is the fact that most studies in the field are violently partisan in attitude.

By the mid-nineteenth century a quasi-Negro style of dance and song was widely composed and disseminated by minstrels, groups of white performers made up with burnt cork to resemble Negroes, as well as Negro troupes. Such well-known songs as the "Camptown Races" of Stephen Foster or Emmett's "Dixie" will illustrate the type. The minstrel show also featured certain types of theatrical dancing. In at least one instance (the "Jump Jim Crow" dance made famous by Thomas D. Rice) it is said that the dance was based on the observation of a characteristic movement made by a Negro.

Two other characteristics gradually made themselves felt in later popular music. One is the "blues" strain, the other the advent of tunes which were markedly syncopated in character. The Foster songs, like most "composed" popular songs of the period, were transparently simple in harmony; but the livelier airs, like "Oh Susanna," show a marked use of syncopation. The same qualities may be observed in early harmonizations of Negro spirituals.

Syncopation is a familiar word the meaning of which may be clarified by a short explanation. The emphatic metric movements 1-2-3-4 and 1-2 which are characteristic of simple marches and quicksteps alternate accented and unaccented counts. These accents may be made emphatic by actually playing the note on the first count louder than those which follow. In an even more fundamental fashion an accent is produced by making the note on the first count longer than those which follow it. This is the usual procedure. Syncopation is the exception to the rule, for the accent is shifted to a normally unaccented beat, usually by one of two devices. The long note may be placed on a beat which is normally unaccented. But since the fact that it is longer than the adjacent notes tends to create an accent, the auditor will think of it as a stressed tone which appears at an irregular time. A note in the preceding measure may also be prolonged past the first or accented count. In this situation the note which carries the accent is delayed until its normal time has passed.

Not only were many spirituals syncopated in rhythm, but such Creole folksongs as "Michieu Banjo" and such dances as the cake-walk show a pronounced use of the device. In Debussy's "Gollywog's Cake-walk," which is, perhaps, the most familiar example, the French composer was working after a Negro pattern.

The "blues" influence is, properly speaking, more a matter of melodic inflection, of harmonic treatment, and mood than a rhythmic factor. A "blues" is often a song of bereavement, of unhappy love. The manner of performance is slow and dragging, and there is a characteristic slide from below into important melody tones. The simple and frank English and Irish folksongs used only the unaltered scale tones. "Blues" tunes often slide through intermediate sounds in passing from one scale tone to another, or dwell on tones which are foreign to the scale in which they are composed. This is a borrowing not from the folk tradition, but rather from art music which has employed the resources of the chromatic scale since pre-classic times. The use of the device has resulted in a richer and more varied harmony, a more pathetic melodic line, but at the same time it has helped to erase one of the boundaries between folksong and composed song.

To such miscellaneous ingredients was added a style of performance which seems to have originated from musically illiterate performers, many of them Negroes, who played in obscure honky-tonks and bar-rooms. They rediscovered improvisation; they found and exploited a whole repertory of instrumental tricks. They played in a devil-may-care style which was brash and uninhibited, and rhythmically exhilarating.

Such are some of the factors which led to ragtime, the fox-trot, jazz, swing, boogie-woogie. What was at first an individual find became a commercial product. Professionally trained musicians, members of symphony orchestras played dance music which had been cleverly arranged by specialists in the field. Up to the end of World War I, jazz had been largely a domestic phenomenon. The years following the end of the war saw American bands playing all over Europe with profound effects on symphonic music and opera as well as on music for dancing. In our own country, too, our popular music has had a considerable effect on the music of "serious" American composers.

This was a natural transition for a composer like Gershwin who started as a song writer and who reached such compositions as the "Rhapsody in Blue" and the "Concerto in F" only after repeated successes on Broadway. Ferde Grofé, whose "Grand Canyon Suite" remains his best-known work, was an arranger for Paul Whiteman's band before he became known as a composer. Such transitions from Broadway to Carnegie Hall were characteristic of the period.

Composers of more orthodox training, however, were attracted by the peculiarities of our popular music and wrote scores under its influence without handling the idiom with the complete naturalness and ease which Gershwin attained. There was, for example, the ballet "Krazy Kat" by John Alden Carpenter with its fox-trot. There were "Daniel Jazz" and the "Jazzberries" by Gruenberg. Leonard Bernstein treated "Fancy Free" in the Broadway vernacular.

European composers also were enormously interested in this new and disturbing music. Since most of them had never taken the trouble to discover that we produced music of all possible kinds, they seized on jazz as the typical and only American music. A considerable number of works reflect this interest. Though one may say that none of these works really captures more than certain external features of the jazz idiom, they resulted in hybrids which were neither jazz nor European art-music. Milhaud's "Creation of the World," for example, contains a jazz fugue. Auric's impressions of the New World are summed up in a fox-trot, *"Adieu New York."* Ravel included a fox-trot in "The Child and the Enchantments." Stravinsky has written a "Piano Rag-Music," a "Ragtime for Eleven Instruments," and (more recently) a "Concerto in Ebony" for Woody Herman's band. Hindemith included a "Ragtime" in his piano suite entitled "1922."

Such are a few of the transformations and adventures of

American dance rhythms. If our own dance music has invaded the rest of the world, we have in turn welcomed the popular music of Cuba and South America. To many listeners such an orchestra as that of Xavier Cugat, such a singer as Carmen Miranda represent Latin America just as Frank Sinatra and Bing Crosby represent us to the outside world. A whole series of dances have reached us, the tango, the rhumba, the conga. Folk instruments like the *marimba, maracas, claves* have become familiar to us, as have the intricate cross rhythms which they play against the sentimental simplicity of the melodic line. Such a development shows a considerable parallel to our own musical relations with Europe. In both cases popular music was able to cross frontiers more easily than symphonic music. Indeed, few musicians of the United States had any knowledge of the composers of South and Central America until the advent of World War II made a more intimate cultural exchange a matter of political expediency. Some of our own composers have seized on the picturesque qualities of the popular dances of the South Americans, notably John Alden Carpenter in his "Tango," Harl McDonald in his "Rhumba Symphony," and Paul Bowles in his *"Huapangos"* for piano.

Much early music was related in rhythm to movements in the outside world by the simple fact that the music developed as an accompaniment to the movements. Perhaps the simplest example (if we exclude the dance) is the worksong. In the true worksong (as distinguished from a song sung merely to pass the time while working) the pauses, the stresses, and the very form of the song are molded by the nature of the work which is performed while it is sung.

If we except the marching song, little labor is now performed to music in the industrialized countries. The need for organized gang labor has diminished as machines have gradually taken over work that was once performed by the rhythmic efforts of gangs of laborers. Yet, if fewer agricultural laborers actually cultivate the fields to the beat of drums, if fewer oarsmen pull to the accents of their leader's song, nevertheless, the long association of music and bodily rhythm has provided the musician with a vocabulary of musical figures which suggest a given movement, and hence the mood which is associated with the movement.

Though the boatsong has largely vanished as a way of lightening monotonous labor, it survived as a musical type. The Venetian composers of the seventeenth century had already written a type of movement in a broad ternary metre which was an early barcarolle. More recent examples such as the famous barcarolle from Offenbach's "Tales of Hoffman" or the Tschaikowsky "Barcarolle" will be more familiar. The "Venetian Boat Songs" from Mendelssohn's "Songs Without Words" cannot be included here since Mendelssohn did not give them this title.

In a similar fashion the rhythm of hammering passed from the worker to the singer and then to the composer. Many of our folksongs about "John Henry," the steel-driving folk hero, move with the swing of hammer blows. Rameau, in the early eighteenth century, had already caught the characteristic iterations of the blacksmith's hammer and put them in his harpsichord piece, *"Les Cyclopes."* Wagner's *"Siegfried"* contains both the repetitive motive suggesting the metal-working of the Nibelungs and the grandiose scene in which Siegfried forges his own sword, *"Nothung."*

The catalogue of movements reflected in music would be too long to complete here: the turning of the spinning-wheel, the rocking of a cradle, the to-and-fro of the swing. Not only were the movements of human beings translated into musical rhythms, animal movements were also transplanted into music. There is the movement of a galloping horse in "Mazeppa's Ride" by Liszt, in Schumann's "The Rider's Story," and in the twice familiar "Light Cavalry Overture" of Suppé. The "Little White Donkey" of Ibert moves at a brisk pace, the cow-horse of Grofé's "On the Trail" at a more leisurely gait. Even vehicles have their characteristic movements: the post-wagon of Schubert's song, the great ox-drawn Polish wagons (*"Bydlo"*) from Moussorgsky's "Pictures from an Exhibition," the *"Troika"* with its bells in Tschaikowsky's attractive piano piece, Honegger's puffing locomotive, "Pacific 231," and Villa Lobos' *"Caipira, Little Train of the Andes."* A modern age finds symbols in machine rhythms. Indeed composers had discovered them long before the present day.

It must be confessed that the symbolism of musical rhythms is sufficiently vague unless they are defined and clarified by other musical factors or by a text. The cycle of preparation, movement, and impact occurs in many types of movement, in the blow of a hammer, the sweep of a scythe. Clearly if one basic rhythmic cycle can apply to several different activities, there is a considerable area of ambiguity. Even the rocking of a cradle and the movement of a steel-drilling man might have a considerable resemblance in their rhythmic patterns.

The composer, however, can call on other musical factors. The cradle song will be hushed and gentle in style where the song of steel is boisterous and rude. If the orchestra is employed, the composer might use muted strings with flute and clarinet tones for the cradle song, brass instruments with the accents marked by drums and bells to suggest the ringing of steel under the impact of the hammer. If the composer calls on the aid of words as in the forging scene from *"Siegfried"* or the "Cradle Song" of Brahms, his intention becomes entirely clear—if the audience understands the words. Bach was able to develop an elaborate symbolism in his cantatas by combining an appropriate rhythm, a characteristic melody, and a text which contained the final key to their significance. Any operatic score will contain examples of the same threefold association.

The artists of China drew pictures of the lion, not from any actual acquaintance with lions, but from a study of pictures by earlier artists. The lion does not exist in China though it served them as a symbol of courage. In music there have also appeared certain musical rhythms and melodic figures which are accepted as a portrayal of external movements. Such associations are better understood by recalling other pieces of similar character and their titles than they would be by comparing the piece directly with the subject which is presumably described.

Much romantic music which suggests the turning of a mill-wheel, the rustling of leaves, or the movement of a boat is of this kind. Many barcarolles have been composed with so little reference to the rhythms of rowing that the musician does no more than write a piece which moves to a count of six and has a gentle lyric melody. Pieces which suggest the rustle of leaves or the coming of spring employ fluent and undulating passage work which is not unsuitable to the title, but which might be placed at the service of many similar poetic ideas.

Up to this point we have outlined the relationship between music and the dance, between music and the movements made by the worker, between music and the rhythms of the machine.

The musician has preserved dances which have been forgotten by the dancing master. Writing music for the dance as well as music which is the equivalent of the varied movements and moods suggested by the texts of operas and cantatas has provided the musician with a large rhythmic vocabulary. Many of these rhythms possess a fairly well-defined character, and are capable of affecting an audience in a given way. It was music with a text, the song, the cantata, the opera, which was the best school for both composer and audience. Once the emotional suggestion of an effect had been established, it might be transferred to instrumental music with some assurance that it would establish a comparable mood.

When an audience hears a slow and repetitious figure and sees on the stage the blind Sampson turning the millstone, it will be more apt to accept similar rhythmic patterns without the help of stage and declaimed text as expressions of hopeless despair. Indeed, if the opera had not existed, the symphonic poem, which undertakes an instrumental illustration of a text, would be incomprehensible. In the opera the action and the text explain the nature of the music, and usually do so simultaneously. In the symphonic poem, however, even where the audience reads the program or poem on which it is based, they must understand the implications of musical movement sufficiently well to recognize that the appearance of a given musical rhythm is intended to correspond with a given portion of the program.

The composer, however, frequently writes passages where no actual motion is depicted, but rather a given mood or character. The rhythms chosen for the purpose are used in a symbolic sense and are intended to convey the emotional tone suitable to the type of rhythm employed. The movement of the sarabande might suggest dignity, pride, nobility. It is curious to see the characteristic rhythm of this dance employed by composers who, in all probability did not think of it at all, but were merely searching for a theme with a majestic and noble character. The opening chords of Beethoven's "Egmont Overture," which suggest the character of the hero, are in the characteristic rhythm of the sarabande as are the chords which accompany Tristan's entrance in the first act of "Tristan and Isolda."

In the preceding discussion rhythm has been considered in a rather detailed and specific fashion. There are broader and more general characteristics of musical motion which are nevertheless of great importance. A given kind of musical movement may continue for a long time. Such a treatment will give a kind of persistent character to the music which may have a variety of emotional suggestions depending on the nature of the other musical resources employed. It may suggest patient endurance if the music is melancholy, an obsession if it is fantastic and spectral, heroic fortitude if it is broad and sonorous.

Well-marked changes of musical motion within a piece suggest discontinuity, interrupted progress. A striking example of such a marked change is the repeated appearance of the "fate motive" in abrupt contrast to its musical environment in Tschaikowsky's "Fourth Symphony." On the other hand the motion of the music may increase; notes of longer duration may be followed by tones which move with greater rapidity. When combined with an increase in loudness such an alteration of rhythm gives the impression of a climax, of a building up of musical tension. Where a symbolic interpretation is justified, it may suggest conflict, a struggle against fate.

At the end of a composition the opposite may occur, a gradual cessation of motion, decrease in psychic tension. Here too the effect is often justified only by musical and formal considerations. In program music, however, such a treatment might suggest repose, death, or transfiguration after a heroic struggle.

Rhythm is the primordial musical factor, deep-rooted and primitive and at the same time capable of the most subtle suggestions. It may, in its later manifestations, seem to be a purely artistic means of expression which appears to have its origin nowhere save in the imagination of the composer. Even in such a case the composer is likely to draw on the associations that have been created out of its long development in connection with bodily movement. It may mimic the rhythm of things in the external world, the periodic songs of nature, recurring gusts of wind, the surging of waves up the beach, the rustle of leaves. It may reproduce the rhythm of man-made machines, the gradual acceleration of a locomotive, the heavy turning of a mill-wheel. In a still broader way all nature is rhythmic in the sense of a measured recurrence of things. It is then natural that the movement of music which man has made for himself should be measured, both in its movement in detail and in its broader flow.

CHAPTER XIII

THE EFFECTS OF MELODY

MUSIC has a twofold nature, a twofold development. On the one hand, music arouses our emotions. That is a basic fact which everyone sensitive to music must have experienced for himself. On the other hand, it depends for its effect on our response to the relationships of the tones employed. This response is not an act of conscious analysis at the moment when a melody is experienced. It depends rather on the cumulative effect of past experiences. These experiences lead to a simpler system of relationships than might be anticipated, for, though melodies are different as wholes, their elements do repeat themselves. Thus the round "Three Blind Mice," the folksong "Sleep Baby Sleep," and Stephen Foster's "Old Folks at Home" all begin with the same tone sequence. Yet each melody has a perfectly distinct character in spite of this initial resemblance.

The note groups which are used to end a melody or a section of a melody are especially likely to display resemblances. That this is true of tunes which will be familiar to every reader may be illustrated by three well-known examples. A mental review of "America," "Old Hundred," and "Oh Susanna" will show that each tune ends with two final notes which form one of the most usual cadences or closing formulas. In other respects the tunes are markedly different. Thus it is apparent that many familiar melodies display similarities of melodic movement, and that these likenesses are most exact at the points where a melody or a part of a melody reaches a close. In most of our melodies one tone is of special importance. This is so, not only because it usually occupies the important positions at the beginning and end of a melody, but also because it is used

[261]

more frequently than other tones. An example may illustrate the prominence of this tone, which we may call the "tonic" or the "keynote." The sturdy old psalm tune "Old Hundred" contains thirty-two notes. The "tonic" appears nine times. The melody begins with a repetition of this note and it appears again at the end. It is possible to see an early stage in the evolution of the concept of a central tone in primitive music in which only one or two tones are well defined and all others are shifting. Indeed, in certain oriental performances only the closing formulas are fixed and all else depends on the fancy of the player.

The fact that melodies move in ways which are habitual within a given culture area has resulted in the setting up of a system of expectations based on the fact that we anticipate that a given tone or group of tones will proceed as it did in similar melodic situations which we remember. This is not summed up in a conscious comparison of past and present experiences. Frequently, we only realize that a familiar opening has had an unexpected conclusion by our feeling of vague disappointment or bewilderment. A pianist was practicing a composition which concluded with two long notes. The piano, however, was an old one and the second tone remained silent. The other members of the household, busy about their respective tasks, were aware of something baffling about this close. Finally one of them approached the pianist. "Isn't there something odd about the ending?" She had realized that the first note was usually followed by the second and had been puzzled because the familiar sequence was left incomplete. Thus, our musical experience has trained us to expect certain tones as ending tones, to realize that other tones lead to them.

The tones on which compositions end impress us as having a restful quality, the others (and particularly those used just before the final tone in a closing formula) produce an effect of activity. This impression of tension and relaxation as embodied in these tones may be explained

[262]

(as we have explained it here) by the fact that the composer conceives in terms of a traditional and habitual movement and sequence of tones. The listener becomes familiar with such sequences and eventually anticipates their development. Other students have wished to place the matter on a scientific basis and have attempted to show that the movement of tones and our impression of activity and rest are based on the laws of sound. The matter is too complex to be considered here, but the conclusions to which these two views lead are far-reaching in their importance and must be briefly stated.

The facts about melodic behavior which have been discussed are valid for the simple melodies which were used as illustrations and for Western art-music from Bach to Brahms and Wagner. They are not necessarily valid for the many and varied systems of melody which have emerged at other times and other places. Some of these systems have impinged on and have influenced music with which we are familiar, and they will be considered in the following pages. Those who accept our system as scientifically justified must note the existence of other systems. They are likely to regard them, however, as imperfect experiments which are of value only when they approach the standards of Western music of the nineteenth century (or any other recent stage in the development of our music which might be chosen as a climax period). Not only would this necessitate the placing of such masters of the sixteenth century as Victoria and Palestrina in an inferior position, but it also would make it necessary to regard such facts as the interest in ancient scales manifested by Debussy or Ravel as departures from a norm. The materials of music lend themselves to developments which vary from culture to culture. Each variant possesses its own interest, its own means of effect. Each should be judged as far as possible on its own terms, not by its likeness or lack of likeness to the music with which we are most familiar.

In our previous discussion of tones as restless or restful

we have regarded this quality only as a factor which determines in a general way how notes follow each other. We have seen it as a structural factor defining the closes of melodic sentences or entire melodies. But the fact that tones impress us as "satisfied" or "unsatisfied" could be and was transferred to the emotional realm. The movement downwards at the end of a melody might symbolize rest after effort, transfiguration after conflict. If this is so, it is easy to see that melodies of a peaceful or pastoral character would contain more tones of repose, those with a troubled character more active tones. It is thus no accident that Tschaikowsky's famous song "None but the lonely Heart" should begin with a series of four active tones. Brahms' "Lullaby," on the other hand, achieves its gentle and tender effect in some measure from its use of tones of rest. Its nine opening tones belong to the tones of repose of its scale. Thus the pangs of love, the struggle towards an ideal are mirrored in a group of tones which leave us unsatisfied. Their movement towards the nearest tones of rest may symbolize peace, self realization, transfiguration.

The movement of tones is limited by the principles which have been stated, but within these principles a great variety in melodic contour is possible. A composer may move smoothly from a tone to adjacent tones. Such melodies as the choral theme from the last movement of Beethoven's "Ninth Symphony" or the familiar Welsh folksong, "All Through the Night," show a predominant use of this type of movement. Quite a different effect is produced if, instead of moving to adjacent tones, the composer proceeds by skip. The cry of the Valkyries from Wagner's music-drama of the same title, the opening of the "Star-Spangled Banner," and the initial theme of Brahms' "Fourth Symphony" are themes of this kind. It is easy to experience the boldness and strength of music of this kind, less simple to analyze the reason for the difference in effect. We may perhaps transfer our consciousness that small intervals are sung with little effort, large intervals with a greater expenditure of energy, from the sensation of singing to the music which we hear. In this way we have come to feel that melodies which move smoothly are tranquil and gentle, those that move by large skips energetic and intense.

A similar transfer seems to take place in our associations with musical passages composed of high or of low tones, with what the musician calls "register." Two people engaged in an animated discussion are not only likely to talk louder as the argument reaches its climax. They will also "raise their voices." While the smooth or disjunct movement of a melody remains a general characteristic which determines its mood and character, the undulations of a melody from low to high form an important element in the dramatic pattern, the structure of music. It is a major factor in holding the attention of the listener.

In early times this factor was less artfully or perhaps differently employed. It has been remarked that certain Gregorian melodies start high and move downwards to a close. The same observation applies to many American Indian tunes. Such a pattern is an artistic version of the "descending howl" which has been noted in the calls of certain primitive tribes. It corresponds to a natural exhalation and perhaps requires less of forethought, of conscious organization than the schemes which have prevailed in our own music. Only in an occasional composition of recent times do we find a recurrence of this old and primitive trait. Such an exception occurs in one of Ravel's "Songs of Madagascar" where a high note, a climax tone, is the first of the composition.

Our recent music tends to follow a pattern of gradually rising melody, point of climax, and descent from the climax tone. The pattern is perhaps most stereotyped in the operatic aria where the singer's highest tone just before the close of the composition is so usual a feature that its approach (at least in pre-Wagnerian examples) will be anticipated by the audience. On a smaller scale, many of our familiar songs

[265]

will show some variant of the standard pattern. "America," for example, follows a rather gentle ascent and descent in the first phrase which closes with the words "Of thee I sing." The second part starts more vigorously and the tune reaches its climax on the word "let" in the final phrase, "Let Freedom ring." The Welsh folksong "All through the Night" is so constructed that the initial melodic sentence is stated ("Rest my child and peace attend thee, All through the night") and then repeated. Then follows a contrasting melodic phrase in which the climax is attained ("Soft the drowsy hours are creeping"). The melodic line descends to lead into a final return of the opening phrase.

It is interesting to note that in tunes where the climax tone appears twice we are so conditioned that we feel the later appearance of the tone as the real climax. We refuse to accept a high tone as a climax if it arrives too soon, or at a weak point from a rhythmic point of view, but wait for the critical time as well as the climactic tone. Any reader may test this for himself by singing through the well-known patriotic air "Columbia, the Gem of the Ocean." This tune really lacks a strongly developed climax. The highest tone, moreover, appears twice, on the word "of" in the phrase "The home of the brave and the free" and later, on "when" in the final line "When borne by the red, white, and blue!" The first high note, however, is not felt as climactic; indeed, it is passed by without assuming any special importance. The second high tone does convey a certain sense of heightened tension because, though it is no higher than the other, it does come at the moment when previous experiences have taught us to expect the culminating moment of a melody.

A similar effect may be noted in the "Star-Spangled Banner." All patriotic Americans of limited vocal compass will recall the sudden silence or the brave attempt at the high tone which occurs on the words "the rocket's red glare." Yet this phrase, however trying to untrained vocal chords, makes the impression, not of climax, but of a lyric phrase which has just begun to unfold. When we reach the same tone on the words "land of the free," it impresses us as the point of maximum tension, an effect which is usually reinforced by the other means at the disposal of the conductor, an increase in loudness, an impressive "slowing down" and a more emphatic utterance. This excitement-generating factor which is so usual in recent music was probably, to a considerable extent, an outgrowth of opera where both the individual arias and the development of the libretto must lead to a culminating point to hold the attention of the audience. Some of the older melodies have little in the way of a constructed climax. It is not necessary to turn to certain Russian dance tunes (like the one used in Glinka's *"Kamariskaia"*) which consist largely of repetitions of a brief musical idea. In such a case any increase in intensity will be due to an increase in loudness, an accelerated tempo, to the cumulative effect of persistent repetition. A familiar melody like "The Blue Bells of Scotland" is an example of a melody which hardly displays any real climax. At the moment where the text is most poignant, "And it's oh! in my heart, how I wish him safe at home," the music simply repeats the opening phrase. What intensity is achieved in this phrase is due to text and manner of performance, not to the development of the melody. The earliest patterns of climax, then, were conditioned by physiological considerations rather than by a well-formulated artistic plan. The role of the consciously achieved climax becomes more prominent as we approach the present.

Melody, however, consists of more than a sequence of related tones, following a well-understood plan of sequence, and rising to and falling away from a point of climax. Tones in most melodies are so grouped, repeated, and varied that the recognition of the re-appearance of these groups or motives is an important element in melodic effect. Such a device has no exact counterpart in the other arts. If we compare it to a repeated design in a textile, we suggest a rigid repetition which is far from the free and varied treatment of a melodic motive. If we compare it to a verbal refrain in such forms as the ballade (for example Villon's poem with the recurring "Where are the snows of yesteryear?"), we compare the return of something fixed with something which can be varied in many ways without losing its identity. Perhaps only in a moving picture where visual patterns repeat themselves in time, sometimes the same, sometimes altered, could an analogy be found.

The origin of groups of tones which were remembered as a group and could therefore be repeated is a matter for speculation rather than scientific demonstration. Certainly a number of causes might induce the appearance of such a factor. In chanting the psalms to the ancient Gregorian melodies the musically characteristic formulas appear at the beginning, middle, and end. The remainder consisted merely of a recitation in monotone. Here we see in the use of a simple closing formula, repeated at the end of each section of the text, an early use of motive repetition. Yet it is possible to go back in primitive folksong to a still more primitive stage in which a melody is built up of the repetition of a simple group of tones, perhaps with some more or less random variation. Psychologically such a process is based on the fact that early peoples possessed a short attention and memory span and that there has been a historical evolution of the ability to remember and repeat tones.

Though such a practice may have developed because the simple repetition of a short group of tones was easier than more elaborate methods of melodic construction, such repetitions did lend unity to what might otherwise appear to be a random improvisation. But a unity gained by countless repetitions of a limited group of tones was a unity gained at the expense of what seems to be intolerable monotony.

The next stage in melodic development depended on the fact that simple repetition did indeed produce satiety, weariness. The element of variety may at first have entered in a purely accidental fashion. Instead of repeating his melodic motive exactly, the performer may have added or repeated a note or have made some other slight change. What may have happened at first as the result of chance produced a pleasing effect and was repeated by intention. Such an evolution would not only lead to the ornamentation and transformation of motives but also to a wider application of the idea of transforming melodies in the variation forms.

Another kind of melodic construction may have had its origin in a situation in which a brief phrase enunciated by a priest is answered by a response on the part of the worshippers. This might result in an alternation of two different musical figures. In some such way the second basic element in melody, the introduction of figures of contrast, may have entered our musical language.

These, then, are the basic elements in the formation of melody as we know it: the creation of a characteristic group of tones or a motive, the repetition and the variation of the motive, and finally the alternation of one motive with another of contrasting character, or (on a more extended scale) the interplay between a section unified by the use of one motive and a section dominated by another. An example may make the interaction of these factors clearer. The Russian folksong, "The Birch Tree," is not only familiar in its simple form, but also in the symphonic treatment accorded it in the finale of Tschaikowsky's "Fourth Symphony." This melody naturally divides into two halves. Each half may be further analyzed into two smaller and equal parts. But if we consider the first half of the melody, its subdivisions are not really different. The second is merely variant of the first. Moreover, each of the subdivisions, or smaller parts of the melody, ends in the same way. A diagram may show the way in which the tune is organized: A-Á-B-B. This is a very simple example of "binary" or two-part form.

A more usual plan for melodies of recent date is to follow the first part by a second and contrasting part and then to round it off in a satisfying fashion by repeating the first part once more, sometimes with some variation. This is the "ternary" or "three-part form" of the musician which might be represented by the formula A-B-A. Quite commonly A is repeated on its first appearance, but not when it recurs at the end: A-A-B-A. The familiar tune *"Au clair de la lune"* follows this plan as does the "Blue Bells of Scotland."

Most of our recent popular songs have followed this ternary or three-part plan with certain peculiarities which deserve mention in view of the domination of the radio channels and of the record business by popular music. In most instances the popular song begins with an introductory section for the piano. Then follows the first part of the song, the "verse," which usually narrates the story or presents the facts which explain the mood of the "chorus" which follows. The verse is frequently informal and conversational in style and less melodious than the chorus. Indeed, the chorus is likely to be played without the rest of the song since it sums up in melody the mood suggested by the verse. The chorus is regularly composed of three equal sections of which the first is repeated. The middle section forms a contrast. The last section is a return of the first. Critics have spoken of the tyranny and the monotony of this fixed plan, the "thirty-two measure chorus," since each part normally consists of eight time units or measures. If the custom of introducing brief improvised passages or "breaks" in popular music was, on the one hand, an opportunity for a soloist to display his virtuosity, it was, on the other, a partial escape from the monotonous symmetry of the form.

The use of characteristic tone-groups or motives thus stems from a long historical evolution. Man at an early stage of development could only conceive and repeat relatively short and simple groups of tones. What was at first a psychological necessity gradually became a means of artistic expression as he found ways of varying and transforming these note-groups and of alternating them with contrasting note-patterns. The music-lover is not consciously aware of these factors, but, as is so frequently the case, he is bewildered and annoyed when a tune is either too monotonous or too varied. The effect of monotony usually results from excessive repetition. "Love's Old Sweet Song" illustrates both the monotony caused by undue repetition and the fact that a tune may be sung with much satisfaction in spite of its defects. A mental review of its refrain will show that the rhythm of the opening reappears seven times before it is changed by the composer. From the point of view of the musician its contruction is over-obvious, repetitious, and lacking in inventiveness.

Undue repetitiousness is much more common in familiar melodies than too great a variety in melodic motives. Indeed, it is difficult to point out a tune which is generally known and at the same time so varied as to be unsatisfactory from the point of view of unity. The obvious deduction is that such tunes simply do not attain a wide circulation. It would be easy to find primitive or oriental tunes which strike a Western ear as too varied.

In general an attentive hearing of the music which has gained and retained a considerable measure of popularity would indicate that short motives rather persistently repeated are still the rule. The future evolution of music in these respects is inextricably connected with more general considerations. How long a melodic series can the members of our audiences remember? Are our composers to write for a limited audience composed of especially musical and especially prosperous listeners or for our whole people? Will our workers attain a sufficient measure of economic security and leisure to make a more general enjoyment of symphonic music and opera possible for them?

Our own familiar tone patterns are not the whole of music though they do constitute the whole of music for many of our people. The melodies which are most familiar to us are written in one of two scales, the major or the minor scale in its varied forms. Most readers will have some experience with scales either from their personal encounters with the piano keyboard or as an auditor of the efforts of others. The basic concept gained by such experiences is the fact that a scale is an ordered series of tones proceeding from the lowest to the highest tone and returning to the lowest again. It is in fact a synopsis or summary of the chief tones which a composer might use in composing a melody or a composition. But these scales of ours are not by any means the only scales in use today and they came into being only as the result of a long historical evolution.

Most listeners know some tunes which belong to systems foreign to our own, and recent composers have tended to borrow or imitate such tunes to color their own music. Many Negro spirituals are conceived in terms of the old gapped scale of five notes, which sometimes proceeded from tone to tone, sometimes moved by skip in the pattern formed by the black keys of the piano. Such a tune is "Lit'le David Play on yu' Harp." The Largo from Dvořák's "New World Symphony" (subsequently arranged as a song with the text "Goin' Home") and "Old Man River" from Jerome Kern's "Show Boat" both conform to this tradition though in these instances the scale was adopted by the composers to obtain a special effect. The American folksong "I Wonder as I Wander" which is so widely performed at the present day belongs to an older tone-system than our own. Such melodies and others like the oriental melodies dear to the Russian composers of the nineteenth century (Rimsky Korsakoff's "Scheherazade") remain on the periphery of the musical consciousness of the great audience. So indeed do the experimental scales of the modern composers. They form a sort of musical paprika, but music's main course is still served up largely in the major and minor scales.

The influence of instruments, and particularly of wind instruments, on early music must have been great. The human voice can (and usually does) slide from one vague pitch to another. A lyre or harp could be tuned in a variety of ways. A flute, by its very construction, was best adapted to produce

[272]

a particular series of tones. It could hardly appear unless the idea of a stable series of tones was developing and, once invented, it was a method of confirming and standardizing such a tone series.

Another simplification of the infinitely complex matter of evaluating the various tone systems is the result of the attempts of scholars of the period after Darwin to apply the Darwinian findings to other fields. In music this led to an attempt to regard all other tone systems as successive approaches to a perfection represented by our major and minor scales. Such an attempt must result in an over-simplification which nevertheless had an obvious appeal for those whose musical system was thus placed at the apex of the evolutionary process.

Such a philosophy overlooked the fact that a musical system is an expression, an expression which is completely clear only to those who have grown up with it and have completely absorbed its every implication. The difficulty of absorbing a tradition which is after all not very remote is shown by the efforts of European composers to assimilate our jazz idiom. Many French composers in the period following World War I wrote pieces which were directly inspired by our popular music. Many piquant and amusing pieces were the result of this interest; yet of the hybrids thus formed it would be difficult to find one which did more than reflect certain external mannerisms of jazz. In the same way an educated Persian or Chinese musician might regard our treatments of oriental folk melodies as we regard a tribal chieftain wearing a stovepipe hat. Few people possess one musical culture with any approach to completeness. Fewer still can claim a deep understanding of an alien system.

If we are to arrange musical systems in order on a scale of development, what criteria shall we employ? A Hindu musician or the church composers of medieval Europe possessed a greater variety of scales than the two which form the chief basis of our music. The rhythms which we most generally employ are primitive compared to those employed by skilled Arab musicians. What can be claimed for our system with all justice is that it has led to the development of harmony, while the Eastern systems have in general drawn their effects from melody and rhythm. This is not to say that the use of simultaneous sounds is confined to European music, but the interest and complexity of our harmony is perhaps the most significant factor in musical development since the early Middle Ages.

It is, in the final analysis, a vain effort to attempt to evaluate the music of remote and alien cultures without a more complete understanding than that which we have attained. Musical systems must be understood in terms of what they express and how they are suited to produce that expression. This is at once a more difficult and a more fruitful approach than a mere analysis of external factors.

Though the chief emphasis in this chapter has necessarily fallen on the music closest to us, some discussion of other scales seems pertinent since many of them underlie and lead to our major and minor scales. Others have been absorbed into our music. They furnish special colors to the composer and add variety and a suggestion of remote places or periods to his music.

As man became capable of a more careful analysis of his emotions, certain tone series, certain scales, were felt to be appropriate to certain emotions. We may speculate that tones and words may have been born together in the mind of some forgotten singer and that the music thus created may have been accepted thereafter as an expression of similar moods. However this may be, certain scales were from very early times employed for definite expressive effects. The accounts of early musicians who aroused martial ardor and extinguished it, who lulled their hearers to sleep or roused them to the wildest excitement by the use of the appropriate scale are a testimony to this belief. A little volume of psalm tunes in the church modes in settings by Tallis (c. 1505-1585) puts this belief in a series of very amusing explanatory statements. "The firste (Dorian) is meeke: devout to see." "The third (Phrygian) doth rage: and roughly brayth."

Such beliefs were stronger in the older cultures than in those of more recent date, though some traces linger in our feeling that the minor scale is sad, the major cheerful. Other scales convey suggestions of remoteness, of far lands and peoples, of that special charm which clings to the exotic and remote.

Thus the scale which may be obtained by playing the black keys of the piano (G flat A flat B flat D flat E flat G flat) carries a suggestion of Chinese, or perhaps Scottish music, to the average listener. It is a curious scale which, unlike our own major scale, has a gap between the third and fourth as well as between the fifth and sixth tones. This results, as a glance at a piano keyboard will show, in a group of three and another of two closely spaced tones separated from each other by a gap. Any of the notes of the scale may assume the role of final or closing tone. Many Chinese melodies are in this scale, though it is employed in Scotch, Negro, and American Indian music as well. Such a familiar tune as "Coming Thro the Rye" and the Chinese folksong "The Jasmine Flower" as well as Ravel's *"Laideronnette"* (from his "Mother Goose Suite"), Novak's *"Printemps"* (from his *"Exotiken"*), Casella's "Canon" (from his "11 Children's Pieces"), the Chopin "Etude" Op. 10, No. 5 (on the black keys), and the March from the "Song of the Nightingale" by Stravinsky derive their special effect from the use of this scale.

Piano keys separated by an intervening key produce sounds which have a relationship or interval which the musician calls a tone. In terms of the piano a half tone is produced by striking a key (either black or white) and the key nearest to it. In the pentatonic scale, for example, each note in the group of three closely spaced black notes is a tone from its neighbor since between each black key is an intervening white key. Occasionally an especially large step measuring three half tones is used. This interval is the "augmented second" of the musician. It is used in one form of our minor scale (the harmonic minor) and also in certain Gypsy and oriental scales. A particularly clear example is the Serbian marching tune used by Tschaikowsky in his "Marche Slav." (Here the interval appears between the second and third notes of the tune.) The florid passages in the "Hymn to the Sun" from Rimsky Korsakoff's "Golden Cockerel" owe much of their exotic effect to the presence of this interval.

The Gregorian modes constitute a scale system with a whole range of color possibilities. They have a more complete recorded history than any of the other remote scale systems. They were first formulated by the Greeks. They passed from the Graeco-Roman civilization to the Christian church which adapted them for its own purposes. The reader who may wish to experiment at the piano may gain an idea of their effect by playing eight-note scales using the white keys only. The scale on D was called the Dorian mode, that on E the Phrygian, that on F the Lydian, that on G the Mixolydian, and that on A the Aeolian mode. An examination will show that these scales are not alike in structure. The sequence of half and whole steps is different in each scale as can be seen at the piano keyboard. Ancient composers felt that the mood of each scale and its range of expression were different. Since our contact with these scales is slighter, we are likely to feel their effect as minor, with a certain added undertone of ancient gravity or melancholy.

Respighi has attempted to reflect the grave remoteness which these scales possess in his "Pines near a Catacomb" from his "Pines of Rome." Debussy, in a very different fashion, has evoked the magic of an ancient mode in his "Submerged Cathedral." Ravel has wedded one of these scales with the movement of a dance of former times in his "Pavane of the Sleeping Beauty" from his "Mother Goose Suite." Such works as Moussorgsky's *"Boris Godunoff"* and his Prelude to *"Khovantchina"* are conceived in the spirit of the ancient folksongs of Russia. Such diverse tunes as the ancient hymn "O Come O Come Emmanuel," the English folksong "The Keys of Canterbury," and the beautiful folk-hymn "Poor Wayfaring Stranger," all are conceived in terms of the same scale (in this case Aeolian).

The major and the minor scales developed from the old church modes. Over a considerable period singers tended to make the close or cadence of melodies where the final was approached from below by singing a half step even where the original interval was a whole step. The singer thus tended to reduce them all to half steps, the "ti do" of public school music. The white note scale beginning with D, for example, has C and D for the two highest tones. Since a black key (C sharp) separates C and D, these two tones are a whole tone apart. In a scale like this, it became customary to substitute C sharp for C. As a result of this change the various modes tended to lose their individual characteristics. After a period which mingled old and new scales in a hesitant fashion, the major and minor scales emerged and were arranged as a series built on every possible note. Not only was "ti" a half step from "do," but every major scale was constructed on the same pattern of whole and half steps. With this change disappeared most of the variety of color and the consequent variety of expressive possibilities possessed by the old modes. So far as the major scale has an individual character, it expresses joy, rejoicing, triumph. Since it is also the common vehicle for musical speech, it assumes the most varied aspects depending on the character of the melody, the harmonies, and the instrumental color. Compare for instance Handel's Funeral March from "Saul," the Finale of Beethoven's "Fifth Symphony," and the introduction to the first movement of Mozart's "Dissonance Quartet." These three movements are all in the key of C major, a funeral march, a joyous and epic hymn of triumph, a brooding reverie. Obviously a scale which is capable of such a variety of musical speech can hardly be said to have a very fixed character of its own.

[277]

We have said that all major scales have the same arrangement of whole and half steps. The pattern is whole step, whole step, half step, whole step, whole step, whole step, half step.

do	re	mi	fa	sol	la	ti	do
		half step				half step	
1	2	3	4	5	6	7	8

The adoption of this system involved, as we have said, a certain loss of expressive possibilities. It brought with it compensating gains. Composers found that a certain amount of color and drama could be achieved by so altering the notes of one scale that it became identical with another. The ear followed this process, and, once it had been achieved, demanded that the melody revert to and end in the original scale. Thus a tonal drama took shape involving a departure with heightened interest, followed by a return to the original scale. A specific example may make the process clearer. A composer may wish to make a "modulation" from the scale of C to the scale of G. If we compare these two scales, we can see that they differ only in respect to one note. The fourth note of the C scale is F. The seventh note of the G scale is F sharp. Our composer would therefore, write a part of his melody in the scale of C. Then, after avoiding the note F for a time, in order that the hearer might forget it to some extent, he would introduce the F sharp to make a cadence, let it move to G, and thus establish the new scale. Nevertheless, the ear still retains the memory of the original key sufficiently to realize that this new scale represents a departure which must be balanced by a return to the scale of C major.

The minor scale is commonly thought of as the melancholy counterpart of a major scale. It shares with the major the cadence of the half step between ti and do, but differs in the construction of the remainder of the scale. Our pattern now becomes (harmonic minor scale):

la	ti	do	re	mi	fa	si	la
	half step			half step		half step	
6	7	8	2	3	4	#5	6

This is not the only form of the minor scale, however, for it exists in several forms. Composers may also modulate from a minor to a major scale (or the reverse) in order to gain in contrast of color and mood.

All of the great composers of more recent times have derived many of their effects by utilizing the tones which exist between the whole steps of the melody or, more precisely, by dividing the whole steps into half steps. Such tones are called chromatic or color tones, and when this process is carried out systematically throughout the entire range of the scale, the result is a chromatic scale. Such notes are truly color tones and add to the intensity of the moods of the scale since they alter the less colorful movement of the whole step to the more intense half step, just as in early times the cadence was made more urgent and more intense by approaching the final tone from a half step below. In recent times composers have claimed this scale of half steps as a real basis for composition, thus forming the so-called twelve-tone system.

A strange scale which is associated with French impressionist composers of the late nineteenth and early twentieth centuries is the whole tone scale. It differs from most of the scales discussed in this chapter because all the adjacent tones are equidistant. Pianists may play the series C-D-E-F#G#-A#-C to gain an idea of its special character. Debussy imparted a characteristic coloring to certain passages by the use of this scale. In one instance ("Veils" from the "Preludes, Book I") he creates a piece within the limited color range it affords. It should, however, be remembered that he also drew novel effects from the old church modes and from other sources. "Whole tone scale" does not by any means explain Debussy though it is the basis for certain of his characteristic passages.

[279]

CHAPTER XIV

THE LOGIC AND THE COLOR OF HARMONY

THE tones used in music or stated in the scale have two modes of employment. Stated successively in time they constitute what we know as melody. Sounded simultaneously they form harmony. The simplest example to illustrate the difference between these two elements might be found in the music the Mexican makes when he sings to the plucked chords of his guitar, or the ballads sung by the Southern mountaineer to the accompaniment of banjo or dulcimer. In both examples the tones successively produced by the voice are reinforced by groups of tones from the same scale which are played on the accompanying instrument.

The idea that a melody must have an accompaniment of this kind has become part of our conception of what music is. The appearance of a single performer on the concert stage to play Stravinsky's "Pieces for clarinet solo" was received by the audience with incredulity and amusement. The lonely flute of a shepherd on some far-away hillside, the song of the plowboy are remote from our experience. When we transfer folk melodies to our concert halls, we provide them with an accompaniment for piano.

We regard the harmonization or accompaniment of melodies as obligatory. Our melodies develop in conformity with habitual chord-successions in the accompaniment. They develop not merely as melodies but also as expressions of these underlying chord-successions. Thus harmony and melody mutually reinforce and intensify each other.

This fact is even more obvious in certain modern systems. Scriabine has built entire compositions from a special group of tones, the so-called "mystic chord." From the notes of this chord both the themes of the composition and the accompaniment are derived. In fact, in a real sense, the selected tones are both his theme and his harmony.

The process is in fact not essentially different from the practice of classic composers who wrote so many melodies which evolve from simultaneously conceived chord successions. It is, however, more deliberate, more contrived. With Scriabine, too, the "mystic chord" was to a considerable degree a personal and arbitrary selection of tones which was designed to produce new harmonic effects. With the classic composers, however, the chord movements which guided the progress of their melodies were, for the most part, traditional and might be found both in the works of their contemporaries and their predecessors.

One of the primary facts about a melody, as has been demonstrated, is its return to a central tone or tonic. The desire to emphasize this tone appears at a very early time in a device which was also a step towards the development of harmony. This device, which was known as a drone, was produced by sounding the tonic continuously against the melody. In many instances both the tonic or first scale tone and the dominant or fifth tone were sounded.

We generally think of this as an instrumental effect. Yet if we read a medieval treatise (*"Musica Enchiriadis"*) which discusses the various methods of accompanying a vocal melody, we find that one of the examples corresponds exactly to our idea of the drone. One voice sustains a single tone. The other begins with this tone, and, after singing the varied tones of the melody, ends, as it began, with the drone note or tonic.

If, however, we turn to the realm of instrumental music, we are impressed with the number and the variety of the instruments which were constructed with drones. There are the Greek double-pipe, the Indian double-oboe, familiar as a snake-charmer's instrument, the *lira da braccio,* which is represented in paintings of the Italian Renaissance, the bagpipe, the *organistrum,* that remote ancestor of the hurdy-gurdy. The list might easily be extended.

THE LOGIC AND COLOR OF HARMONY

The means for attaining a sustained tone varied. The double pipes were often so contrived that the performer fingered and produced various tones from one pipe while the other was adjusted to produce only one note. The bagpipe was somewhat more complicated. We have all noticed the pipes which protrude from the bag of the instrument. Only one of these is fingered. This is the "chanter" and on this the melody is performed. The other pipes contain reeds like those of the "chanter," but their lengths are calculated to produce the first and the fifth notes of the scale. Certain highly developed bagpipes even possess the possibility of a somewhat more elaborate accompaniment to which we shall refer later in the chapter.

The *lira da braccio* was a stringed instrument played with a bow and employed chiefly to accompany the voice. One of its peculiarities was that the bridge over which the strings passed was flat so that they sounded together. There was also (at least in certain examples) one string which did not pass over the fingerboard but was fastened to and held tense by a peg at the side of the diamond-shaped peg-box. This string was the drone, and its position shows that it could not be fingered but produced only the tone to which it was tuned. It could be touched with the bow or perhaps plucked with the left thumb.

It is easy to see the importance of these practices in developing the feeling for a tonal center.

The habit of sustaining a tone throughout a composition has passed into music as an expressive device, one that conveys a pastoral flavor, the atmosphere of the countryside, the spirit of rustic merriment. Examples of the pastoral drone-bass are numerous from the keyboard music at the time of Queen Elizabeth to the compositions and arrangements of Bela Bartok. No longer necessary to remind us of a tonal center, it is used to impart a touch of bucolic wistfulness to compositions and to folksong arrangements.

If we except the miracle of the scale, nothing seems so

[283]

utterly impossible of attainment through a long historic evolution as the web of combined sounds woven by the musician. Even the fabulous colors and the fantastic plumage of a bird of paradise seem more accountable as a product of gradual evolution. Their plumage at least has a value in seeking a mate and in insuring the survival of their kind. The idea of evolving pleasing combinations of tones and of employing them in accordance with their essential nature and in terms of a given cultural tradition seems so far removed from any purely practical end, so difficult of explanation, that the student is baffled in seeking a reason for its development. It is obvious that the magic chant, the hymn to the gods seemed vital to man. But why did he need harmony?

The historical record is fragmentary, and the few accounts we have of early singing in harmony are enigmatic and inconclusive. For that period in the early Middle Ages when undoubtedly the feeling for tone combinations was evolving we have almost no sources. We can only guess at a period of hearty experimentation and joyous improvisation which undoubtedly preceded the first written monuments.

Something may be learned if we study the group singing of primitives. To go back to this realm of music we must leave our exactly regulated choral song behind. We must forget the completely fixed character of our music where even a small deviation from the rhythms or the pitch pattern prescribed by the composer is regarded as a mistake. We are proud of our self-abnegation. We are carrying out the intentions of the composer. We even bewail the fact that the finest interpretative shadings still cannot be adequately fixed by our notation.

If one listens attentively to a group of young people singing popular songs together one gains other ideas about group singing. Some youths sing somewhat higher and some lower. Others find the mere singing of the melody too uninteresting. They add improvised melodies, each more or less without reference to the others. At the end of a stanza the impatient ones plunge into the next repetition of the tune while the more placid vocalists are still holding the last tone of the melody. Here we have a process which is not without a relationship with primitive music. In 'both we gain hints as to the paths by which harmony was achieved.

To sing with others in such a way as to obtain an effect of a given kind required a group consciousness, a control over the individual voice, the knowledge of a musical tradition, and the ability to cooperate. It is not difficult to see that harmony of a sort is generated when one of several voices fails to find his tone, but follows the tune in a comfortable register at a somewhat lower or higher pitch. Similar practices actually did crystallize during the Middle Ages and were conducted according to quite carefully formulated rules.

Overlapping was most likely to appear in antiphonal singing where one group answered another. Inevitably a moment would occur when one chorus began its response before the other had quite finished, thus producing an impromptu harmony for a brief period. If we increase this overlapping and employ it consciously as an effect we have something which utilizes the principle of the round. No doubt most readers of this chapter have taken part in performances of "Three Blind Mice" or *"Frère Jacques."* They will recall that in such compositions one voice sings the opening of the tune and, as the first voice continues, the second voice enters singing the same melody. It is not difficult to imagine that here, as in so many other cases, the accident of performance may, in the course of a long historic development, have crystallized into an artistic form.

Percival Kirby has given a most interesting account of a Bantu song which shows how a kind of harmony could arise from ceremonial rather than purely musical considerations. The men of the tribe praise their chief in song. From time to time the women urge the men to continue their efforts by singing to a somewhat similar melody the words: "O sing, O company!" Here an impromptu harmony arises from the fact that men and women are expressing two different though related ideas at the same time.

Evidently the impulse to sing in harmony was felt early in England and perhaps elsewhere in Europe. A passage from Giraldus Cambrensis (end of the 12th century) speaks of the Northumbrians who, though uninstructed, sang in two parts. Not only adults but children were skilled in this manner of performance. An obscure and much disputed passage describes the manner in which Welsh singers performed in harmony. Each singer performed an independent part "uniting these diversities under the soft sweetness of B flat." No attempt will be made to clarify the obscurities of this passage. The one fact which interests us here is the presence of a tradition of improvised part-singing in Wales during the twelfth century.

The ultimate fixing of improvised part-singing by writing it down involved a great struggle for precision, clarity, exact synchronization of the various parts. Even now the difficulties of writing down an improvised performance exactly as it happened are formidable. All that musicians could manage for a number of centuries was to get a rather vague outline or sketch of the music on the paper. The very fact of writing the tones down on paper, however, provided a standard from which deviations could be detected and corrected. We may be sure that many early singers must have resisted such an encroachment on their prerogatives.

Little by little, however, the margin of interpretative freedom diminished as the chapelmaster appeared and as the increased adequacy of notation made it possible to fix finer details of performance. First, random improvisation or accidental harmony, then improvisation within the bounds of a traditional style. The singers gathered around a huge volume of church songs and, while some sang the traditional melody, the others added parts which, to be sure, were improvised, but improvised in accordance with fairly well regulated principles.

At length all the parts were written down. The singers, however, retained and on occasion perhaps abused the right of extemporaneously ornamenting and elaborating the written tones. This was opposed by composer and conductor, but it passed from the madrigal singers of the Renaissance to the opera singer. As late as Rossini the issue was a live one. That composer spoke with indignation of a singer who had taken more liberties than was usual with his melodies. "I am fully aware that arias should be embellished. That's what they are for. But not to leave a note of them . . . that is too much!" Ultimately the victory over improvisation was complete, or nearly complete, in the field of vocal music.

The instrumentalist, too, has found that his freedom to play according to the dictates of his own fancy has been gradually restricted. The earliest instrumental music was improvised. Lute players, for example, were expected to be able to improvise extemporaneous accompaniments to songs. Many of them, no doubt, were capable of inventing little preludes of the kind that we find in the first printed volumes of lute music.

English string players of the seventeenth century made a specialty of improvising passages over a theme in the bass which was repeated again and again. This was the art of playing divisions over a ground. The passages improvised were "divisions" in the sense that the long notes of the bass theme or "ground" were divided into notes of smaller and smaller value. Thus, there was a feeling of increased motion and climax as the improvisation approached its close. When we reach the period of the great violinists of the seventeenth and early eighteenth centuries, we may consider that the simple melodies of the slow movements which they played were to be performed exactly as they appear in the engraved copies. When, however, by some curious chance a violinist wrote down such a movement as he actually performed it, we see how great a difference there might be between the simple sustained melody as it appears in the published copy and the improvised embellishments which the virtuoso violinist habitually added. The solo instrumentalist, like the opera singer, frequently regarded the notes written by the composer as a basis for improvisation rather than as a text which must be literally respected.

The art of extemporizing a composition on a well-known theme or one supplied by someone in the audience was a regular resource of the performers of the past. The Lutheran organist was expected to be able to extemporize a fugue on a given subject. Indeed, this was a usual feature of the competitive tests by which a candidate for a vacant post was chosen. Mozart frequently improvised both in an intimate circle and in public concerts. Beethoven in his younger days was famous as a fiery and impassioned extemporaneous player. Several of his published works give hints as to the nature of many other performances which were never written down, and hence are lost to us.

Audiences demanded that Mendelssohn improvise for them, but we can see from his letters that he was doubtful of the value of the practice. He speaks of an organ improvisation as the only one which he would like to have committed to paper. On another occasion he regrets that he was forced to improvise on the piano at a public concert. "When I appeared to extemporize, I was again enthusiastically received. The King had given me the theme of '*Non più andrai*,' on which I was to *improviser*. I have seldom felt so like a fool as when I took my place at the piano, to present to the public the fruits of my inspiration; but the audience were quite contented, and there was no end of their applause . . . but I was annoyed, for I was far from being satisfied with myself, and I am resolved never again to extemporize in public, — it is both an abuse and an absurdity."

The scope of this ancient art was finally reduced to the brilliant display passage in the concerto which we call the "cadenza." From the time that the classic concerto appears with the predecessors of Haydn and Mozart, it had been usual to provide opportunities for the soloist to display both his technical brilliance and his musical imagination. Not many composers went as far as Handel who, in one of his organ concertos, omitted the slow movement altogether, merely noting on the score *"Organo ad libitum."* After all, Handel was the soloist as well as the composer. Why then should he trouble to note down a movement when he could rely on the inspiration of the moment?

In the classic concerto the most elaborate cadenza was normally placed before the end of the first movement. The orchestra played a loud chord and then remained silent as the soloist improvised with as much brilliance and ingenuity as he could summon on the themes of the movement. He ended on a trill which led to a closing passage for orchestra.

In the course of time soloists who were also composers were tempted to write down cadenzas which were particularly effective. Thus we have cadenzas composed by Mozart for his own works as well as two which Beethoven composed for the D minor Mozart piano concerto (Köchel 466). Finally the composer, anxious to insure the best treatment of his own themes, wrote down his own cadenzas. In such works as the Schumann "Piano Concerto," the Grieg "Piano Concerto," the Brahms piano concertos, the cadenzas were completely written out by the composer. The soloist has only to study the score and to perform it exactly as it is written.

Thus the last trace of improvisation vanishes from the concert hall,—vanishes from the concert hall, but not from the world of music. In honky-tonks and bars American players tried their hands at playing our popular tunes by ear with a great amount of freedom in a style which was quite different from that cultivated by players with a conventional education. They developed a repertory of special devices, rhythmic tricks, improvised countermelodies, a moment of free fantasy which was the "break" before the background instruments resumed their steady rhythm. In the beginning most of them were underprivileged players who had picked up their skills and their performing ability in the school of hard knocks. They were unhampered by the tradition of art music because they had no knowledge of it. Later, conventionally trained musicians entered a field which had become lucrative. As the commercial rewards increased, however, the element of improvisation tended to decrease here as it had previously diminished in classic music, but at a much more rapid rate. At the present day dilettantes of "swing" tend to distinguish between the commercial bands which play the notes written in their parts and the small "chamber" swing groups which improvise in a more spontaneous idiom.

The element of improvisation in both vocal and instrumental music was of incalculable importance in discovering, repeating, and fixing effective tone combinations. No doubt the chord first emerged as a happy discovery, as the result of the struggle of two voices to find notes which would go well with a melody tone. As the organization of music became more complicated, as effects were more precisely calculated, the creative role of the individual performer diminished progressively, and finally improvisation vanished from concert and opera altogether. Such enterprising individualists as the oboe player encountered by Berlioz in Dresden would be unthinkable in a modern orchestra. This performer had a habit of adding little trills and embellishments to his part. When he was reprimanded for these additions at the rehearsal, he submitted without protest. At the concert performance, however, he calmly proceeded to ornament his part in his usual fashion to the chagrin of the furious but completely helpless conductor.

The music theorist examined and clarified the musical procedures which had been embodied in music in terms of individual instinct and group tradition. The composer was separated from the performer. He set himself the task, not only of writing down beautiful melodies and harmonies, but of working out and specifying the details of performance in the most careful fashion. The performer has become less a composer and more the sensitive and accurate interpreter.

In some such fashion, by practice and by instinct, musicians laid the foundations of the styles which succeeding composers have so wonderfully developed. They evolved a mode of combining and of using tones which almost seem to have an independent life of their own independent of human creators. Harmony has acquired subtle emotional implications which reinforce and color the melodies. It is, in addition, an important and indeed indispensable factor in constructing compositions, and particularly compositions on a large scale. It is to a consideration of harmony and its use as a color factor and a constructive factor that we now turn.

The harmonies employed by composers from the sixteenth century to the period of Wagner and Brahms at the end of the nineteenth century were, broadly considered, in one line of development. In this period the basic harmonies each consisted of three tones selected from the scale employed. Any tone might be chosen as a foundation tone for such a chord. (In musician's language the foundation tone is called the "root.") The other two tones were selected by taking alternate tones above the root. Thus, if the scale contained the series C-D-E-F-G-A-B-C, and C were the root, D would be rejected, E selected, F rejected, and G selected. The chord would then be C-E-G.

Chords constructed in this fashion had several functions. The simplest purpose of the chord was to underly and to reinforce the melody and to make its harmonic implications clear. In a broad sense many melodies do express a harmony since they either move from one chord tone to another or stress the various tones of the chord. The actual presence of the harmony emphasizes this fact. Thus, if the right hand of a pianist plays successively C-G-E-G, the left hand might sum up the total effect of these tones by playing C-E-G simultaneously as a chord.

Harmony also increases the effect of finality at the end

of a part or the end of a composition as a whole. A succession of chords or harmonies which produces the impression that a piece has ended or that a portion of a piece has been completed is called a "cadence." Cadences are of two kinds. One type makes us feel that we have reached a point of repose. This is a full cadence. The other marks the end of a section, but, at the same time, makes us anticipate that more music must follow since the cadence ends on some other chord than the rest-chord or "tonic." This is the semi-cadence of the musician.

This distinction is a very ancient one. It first appears at a time when poetry and music were more intimately related than at present. In some early compositions we find that where the sense of a line of poetry is left incomplete, the music ends on another note than the key note. When the sense of a line is complete, the music, too, ends on the keynote and thus agrees exactly with the poetic line-structure.

Even where the musician uses a full cadence to close a composition, he can make the ending more or less decisive by varying the note on which the melody ends. If we assume that the rest-chord of a composition is the chord C-E-G which we have already constructed, the composer may allow the melody to end with any one of these tones. If a piece is of a decided and positive character, the choice is likely to fall on C since that is the key note and will make the strongest ending. Beethoven's "The Glory of God in Nature" with its tremendous affirmation of divine greatness ends in this way. If on the other hand a composer wishes an effect of poetic revery, of questioning, of hesitation or uncertainty, he may choose to end with the tone E. This tone belongs to the rest-chord and thus conveys an impression of finality, but, since it is not the key note, the impression is less emphatic than that produced by C. A familiar example of a piano composition which uses an ending of this kind is Schumann's *"Warum?"* or "Why?" Here the effect of an unanswered question is admirably expressed. In all such cases, however, it is well to remember that the cadence is only one element in an effect in which the movement of the composition, its shadings of loud or soft, and its rhythm, all play important parts.

In the type of harmony which evolved in the course of the sixteenth and seventeenth centuries and which dominated Western music to the period of Wagner and Brahms in the nineteenth century, two tone groups or chords were of special importance. These were the chords built on the first and fifth notes of the scale. As we have already seen, the chord on the first tone of the scale serves as a point of repose. A composition normally begins with this chord and, when the composer is through with his musical adventures, he ends with the chord with which he began. The chord on the fifth note of the scale (it would consist of the notes G-B-D in the scale of C) has quite a different character. It is active, restless, dynamic.

If we imagine a brief melody which pauses at its mid-point, as many recent melodies do, we can see how appropriate this active harmony would be for the semi-cadence at the half-way point of the melody. We may pause on this harmony, which we may now give its usual name of "dominant," and thus punctuate the melody without any danger that our listeners will feel that the melody has ended. On the other hand, when the melody does reach its conclusion, our active dominant chord followed by the tonic harmony will bring it to a satisfactory close.

Another function of harmony, and more particularly of the harmony of the romantic and modern periods, is to lend an appropriate richness and (in a figurative sense) "color" to the melodies of a composer. One might indeed say that harmony has two different functions. One is to express in simultaneous sounds what the melody expresses in successive sounds. Such a harmony adds no really new factor. It simply reinforces and makes clearer and more intense the structure of the melody. More recent composers, however, tend to write accompaniments which go beyond a simple reflection of the melody.

In such treatments the harmony adds to the emotional effect of the melody which appears to be more varied, more melancholy, more passionate. It goes beyond the simpler task of merely accompanying the melody and becomes an element in musical expression. Listeners who praise the beauty of Tschaikowsky's melodies would be surprised to find how much of the expressive quality of his music stems rather from his rich and varied harmonies. In a Mozart sonata many passages will be simple accompaniment of a kind which merely supports the important tones of the melody. If we then think of the relative importance of the harmony in a composition by Tschaikowsky or César Franck, we can see that here the expressive role of the harmony is more prominent. Yet Mozart was far in advance of most of his contemporaries in his use of varied and expressive harmonies.

Certain chorale preludes of Bach show admirably how varied an expression can be derived from harmony. These compositions were elaborations for organ based on the familiar chorale tunes which were sung in the Lutheran churches of his day. Frequently the chorale melody floats above a complicated accompaniment. In some of Bach's treatments, however, the melody is repeated. This repetition is not a literal one, but is so varied harmonically as to correspond with the content of the successive stanzas of the chorale text. It is easy to see that the difference in effect is due to the harmony and to the varied interweaving of parts in the accompaniment since the melody is, of course, the same for each repetition.

Bach's boldness of harmony was indeed already evident in his arrangements of chorale tunes for four voices. In these, the severe and traditional melodies adopted by the Lutheran church were so harmonized as to assume a new and colorful aspect, but one which evidently was not a little disturbing to the good church-goers of the period who were sometimes hard put to it to find the tune when Bach was at the organ.

Harmony was also employed as an important element in musical form. To understand this function of harmony, we must first consider briefly what is understood by "key" or "tonality" and by the term "modulation." We have already seen that composing a melody and furnishing it with an accompaniment presupposes the selection of a certain group of tones. In our major and minor scales (which still are the most usual tone-selections for our culture and period) the tones are not static. As has been pointed out, they start from a point of repose, develop as a more or less extended tone-series or melody, and then finally close with another rest tone.

Such a scheme sufficed for short and simple melodies. For extended compositions something more dynamic and dramatic was needed. In these large compositions, such as the rondo and the sonata, more than one theme is presented. If all the themes of a composition were to be stated in the same scale, monotony would result. A second theme should appear with a certain drama like the entry of the heroine in a play.

One means which the musician gradually evolved in response to this need for expressing increasing and decreasing tension was modulation. Modulation is the passage from one scale or related group of tones to another. It is accomplished by modifying tones of the first scale till they correspond in pitch and function with those of the second. Our feeling for the original key was made definite by the movement of the tones of the scale towards its key center or tonic, by the sequence of chords which we have called the cadence. In a similar fashion the new key feeling is confirmed by its appropriate cadence, especially if the composer expects to utilize this scale for a passage of some length. If, on the other hand, the composer wishes to create an atmosphere of restless movement, he may pass from his newly attained key to another and still another without confirming any of them with a strong cadence.

In terms of the practice of the classic composers the statement of a theme is made within the limits of a scale or, at any rate, within a group of scales which have many notes in common. The harmonies, highly colored though they may be, are in relative repose. The passage from one theme to another, on the other hand, is active, dynamic, and this feeling is generated by a series of modulations, culminating with a harmony which awakes anticipation of the scale in which the new theme is to appear. Transitional passages seem to be restless because they use notes which suggest one scale, then tones borrowed from another.

Composers, and particularly the earlier classic composers, felt the need of a third type of passage which affirms the end of a section of a composition or the end of the entire work. We have already noted the fact that a theme is largely stated in terms of the tones of a single scale. This is, of course, true in a broad rather than in a narrow sense. It does not prevent the composer from coloring his harmony with tones borrowed from other scales nor does it preclude short transitions to other keys, provided that they are brief and do not really disturb our fundamental feeling for the home key.

At the end of a composition, or, in more extended compositions, at the end of each major division or part, a composer may wish to assure his audience that he is approaching an important cadence. This obviously demands an even closer adherence to the chief tones of the scale employed than the statement of a theme. The early classic composers of the time of Haydn and Mozart wrote passages of this kind which are little more than the repetition of a closing formula or cadence. This is the simplest way of conveying a sense of the approach of the end of a composition, and this is the means which they habitually employ. The musician uses the term "codetta" or "closing section" for passages of this kind. With later composers the treatment of such sections was much freer, but its function remained the same.

We have established three broad structural uses for harmony: harmonies within a single key for the statement of a theme, harmonies in movement from one key to another for passages of transition, and harmonies of finality, cadence repetitions, to bring a composition to a rounded close. The listener does not need to know how to analyze such passages in detail to understand their function. He must simply be conscious of the quality or mood of a passage as in equilibrium, active, or final.

The most vital key relationship is that between the scale in which a composition is written and the scale which may be built on the fifth note of that scale. Readers who have some knowledge of the piano may imagine that the composition is in the scale of C. In this case the related scale would begin on G. C is a white-note scale. The scale of G contains one black key, F sharp. Readers whose education has not included a study of the piano may disregard the example.

What is important, however, is that the transition or modulation from any scale or key to a second key in this relationship gives a feeling of increased activity, of heightened tension. Conversely, a transition from this "dominant" key back to the home key carries with it the impression of an accomplished return, of decreased tension.

A dance by Bach, a gavotte or bourrée, is divided into two sections. In the first part the composer makes a transition from the home scale to that of the dominant. This generates a feeling of activity and movement, and, though the section closes with a full cadence in the dominant scale, it does not convey a real feeling of finality since we are conscious that the closing formula is not the one appropriate to the home key.

The second section of the composition may employ tones characteristic of various scales, but its main line of progress will be from the scale of the dominant to that of the tonic.

We are conscious of a return to the key in which the composition began, a completion of the tonal cycle. Before the end is reached, we already have a premonition of the approach of the final closing formula. Finally the cadence does appear to complete the piece and release the psychic tension generated by this miniature tonal drama.

This tendency of a composition to move away from and then to return to its tonal center might be compared to a rubber band fixed at one end. If we stretch the band by pulling at the free end, it tends to regain its original length. The greater the extension, the stronger is the tendency to retract. It we stretch the rubber band with undue vigor it snaps. Similarly, the auditor who forgets the tonal center of a composition has no feeling of suspense or tension because he has lost his point of reference, and hence cannot judge the extent of the departure. This may be due either to a poor memory or an insufficent acquaintance with the piece. The composer may also have introduced a transition which is so abrupt as to cause the auditor to "lose his way," to forget the scale or key of the composition.

It should be emphasized again that to the auditor this transition from scale to scale is neither a matter of knowledge nor of analysis. The composer, the practical musician, both need a clear and detailed knowledge of the manner in which effects of modulation are produced. For the auditor, however, modulation is a matter of feeling based on musical experience. Broadly speaking, all music from Bach to Brahms follows a single path from the tonic key to the dominant, then back to the tonic once more. Once the broad pattern has become familiar through the hearing of pieces organized in this manner, the hearer learns to anticipate the familiar moves. Deviations from the norm are felt to be strange or even wrong.

This discussion of the role played by scales, scale contrast, and modulation, useless unless given life by actual listening to music, may at least convey some idea of the complexity and subtlety of a factor of which the average listener is barely conscious. It is a means which has added enormously to the emotional expressiveness of music. It has outlined and clarified the structure of compositions even for many listeners who responded to its effects without being conscious of their nature. Perhaps the mere realization that such a system of equilibriums and tensions does exist may justify this discussion of the most elusive factor in music.

So far we have considered the use of harmony from the point of view of the composer of instrumental music. The attitude of the operatic composer towards harmony is likely to be strikingly different. The opera, indeed, was the great laboratory in which the expressive power of harmony was developed. Many early operatic scenes were no more than a series of neatly constructed solos and duets. Yet even here the musician was challenged to discover harmonies which could suggest an enchantress deserted by her lover, a general urging his armies on to victory, a young girl in love for the first time. Always the stage picture, the development of the dramatic moment, the mood of the text were a spur and an incentive for the musician.

The earliest Florentine music dramas exhale a sort of pastoral poetry in spite of their stiffness, their stylistic poverty, and their self-imposed limitation of musical means. In the work of Monteverdi, however, the passionate expression of human deprivation and sorrow reaches a poignancy which has not since been surpassed. Once the lament had been discovered, it was echoed by many other composers till it hardened into a convention. Composers represented the voices of condemned spirits by monotonous uninflected tones. Martial airs borrowed the iterations and the simple harmonies of military music. Always grief was more richly and profoundly expressed than the brighter emotions. Perhaps this was so because the minor scale possessed richer and more varied resources.

At a later period the resources and possibilities of harmony and more particularly of modulation were so varied that it is hardly possible to do more here than enumerate some of the many ways in which they served to color and heighten a stage situation. If we turn to one simple factor, for example the light effects which accompany the stage scenes, it is easy to show that modulation often is an important factor in the impression of brilliance or gloom which the auditor receives.

In the third scene of Wagner's "Valkyrie" we find Siegmund weaponless in the house of his enemy Hunding. Siegmund knows that Hunding will slay him in the morning if he fails to find a weapon with which he may defend himself, and he calls on his father, Wälse, who had promised him a sword in his hour of greatest need. At this moment the fire, which had been smouldering dully on the hearth, breaks into flame. As the light increases, Siegmund sees the glitter of a sword blade thrust deep into the trunk of the great ash tree about which Hunding's dwelling was built. As the light increases, three accompanying and reinforcing effects occur in the orchestra. The instruments move from the lower register into a higher and more brilliant range, the music shifts from a minor scale to the major, and the composer modulates to successively higher keys. (The scene, which begins in A minor, moves on to climactic statements of the sword motive in C major and G major.) The flame subsides; the sword blade fades into darkness once more. As the light grows dimmer the instruments sink once more to the lower register, and the scene ends as it began in a sombre mood. No clearer example could be chosen to show how the orchestral score reinforces an effect of light.

Wagnerites among the readers of this volume may also recall the scene at the bottom of the Rhine ("Rhinegold," Scene I) in which the treasure guarded by the Rhine Maidens begins to glow, as they sing its praises and Alberich looks on with wonder and greed. In this scene, as in the episode from "The Valkyrie," various means are employed, but among them are those we have already noted: movement to a high register, a shift from a minor to a major scale, and modulation to a higher key.

Frequently a composer will introduce a dramatic change of key accompanying the appearance of a supernatural character on the stage. Most modulations in instrumental compositions connect keys which possess many notes in common. What is desired is a smooth transition from one scale to another. A sudden and startling stage apparition, however, can best be interpreted musically by a shocking or highly dissonant chord or by a transition so abrupt as to startle us. The sense of discontinuity, abruptness, of shock produced by such a transition is a psychological equivalent of the feeling of fright and unreality which the spectator of a satanic apparition might be supposed to experience.

Mephistopheles has been a frequent performer on the operatic stage. In Gounod's "Faust," for example, the aged philosopher sits in his study while outside he can hear the joyous voices of youths and maidens. In despair he calls on Mephistopheles. "Appear Satan!" Gounod, who composed the preceding passage in the key of C, passes abruptly to a fortissimo chord built on B. If we adopt the method of calculating the relationship of scales by counting the tones which they have in common, we find that of seven only two belong to both scales. This is a simple way of indicating the very remote relationship between the two scales. The composer has made the transition more emphatic by indicating a gradual crescendo which rises to a sudden climax as the remote chord is reached.

The same subject had been treated at a somewhat earlier period by Hector Berlioz in his dramatic cantata "The Damnation of Faust." Here, too, the advent of Mephistopheles is characterized by abruptness of rhythm, by a sudden increase of loudness, and by harmonies chosen because they are at variance with the preceding tone-impressions.

It would be easy to extend the list of ominous and supernatural operatic visitants, but here, too, we would find a frequent similarity of means with, of course, infinite variety in the manner in which the general principle is applied.

These two specific situations may be sufficient to emphasize the manner in which harmony reinforces and lends life to the stage action in opera. We have already noted that even in instrumental compositions the color effects of harmony play an important role, especially in more recent music. In opera, the nature of the form serves as an incentive and a direct stimulus to the composer who is required to play his part in heightening dramatic situations and reinforcing scenic effects. Moreover, this use of harmony, though it developed through the practices of the operatic composer, has in its turn reacted on instrumental music. This is most evident in the symphonic poem which combines picturesque and descriptive elements with purely musical developments. The same influence may also be traced in music which has no overt programmatic intent. The growth in subtlety, variety, and psychological suggestiveness of modern harmony is perhaps the most remarkable fact in the development of romantic and modern music. To those who may feel that the first place should be conceded to melody one may answer that modern melody itself is generated by and conditioned by the harmonies which the composer has conceived.

CHAPTER XV

THE CONSTRUCTIVE ELEMENT IN MUSIC

THE musician who writes music of considerable duration faces problems of great difficulty. The reduction of the formless world of sound, shifting and intangible, to the magnificent and ordered sequence of the symphony must rank as one of the most remarkable achievements of the human mind. The effects of a musical composition are due to pleasure in recognizing melodic returns and recurrences. They depend on the basic sensations of repose and activity produced by a succession of harmonies. They depend, but perhaps in a more tenuous fashion, on our feeling for balance, our pleasure when one melodic sentence answers another in an effective fashion, or, on a larger scale, when larger sections are placed in a satisfactory relationship.

Broadly regarded, the patterns used by the musician are simple though they are subject to a tremendous amount of elaboration and variation. An audience listens with satisfaction to music of a given pattern. If the composer is skilful, he will have introduced some element of contrast before it becomes weary, at a point when it is ready to welcome a change of musical mood. After such a diversion the audience receives with renewed pleasure a recurrence of the music which was first heard. Two simple and basic principles are involved here. Pleasure in a given musical pattern is of limited duration. Once that limit is approached, the composer can only sustain interest by the introduction of music of a somewhat different character. However, a continual shift to new material tends to convey a feeling of vagueness, of a lack of coherence. The composer gratifies the listener's pleasure in the recognition of familiar material by returning at intervals to themes which have been previously heard. Musical form depends on the proper balance between familiar material, which will include the composer's main themes, and material of lesser importance which is introduced for the sake of variety and contrast. It is clear from what has already been said that musical compositions of considerable length are not continuous in texture. They tend rather to be organized in parts, and these parts are punctuated by cadences. By musical form a musician means the arrangement, the balance, and the interrelationships of the parts or sections of a piece. A part is closely related to another if it is based on the same melody or a transformation or alteration of a melodic fragment derived from the melody. Such sections represent the element of sameness, reiteration, unity. Sections may also be distinguished by their lack of melodic relationship, by contrast, difference of style, variety instead of unity.

The "minuet" shows the principle at work in a composition of very slight duration. The minuet usually possesses a considerable internal similarity of style. It is followed by an independent composition, the "trio." The trio, though it also possesses internal unity, is planned as a contrast to the minuet. Quite commonly the minuet will be vigorous and rhythmic. If this is the case, the trio may be gentle and lyric. Each of the two pieces thus displays a unity of style within itself, diversity of style when contrasted with the other. The minuet is played again after the trio. Frequently, however, the composer writes down only the minuet and trio, indicating the return to the minuet by the Italian phrase *"Da Capo"* (i.e. "from the beginning").

By balance a musician understands the relative proportions of the various sections of a composition, and, on a smaller scale, the division of a melody into the phrases of which it is composed. In general this factor is less noted by the casual listener than any other basic element of music. When it is perceived at all, it is because of some real or imagined shortcoming of the composition in this respect. The composition "ends too soon." A composer may suggest a close so decidedly that even a sophisticated audience is deceived and bursts into applause which subsides when the conductor looks annoyed as he proceeds with the remainder of the composition. Yet even when we are not conscious of it, the balance and the proportions of a musical composition contribute to the feeling of perfection which is our response to musical masterpieces.

Most listeners think of music as made up of melody and accompaniment. Music of this kind is "homophonic." One melody is of chief importance, and the others are subordinated to it. In such music, the melodic repetition which lends it unity occurs at a later point in the progress of the piece and frequently in the same voice. The factors of variety and unity present a somewhat different aspect in music for several voices where each part is equally interesting and important. Such music is "polyphonic," many voiced. In polyphonic music a melody or "subject" is frequently sung in what we may call overlapping repetition by each of the voices in turn. Here the desired element of unity, produced by each successive announcement of the melody in the various voices, is combined with a new element of variety. Such a passage is called "imitation," as if each singer listened to the preceding performer and imitated the melody which was just heard. The fact that the melody is repeated not by the same voice but by different voices produces a certain change of character. A kind of simultaneous variety results from the circumstance that when the later voices sing the principal melody, the other voices have proceeded to other and frequently contrasting phrases.

The polyphonic manner may be applied to many musical forms. Certain forms such as the "fugue" (and the forms related to the fugue) are its peculiar province. Many of the Bach inventions, in spite of certain technical pecularities, have the effect of fugues with a slight and playful development. The fugue was most intensively cultivated by Bach and his predecessors. The nineteenth century witnessed the most complete deviation from the principles of polyphonic music in favor of a single expressive melody with accompaniment. But the same period witnessed the rediscovery of Bach by Mendelssohn and Schumann. With the Bach revival came a renewed interest in polyphonic music which has increased up to the present.

The peculiar interest of music in which the various voices enter successively with announcements of the same melody was early realized. Early examples were developed in two ways. The leader (i.e. the voice which entered first) might be completely reproduced by those which followed. This is the procedure followed in rounds such as *"Frère Jacques"* where, indeed, each voice may read from the same music. The later voices simply wait until the apropriate moment for their entry arrives. The term which designates such a composition is "canon." The most famous early example is the English composition "Sumer is icumen in." Later composers wrote such works either for voices or instruments. The opening melody of the finale of César Franck's "Violin Sonata," for example, is treated in canon.

On the other hand, a composer might allot to each voice an announcement of the subject after which each part in turn went on with new material. Earlier composers, however, lacked the power to continue and, after the theme had appeared a sufficient number of times, they united the voices in a cadence and proceeded to treat a new theme in a similar fashion. Perhaps, for the sake of variety, the voices moved together in chords in certain sections without any attempt at imitation. Where the composer was writing for voices, each section corresponded with a phrase of the text. A sixteenth century vocal composition built on such a plan was a motet if the text were sacred, a madrigal if the words were gallant or courtly. When these procedures were applied to instrumental music in the sixteenth century, the *canzone* and *ricercar* appeared. Imitative compositions for instruments which appeared chiefly during the seventeenth century were fantasias or fancies.

The difference between such early compositions and a fully developed Bach fugue is largely due to the fact that where the older composers were likely to construct a longer work by building it up in small sections, each with its own theme, Bach found a single theme sufficient for the elaboration of an extended work. In place of a musical patchwork quilt, a movement unified by the entries and the metamorphoses of a single theme.

The imitative opening (the "exposition") is retained by Bach. After he presents his theme a satisfactory number of times, however, he constructs a passage of contrast, an "episode." But an episode in the more closely-knit fugues of Bach is not new material introduced simply to avoid monotony. It is sometimes a transformation of the theme. This is, of course, a subtler kind of variety, and it demands both skill and musical imagination on the part of the composer. The end of an episode is marked by a new entry of the subject, the beginning of the next episode by its disappearance.

The whole structure, however, is more organic, more continuous than most compositions in homophonic style. Most sections do not end with all the parts at rest in a final chord. By the time the cadence has been reached, a voice, which has perhaps been silent for a time, has already announced the melodic phrase which begins a new episode. It is this type of overlapping which makes the texture of a fugue appear continuous until the final close.

A few special devices which have become usual components of more intricate and ingenious fugues may be mentioned at this point. The various entries of the subject, though they may appear on various tones of the scale are not usually radically transformed. The rarer metamorphoses of a subject may take the form of an increase of duration for the tones of the subject ("augmentation"). In such a case the subject is likely to appear as a long sustained line against a web of more rapidly moving parts. The subject may, on the other hand, appear in shorter note values than at its original appearance ("diminution"). A still more radical transformation substitutes downward motion for upward and upward motion for downward motion ("contrary motion"). The composer may even state his theme beginning with the last note and ending with the first ("*cancrizans*"). The danger in employing such devices is that they may well become so remote in sound and character from the original form of the theme that their relationship is no longer apparent. When this is the case, their usefulness has ceased and they have become a sort of composer's puzzle.

Just as the mounting excitement of a conversation may be measured by the increasing rapidity of statement and rebuttal, so the musical tension of the fugue may be increased by allowing the voices to enter with the subject at shorter time-intervals than in the exposition. Such a passage is a "stretto." The composer usually plans the use of a stretto when he composes his subject, although some subjects which were not composed with this in mind will produce a stretto.

Another effect for which composers of fugues have shown a marked predilection is the "pedal-point." An organist finds it simple to sustain a bass tone with his foot while his hands are busy with the development of a theme on the manuals. Once the mind has become accustomed to the presence of the bass tone, this sound is accepted, and it is possible to play combinations above it which would normally clash with it without disturbing the ear. Such a device is a pedal-point or organ-point. It usually occurs somewhat before the close of a fugue. Often it serves as an occasion for building up a climax.

Sometimes, too, a composer will balance the exposition of the fugue with a later passage of the same kind which is then called a "counter-exposition." But the resources of the polyphonic style make it possible to reannounce the subject in a new fashion. The voices may enter in a different order, or they may enter in stretto. In some fugues this counter-exposition takes on the character of a thematic return. In that event the fugue assumes a three-part form.

The simplest and most primitive treatment of a melody is to repeat it tirelessly like a fiddler playing for a country dance. Such repetitions are produced by the practical demands of the situation. They do not constitute an artistic form by themselves, but they lead the way to a group of forms of some importance.

In the *ostinato* a short melody is repeated in this persistent fashion, but the composer adds to this unifying factor a variety of contrasting melodies. This was a procedure which was most usual during the seventeenth and early eighteenth centuries and with the modernists of the early part of the present century. Early composers evidently liked the device because they were able to build up a cumulative tonal structure by gradually increasing the complexity and animation of the added melodies. Modern composers like the device because it was characteristic of the music of primitive people, and "primitivism" in music was a cult of the 1920's. Perhaps, too, the implacable repetitions of the machines which formed so important a part of the environment of modern man turned the attention of the musician to an equivalent musical device. Sometimes the device is employed with a definite expressive purpose. Thus, in Bizet's *"Carillon"* from *"L'Arlésienne* Suite,*"* a pattern of three notes (mi do re) is repeated by the horns to suggest the pealing of bells. Dido's lament "When I am laid in earth" from Purcell's "Dido and Aeneas" is built over a persistent bass which carries the suggestion of a sorrow which constantly renews itself.

The danger of monotony in such forms was clearly great. Composers realized this, and they realized, too, that the only solution lay in a progressively more interesting and more complicated treatment of each appearance of the theme. This method of building up the interest of the auditor through a gradual increase of motion is evident in the *passacaglia*. In this form, which started as a dance and developed into a specialized type of variation, the theme is first announced in the bass. The text-books usually state that the theme is persistently repeated in the bass as the upper parts are varied. This, though often the case, is not uniformly true. The Bach *"Passacaglia* in C minor" for organ (often performed in transcriptions for orchestra) is a wonderful example of the form, though Bach's older contemporary, Buxtehude, also wrote fine but less frequently performed works in this form.

Already we have entered the field of the so-called "variation forms." The repetition of the theme with progressive elaboration and acceleration is also characteristic of the classic variation. In the sets of variations by Mozart and early Beethoven, however, the melody rather than the bass is the theme. It is the melody which is elaborated and varied though the accompaniment also undergoes appropriate alterations. In other words in the passacaglia the theme in the bass remains relatively unchanged. The upper accompanying parts are elaborated. In the classic variation the melody, not the bass, is the theme, and (at least in early classic and all naive examples) it is the melody itself which is varied.

The practice of turning a melody in long notes into a running passage in shorter tones may become a very dull game indeed in the hands of a lesser master than Mozart. With the mature Beethoven a change in attitude towards the variation form is apparent. Beethoven's earlier variations (such as the delightful set on *"Nel cor più non mi sento"*) are completely in Mozart's manner. In his late variations the melody may vanish or at least become less prominent. What remains is the skeleton of the theme, a succession of harmonies punctuated by cadences. With this as a basis, the composer produces a series of characteristic pieces, as varied and as arresting as possible. But such variations have a definite relation to the theme. It is difficult to illustrate this point in words. Beethoven's "Variations on a theme by Diabelli" have a rather feeble little waltz as a theme. The waltz tune begins with the notes C-B-C (do ti do) preceded by a grace note. In the ninth variation Beethoven builds a charming piece in which we repeatedly hear tones in this relationship. In another he reminds himself that Leporello's air *"Notte e giorno fatticar"* from *"Don Giovanni"* begins with a skip from do to sol and that two prominent tones at the beginning of his theme have a similar movement. This inspires him to compose a variation in the style of this Mozart aria (No. XXII). This type of variation appears in the works of later composers, in the "Symphonic Etudes" of Robert Schumann and the orchestral "Variations on a theme by Haydn" by Brahms.

In at least two notable instances the theme with variations has been used as program music. In Richard Strauss's "Don Quixote" each variation represents an episode in the adventures of the mad but chivalrous hero. One shows him vanquishing a flock of sheep, another depicts his tilting against a windmill. Since the Don was accompanied by rotund Sancho Panza, the composer provides a special theme for his companion. The Don seeks Dulcinea. Accordingly Strauss has written the "theme of the ideal woman." With such a wealth of themes at his disposal Strauss weaves a curious and, at moments, moving score.

Sir Edward Elgar's "Enigma Variations" are elaborate orchestral treatments of a theme in which each variation is a musical characterization of one of the composer's friends. The friends are indicated by half-veiled allusions which have given plenty of busy-work to the commentators. ("Nimrod," for example, is the title of a musical portrait of a Mr. Hunter of Elgar's circle.) The warm romantic tone of the work, the effective scoring for orchestra, and the inventive skill of the composer have gained for this work a secure place in the orchestral repertory. It seems strange that so personal a subject should be dealt with in such an elaborate work and one designed for a large concert hall. Probably Elgar felt that a knowledge of the "portrait" aspect of the variations was not necessary to our listening pleasure.

The prototype of the variation was the single group of notes inexorably repeated until chance, boredom, or a happy inspiration brought about a change. Another ancient mode of performance involved a solo phrase sung by a leader answered by a group response. It is easy to see that the idea of solo and response might develop into a primitive composition made up of two different phrases but with a satisfactory balance between the two. On a very simple scale there are the cries of the leader and the response of the crew on the Nile boats, the responsive answers of the congregation to the intonations of the priest. On a somewhat larger scale are the leader's solo and the answering chorus in the chanty or the Negro spiritual.

Dance pieces with a division into two sections are frequent during the seventeenth century and persist through the period of Bach. By this time, however, the simple opposition of early examples was no longer satisfying. Later dances are still divided into two parts. Each part is normally repeated. Frequently the beginning of the second part resembles the opening melody of the piece except that it is usually presented in a different scale. The closing measures of the two parts often reveal a similar parallelism.

Such pieces follow the fundamental pattern of modulation which was sketched in an earlier chapter. The first part moves to the scale of the dominant. The second part may touch on various scales but must close in the tonality of the piece.

It will be evident that, though the "two-part" or binary division persists, these pieces possess new factors of unity through the parallelism of the openings and the endings of the two sections. Modern listeners are likely to note the repetitions of the parts (AA-BB) and the negative fact that the opening theme does not return in the original scale. The three-part pattern is so much a part of our consciousness that we are likely to judge all others by their re-semblance (or lack of resemblance) to it.

By "three-part form" we understand the whole series of compositions of diverse styles and periods which have one musical drama as their basis. First the theme or themes of the composition are stated. Then follows a section of contrast and finally the restatement of the first section. Statement, contrast, re-statement. The section of contrast may either be entirely new or it may be a new treatment of themes which have already been stated. Each part may be diminutive or of considerable duration. Not only is this principle used for entire compositions but also for their parts.

A composition as short as "All through the Night" con-sists of a simple melodic phrase for each part. The first phrase is repeated, but, with this exception, each part is brief, unelaborated. In a composition of the length of the well-known "Minuet in G" by Beethoven each of the two principal parts has reached a length beyond the limits of a simple melody. Beethoven accordingly composes both of these parts, which we call the minuet and the trio, in three-part form. Since in performance the minuet is followed by the trio and this in turn by a repetition of the minuet, the pattern minuet-trio-minuet forms a larger but otherwise similar form. We might express the entire composition in the form of a diagram:

Minuet	Trio	Minuet
A	B	A
a-b-a	a'-b'-a'	a-b-a

Actually, the pattern in performance is somewhat more elaborate since both minuet and trio are divided into sec-tions each of which is repeated (a-a-ba-ba). When the minuet returns after the trio, the repetitions within the minuet are omitted.

Although it is possible to point out very ancient ex-amples of this kind (certain Gregorian chants are in three-part form), it was largely through the opera that it gained its dominant position among the other forms. After the earliest experiments in musical declamation, composers sought a more symmetrical and balanced form to express the emotional moments of the dramatic action. A melody in concise three-part form appears in Monteverdi.

In the operas and cantatas of Alessandro Scarlatti this tendency had crystallized into the *"da capo aria."* The name was applied to these arias because they were habitually written out in an abbreviated form. The first and second parts only were copied out in full. Instead of re-copying the first part after the middle section, the copyist merely wrote the indication *"da capo"* (literally "from the head," i.e. "from the beginning"). The singer, following this direction, repeated the first part.

This form, from the musical point of view a very satisfactory one, crystallized into a convention. In the operas of Handel it became an incubus which hopelessly retarded the movement of the dramatic action, which was already slow because of the simple fact that the sung word moves more slowly than the spoken word. Songs, arias, short instrumental pieces were written in this form. The intimate piano pieces of a later date were all, or nearly all, three-part in form. Familiar examples may be found in the Mendelssohn "Songs without Words," the Chopin "Nocturnes," the Brahms "Intermezzi" and "Capriccios."

We have already seen that a three-part form can be constructed by using the trio as a section of contrast between two appearances of a minuet. It was possible to carry this idea one stage further by composing two different trios and allowing the minuet (or the scherzo in the case of a more modern work) to appear three times. The Scherzo in Schumann's "C Major Symphony" is so constructed. A similar but more ancient form was the "rondo" which differs chiefly in possessing a more unified style and therefore gives the impression of one unified piece rather than a series of rather well differentiated short pieces.

Probably early suggestions for the rondo came from verse forms (which were in many instances associated with music) with a recurring line as refrain. Similar suggestions may have been derived from folksongs with a returning phrase like the well-known *"Ich weiss ein Maidlein"* ("I know a maiden") with its refrain "take care, she is fooling you." The rondo (or *rondeau*) of Couperin was constructed of a refrain and two couplets. The resulting pattern was then: refrain, couplet I, refrain, couplet II, refrain. The rondo of Haydn and Mozart followed the same general plan on a larger scale with gradual transitions leading from part to part in place of the complete stops and starts in the earlier and more primitive form.

The problem of providing music of considerable duration was met by early composers by following one small and well-unified composition by others of the same general type. The process of linking dances together to make a series can be traced back to the early days of instrumental music. It seems to derive in part from the habit of playing the same dance tune in different metres and at different rates of speed to serve for dances of a different character. Thus in old music for lute we frequently find a "dance" in duple metre followed by a lively "after-dance" which is counted in threes. On a more extended scale the same idea was applied to a series of dances of varied character. In this way the variation suite arose. Each dance employed the same tune altered to suit its special rhythmic character. Obviously this gave the "suite" or dance-sequence a closely unified character. Indeed, the danger was rather that it was difficult, if not impossible, to avoid an intolerable monotony.

The dances of the classic suite were discussed in an earlier chapter. What was said there need not be repeated here. The term is now also used for a varied sequence of pieces which may be derived from a ballet (the "Nut-

[315]

cracker Suite" by Tschaikowsky) or incidental music to a play or a moving picture (*"L'Arlésienne* Suite" by Bizet, the music from "Lieutenant Kijé" by Prokofieff).

Another form cultivated by Bach and Handel and by such contemporary figures as Corelli and Vivaldi was the "concerto grosso." The name of this form is derived from the orchestral practice of the period. The concerto grosso ("large concert" or better "large group playing in concert") referred to the string orchestra in which several players joined in playing each of the parts. To this large group, composers of the period opposed a small solo group of performers. This smaller group was known as the "concertino" ("little concert"). Thus the composer could alternate the heavier tone of his large group with the thinner tones of the soloists who in most cases numbered three, two violinists and a cellist. He could accompany the soloists with his orchestral group. He could oppose to a melody assigned to his large group the more brilliant passages allotted to the members of the concertino.

The usual number of movements for the concerto grosso was three, a vigorous and moderately fast movement, a slow middle movement, and a lively finale. This is the same order of movements which we find in certain early symphonies though here the character of the first movement is still far from that of the symphonic first movement as the classic composers understood it. Nevertheless the fact that a theme introduced at the opening of the movement is shifted from key to key, is varied and elaborated does show an approach to the process we shall consider later as musical development.

The "sonata," like the suite or the concerto grosso, is a series of movements, not a single continuous composition. We must, however, except certain one-movement sonatas of recent date. (Some of these really include the usual movements, but they are connected with one another without a complete interruption of the musical thought. Beethoven had already initiated this pulling together of separate movements in the "Fifth Symphony" in which the scherzo is joined to the last movement by a transitional passage.) The sequence of movements might be fast, slow, fast, as in the concerto grosso. In fully developed examples, however, a minuet followed the slow movement. In most later works the more vivacious "scherzo" displaced the minuet. Occasionally the scherzo preceeded the slow movement. The symphony and the sonata assumed their basic form in the period between Bach and Haydn. In Haydn's day the form dominated all instrumental music except actual dance music. A string quartet, a piano sonata, a symphony, considered broadly, differed, not in the musical forms employed, but simply in instrumental medium. A string quartet is played by two violins, viola, and cello, a symphony by an orchestra.

The characteristic movement of a sonata is the first movement which is constructed in what we call "sonata form." Here we find the same broad tripartite division as in the smaller three-part forms. The first section or "exposition" no longer consists merely of a simple melody, but rather of two or even three themes. The composer, however, takes care that these themes are in contrasting keys, most frequently indeed in the familiar relationship of tonic and dominant. Since the two themes are stated in different keys, the composer invents a passage of a less balanced and melodious character which leads from one to the other. Such a passage is a transition. In a piece of large dimensions, at least at the period of Haydn and Mozart, composers felt the need of emphasizing the end of a section by presenting a final theme or passage which was based on the succession of chords which we know as the cadence. If a melody was presented here it was brief and was usually repeated.

The second section of the movement is called the "development." Here the composer follows no conventional plan either in the treatment of his themes or in the succession of keys utilized. Ingenuity in restating, combining, and

[317]

transforming the material is his object. The keys used tend to be varied and shifting. In this section the composer deviates most widely from his tonal center. Here he gains in color and drama by the use of remote keys or drastic transitions. This section closes on a harmony which produces an effect of suspense and expectation.

The return of the first theme which ushers in the last section or "recapitulation" is a crucial point in the unfolding of the form. Here, as in the smaller three-part forms, the hearer must not only recognize that it is the first theme which returns at this point. He must also be conscious that the first theme is restated in the key in which the composition opened. Beethoven sometimes anticipates the real re-entry of the first theme by a false entry in another key. The whole point of such a manoeuvre is lost if the auditor has forgotten the sound of the original scale and cannot tell the false entry from the real entry in the tonic key.

The third section of a movement in sonata form normally follows the same order of themes as the first section. The first section, however, is based on an opposition of two keys. The last section attains tonal unity, by presenting both themes in the tonic key. It is clear that, since the first section ended in the dominant key, it could not also serve as a final section without alteration. The essential alterations involve both the transition passage and the second and closing themes. This transition passage might seem almost unnecessary since it now connects two themes in the same key. The composer, however, manages to imbue what might appear to be a rather tame enterprise with a sufficient feeling of departure to make the entry of the second theme seem fresh and interesting in spite of the fact that it is now stated in the tonic key. In early sonatas the return of the closing theme brought the movement to an end. In later works of this kind a "coda" or terminal section is added to give more weight and importance to the closing measures of the composition and to afford the composer a final opportunity to present his themes in a new light. Tonally considered, however, the last section merely reaffirms the key of the composition with a sufficient use of other keys to make the actual close sound fresh and convincing.

The idea of musical development presents so few analogies with any other art that a special effort may be necessary to understand what the term implies. A musician is likely to open a symphony by announcing a subject rather than a melody. A simple distinction (too simple, indeed) might be established by stating that a melody is complete in itself and has its justification in the pleasurable response of its audience. A subject is usually shorter, more concentrated. Its importance lies less in its own immediate effect than in the way in which it grows and is transformed, the manner in which it is combined with other elements, the manner in which it unifies the whole composition. A familiar example must serve as an illustration.

The famous opening of Beethoven's "Fifth Symphony" consists of three repeated notes followed by a small skip downwards to a longer tone. This is Beethoven's subject. The opening of the Andante of the same symphony is a melody. The idea of the composer, the subject, is a sequence of sounds in time in which the tones vary in length as well as in pitch. What do we mean when we say that such a sequence of tones is developed? It may be subjected to a number of transformations. The subject may appear in different registers which may be higher or lower than its original pitch. It may, in orchestral compositions, be announced by different instruments. The composer may devise a melody which may be combined with the original subject. All these changes, however, are superficial. None of them really involve the transformation, the resulting stimulus to the imagination of the hearer which is the essence of real development. Indeed the fact that a composer has done no more in his development than to restate his themes in different scales is a common critical reproach.

[319]

A composer may make a more drastic change in his material. He may alter the rhythm or the relative lengths of the notes comprising the subject. He may change or even eliminate the up and down movement, the pitch factor of the subject, while holding fast to the rhythm. When reduced to its characteristic rhythms a subject may even be announced by the drums. The composer often concentrates on a single feature of the subject. Even the opening tones of the "Fifth Symphony" might be divided into two typical aspects, the repeated tones and the small skip downwards at the end. At moments Beethoven vehemently reiterates these repeated tones, concentrating entirely on this one aspect of the theme and neglecting the closing skip.

Such a partial and incomplete account of the changes which a subject may undergo during development cannot go far in explaining the interest which such a passage may have for a sensitive listener. In the kaleidoscope the operator looks through the eye-piece and sees a pattern made by bits of colored glass. If he shakes or turns the toy he sees new patterns emerge. Yet they are not really new since they are merely rearrangements of the same units which formed the original design. In the same fashion, a development presents us with a creative play which is new, but at the same time derived from and related to the melodies or subjects which we have already heard.

The satisfaction which the listener derives is thus a product of two factors: pleasure in the recognition of the familiar and interest in the transformation which it has undergone. If this statement seems to reduce a development to an intellectual guessing game, it fails to convey the whole truth. The intellectual demands made by the symphony are indeed greater than those made by any other musical form (except the fugue). But just as the original statement of the themes established a definite emotional tone, so the various sections of a development convey each its special emotional atmosphere. No further proof of this fact is needed than the numbers of ardent concert-goers who manage to enjoy symphonic music but who, at the same time, blandly ignore all intellectual factors.

From the composer's point of view, a development demands an analysis of the thematic material followed by a new synthesis. There is also another process in which a theme seems to emerge from statements of its fragments or sections. This process may be illustrated by the scherzo from Tschaikowsky's "*Pathétique* Symphony." The movement starts with rapid whirling passages in the strings. Then, against this continuing background, the brass instruments play echoing calls. Though the listener does not realize this at the first hearing, these calls are built on the opening notes of the march theme. The calls follow each other at shorter intervals, the music grows louder, and finally the complete march theme is enunciated by the orchestra. Thus, instead of breaking a theme into its component parts, the theme seems to emerge from repeated statements of its most characteristic fragment. It is a process of synthesis which is worked out in a much more elaborate fashion by Sibelius and by other contemporary composers. In the first movement of the "Second Symphony" by Sibelius, for example, the composer builds new and imposing musical sentences during the development from musical ideas first stated in the opening section of the movement.

So far only one movement of a symphony has been considered, the first and most characteristic movement. But, as has been pointed out, the symphony is not a single movement but a series of contrasting movements. The slow and lyric second movement is frequently in a large three-part form. Earlier composers such as Haydn, Mozart, and the early Beethoven wrote a minuet as the third movement of a symphony. The name "scherzo" (jest) does indeed appear as a title for the corresponding movement in certain Haydn quartets. The rhythmic wit and the vivacity of many Haydn minuets, which are not so designated, certainly approach the capricious character which we associate with the scherzo. It is not till Beethoven that the scherzo really replaces the minuet. This, however, represents a change of mood and style only, for the form remains essentially the same. A modern composer has the option of writing a scherzo or minuet or may even substitute another dance (the waltz in Tschaikowsky's "Fifth Symphony," the gavotte in Prokofieff's "Classical Symphony").

The last movement of a classical sonata or symphony is likely to be a rondo. Beethoven frequently used the rondo, but his interest in sonata form sometimes led him to substitute a sonata form for the rondo in the last movement. Sometimes a hybrid form appears which is intermediate between the sonata form and the simple rondo. Such a movement might be outlined as A-B-A-C-A-B-A-Coda. The last movement of Beethoven's "*Pathétique* Sonata" is in this form. In so far as the movement is unified and organized by the returns of the first theme it is rondo-like. The appearance of B in a contrasting key and its return in the key of the composition are traits borrowed from sonata form. The central episode takes the place of, but lacks the character of a development.

The "concerto" as we find it at the time of Mozart is a work for a solo instrument and orchestra which is closely related to the symphony. The normal number of movements is three: a rapid movement in sonata form, a slow movement, and a vivacious finale. The very presence of a soloist caused certain changes. Thus, the first movement usually begins with a passage for orchestra. Only when the ideas of the movement have been stated does the soloist enter to embroider or to repeat them. The brilliant display passages or cadenzas for the unaccompanied solo instrument are typical of the concerto. The most extended cadenza occurs just before the end of the first movement.

In the early symphony the movements, though written in the same or in related scales and composed with a view to variety and contrast, have no closer connection. In the eighth of his "London Symphonies," Haydn prefaced his first movement with a slow introduction built on the theme which later appears in more rapid tempo as the first theme. Most frequently in the classic works the slow introduction is based on its own thematic material which is not utilized later.

The Beethoven "Ninth Symphony," however, shows how a final movement may serve to sum up and restate the themes of the earlier movements. In the introductory section of this final movement Beethoven quotes the chief themes which have appeared in the earlier movements only to dismiss them at last and turn to the choral theme on which the final movement is actually developed. A still closer unity may be achieved by announcing in the first movement a short but striking subject which is then utilized in the course of the later movements. Such a unifying device is used in highly different and characteristic ways by Brahms in his "Third" and by Tschaikowsky in his "Fourth Symphony." Many other innovations in symphonic form have been attempted, such as the symphony in one movement. The continued production of symphonies by modern composers makes it evident that the form remains a vigorous and fruitful force in the development of music.

Index

INDEX

Caccini, Giulio—75, 78.
cadence—261, 278, 292, 295, 296, 298, 304, 306, 317; full—292; semi - cadence — 292; cadence repetitions—297; full—297.
cadenza—288, 289, 322.
Caedmon—92.
"Caipira, Little Train of the Andes"—255.
"Ca ira"—62.
Cambert, Robert—102.
Camerata—75.
"Camptown Races"—250.
cancrizans—308.
"canned music"—206.
canon—275, 306.
cantata—256.
cantatas, Bach's—221, 255.
canzone—306.
"Capriccio on the Departure of his dearly beloved Brother"—84.
"Capriccios"—314.
"Carnival"—112.
carol—55.
Carpenter, John Alden—252, 253.
"Carillon"—309.
Caruso, Enrico—177.
Casella, Alfredo—44, 275.
castanets—237.
"Cathedral Movement"—235.
celesta—237.
cello—229.
censor—154-55.
ceremonial music—50, 57.
Chabrier, Alexis Emmanuel—236.
Chadwick, George Whitefield — 36.
Chaliapin, Feodor Ivanovich—177.
chalumeau—233.
Chambonnières, Jacques Champion de—168.
Champéron—102
Chandos, Duke of—124.
change, musical—43.
chansons à boire—53.
chant, Gregorian — 239; magic — 284
chanter—283.
chanty—51, 54, 312.
chapel—94, 97, 144.
Chapel Royal—172.
chapelmaster—286.
Charlemagne—163.

Charles II—152.
Chavez, Carlos—23, 25.
"Chester"—62.
"Child and the Enchantments, The"—252.
children's games—94.
choice, musical—28.
choirs (of orchestra)—226.
choir school—172.
Chopin, Frédéric François — 14, 33, 108, 130, 132, 134, 248, 275, 314.
chorale—56, 98, 123, 222, 294.
chorale prelude—124, 294.
chord—281, 290, 291, 293; highly dissonant—301; remote—301.
chord-successions—281.
chorus—270.
chorus, opera—81.
chromatic tones — 279; scale — 279
claque—45-46.
clarinet—225
"Clarinet Quintet"—134.
classic—125. 204.
"Coming Thro the Rye"—275.
commercials (radio)—7, 30, 178, 203.
commercial, singing—203.
"Complete Pianolist, The"—vi.
"Compliment Quartet"—146.
composer—290; operatic—299.
Composer's Forum Laboratories — 154.
concert—216.
concert, aristocratic—148, 195; development of—193-94 et seq.
concertino—316.
concerto—125.
Concerto:
  Gershwin, "Concerto in F" — 252.
  Stravinsky, "Concerto in Ebony" —252.
  Mozart, "D minor Piano Concerto" (Köchel 466)—289.
  Schumann, "Piano Concerto"— 289.
  Grieg, "Piano Concerto"—289.
  Brahms, piano concertos—289.
concerto, organ — 12, 289; classic —289, 322.

INDEX

INDEX

guitar—281.
"*Gurrelieder*"—134.
guzlari—73.
Gyrowetz, Adalbert—12.

"Hail the Conquering Hero" — 192.
Hainault—172.
half steps—278, 279.
half tone—275.
hammer—225, 237.
Handel, George Frederick — x, 8, 12, 61, 70, 77, 82, 83, 120, 124, 128, 149, 191-92, 194, 227, 231, 233, 244, 245, 277, 289, 314, 316.
Hanson, Howard—150.
Harald Fairhair—92.
harmonic minor—276.
harmonics—228.
harmonium, automatic—176.
harmonization—281.
harmony—49, 209, 211, 218, 274, 274, 281, 285, 291, 293, 294, 295, 296, 297, 299, 301, 302; as color factor — 291; as constructive factor—291; as color—293; color effects of—302; of suspense—318.
"Harold in Italy"—229.
harp—272.
harpers—93.
harpsichord—40, 76, 188, 244.
harpsichords (automatic) — vi, 175.
Harris, Roy—135, 216.
"Harrison and Log Cabin Song Book"—64.
"Hawaiian music"—25.
Haydn, Franz Joseph—11, 32, 43, 103-04, 113, 125, 127, 142, 195, 197, 232, 234, 244, 247, 288, 296, 315, 317, 321.
Haydn, Michael—143.
heckelphone—231.
Heifetz, Jascha—29.
Henry VIII—185.
"Hero's Life, A"—131.
"high" dances—243.
hill-billy music—25.
Hindemith, Paul—41, 252.
"History of a Soldier"—135.
Homer—73, 91.

homophonic—305.
Honegger, Arthur—255.
"Hopak"—55.
Hopkinson, Francis—19.
horn—224, 233, 234, 235.
Horowitz, Vladimir—29.
"How to Listen to Music"—viii.
"How to Understand Music"—viii.
"Huagangos"—253.
Hugo, Victor—3.
"*Huguenots*"—131.
Hullah, John—viii.
"Humoresque"—117.
Hunding—300.
"Hungarian Rhapsodies"—33.
"Hungarian Rhapsody No. 2" — 175.
hunting horn—235.
hurdy-gurdy—121, 175, 282.
Hutchinson family—19, 64.
"Hutchinson's Republic Songster" —64
Huygens
hybridization of music—36.
hymn—284
hymns, revival—56.
hymn, Sumerian—162.
"Hymn to the Sun"—276.

Ibert, Jacques—254.
Ice Follies—130.
"*Ich weiss ein Maidlein*"—315.
Idelsohn, Abraham—72.
"I know a maiden"—315.
Iliad—73.
imagery, musical—6.
imitation—305.
Immyns—187.
implications, harmonic—291.
impressionist composers—279.
impressionists—230.
improvisation—204, 286, 287, 288, 289, 290.
Industrial Revolution—127-29.
"*Institutio Oratoria*"—92.
instruments—221, 223.
intellectual understanding (of music)—214.
"*Intermezzi*"—314.
interpreter—291.
intonation—73.
introduction, slow—323.

[331]

INDEX

INDEX

INDEX

spiritual—56, 250, 272, 312.
"Spring Song" ("The Valkyrie")
—81.
"Stabat Mater"—58.
staccato—228.
staff, musical—164.
"Star Spangled Banner" — 264,
266.
state as patron—151-54, 156-58.
statement—296, 313.
steps, whole and half—278, 279.
Stokowski, Leopold—40.
Stradivarius, Antonio—4, 200.
Strauss, Johann—242, 247, 248.
Strauss, Richard—113, 132, 134,
135, 216, 221, 229, 231, 235,
311.
Stravinsky, Igor—41, 42, 44, 135,
223, 275, 281.
street cries—69.
stretto—308.
string—225.
stringed instruments—225.
string orchestra—226, 227.
string quartet—242, 247, 317.
strings—226.
strophe—241.
subject—305, 306, 319, 320, 323.
"Submerged Cathedral"—276.
subscription concert—195.
subsidies, government—152-53.
suite—244, 246, 249, 315; classic
—246, 249, 315.
Suite:
Bizet, from "L'Arlésienne" —
138, 309, 316.
Tschaikowsky, "Nutcracker
Suite—237, 315-16.
Prokofieff, from "Lieutenant
Kijé"—316.
sul ponticello—228.
"Sumer is icumen in"—306.
Suppé, Franz von—254.
survey, popularity—205.
"Swan of Tuonela"—231.
Swieten, Baron von—143.
swing—21, 249, 290.
sword dances—55.
symbolism of musical rhythms —
255.
"Symphonic Etudes"—311.
symphonic music—271, 321.
symphonic poem—131, 257, 302.

"Symphonie Fantastique"—222.
"Symphonies for Wind Instru-
ments"—135.
symphony — 125, 242, 247, 303,
317, 319, 320, 322; one-move-
ment—323.
Symphony:
Antheil, "Symphony No. 4" —
217.
Beethoven, "Seventh," "Eighth,"
"Battle Symphony"—13.
Beethoven, "Fifth," Andante —
15.
Beethoven, "Ninth Symphony"
—89, 230, 264, 323.
Beethoven, "Eroica"—129, 139,
231.
Beethoven, "Fifth Symphony"—
198, 230, 231, 277, 317, 319,
320.
Beethoven, "Pastoral Sym-
phony"—222, 231.
Berlioz, "Symphonie Fantasti-
que"—222, 248.
Brahms, "First Symphony"—27.
Brahms, "Fourth Symphony"—
222, 264.
Brahms, "Third Symphony" —
323.
Copland, "First Symphony" —
216
D'Indy, "Symphony on a French
Mountain Air"—133.
Dittersdorf, set of six—12.
Dvořák, "New World Symphony"
—272.
Harris, "Folksong Symphony"—
135, 217.
Harris, "Symphony 1933"—216.
Haydn, "Farewell Symphony"—
142.
McDonald, "Rhumba Sym-
phony"—253.
Mendelssohn, "Italian Sym-
phony"—235.
Mozart, "Paris Symphony"—44.
Prokofieff, "Classical Symphony"
—322.
Schubert, "C major Symphony"
—235, 236, 248.
Schumann, "Rhenish Symphony"
—236.
Shostakovich, "Seventh," or

INDEX

"Two Part Invention in F major"
—83.

"Un Ballo in Maschera"—155.
Underwood, Leon—67.
United States, music in—33.
unity—304, 305, 312.

"Valkyrie, The"—81, 300.
Valkyrie motive—86.
values, musical—13.
valves—234.
Vanhal, Jan Baptist—201.
variants—160.
variation—269; classic—310.
Variations:
  Beethoven, on "Nel cor più non mi sento"—310.
  Beethoven, "on a theme by Diabelli"—310.
  Schumann, "Symphonic Etudes" —311.
  Brahms, "on a theme by Haydn" —311.
  Strauss, "Don Quixote"—311.
  Elgar, "Enigma Variations" — 311.
variation form—310.
variety—268, 271, 304; simultaneous—305.
Vaughan Williams, Ralph—134.
"Veils"—279.
"Venetian Boat Songs"—254.
Verdi, Giuseppe—89, 129, 155.
verse—270.
"Vespri Siciliani, I"—89.
vibration frequency—210.
vibrato—4, 228.
Victoria, Tomás Luis de — 29, 58, 117, 263.
vielle de la rue—121.
"Viennese Carnival Jest"—154.
"Viens mon beau laboureur"—55.
Villa Lobos, Heitor—255.
villancico—56.
Villon, François—268.
Villoteau—162.
viola—288.
viola da gamba—40, 76.
violin—221, 226, 227.
viola—228.
Virgil—94.
virtuosa—101.

Vivaldi, Antonio—173, 316.
vocero—51, 71.
voice types (in opera)—87.
"Volk ans Geweher"—63.

Wabanaki Indians—70.
Wagner, Richard—x, 10, 32, 33, 81-82, 85, 86, 95, 108, 112, 129, 132, 134, 216, 224, 226, 233, 235, 236, 254, 300.
"waits"—99.
"Waldesrauschen"—89.
"Waldstein Sonata"—87.
Wälse—300.
Walton, William—39, 204.
waltz — 210, 242, 247, 248, 310, 322.
"Waltzes," Op. 39 (by Brahms)— 248.
Ward, Ned—99.
"Warum,"—292.
Weber, Carl Maria von—127, 130.
Weill, Kurt—213.
Weinberger, Jaromir—249.
Welte-Mignon—176.
"When I am laid in earth"—309.
"When Johnny Comes Marching Home"—135.
Whiteman, Paul—242, 252.
whole steps—278, 279.
whole tone scale—279.
"Why?"—292.
Wilbye, John—119, 216.
Wilkinson—162.
Williams, C. E. Abdy—168.
"William Tell"—131.
wind—224, 226, 227.
"Wir fahren nach England"—63.
"Wise Virgins, The"—40.
W N Y C—206.
wooden block—237.
wood engraver—170.
Wood, Sir Henry—153.
woodwinds—226, 230.
work songs—51, 253.
W.P.A.—154.
W.P.A. Music Project—24.
W Q X R—206.

xylophone—237.

"Yankee Doodle"—55, 62.
"Yip I Addy I Ay"—202.
"Yip Yip Yaphank"—158.

[341]